A Black Future?

RONALD NICOLSON

A Black Future?

Jesus and Salvation in South Africa

SCM PRESS
London

TRINITY PRESS INTERNATIONAL
Philadelphia

First published 1990

SCM Press Ltd
26–30 Tottenham Road
London N1 4BZ

Trinity Press International
3725 Chestnut Street
Philadelphia, Pa. 19104

British Library Cataloguing in Publication Data

Nicolson, Ronald
    A black future?: Jesus and salvation in South Africa.
    1. South Africa. Christian theology
    I. Title
    230′.0968

    ISBN 0–334–00120–X

Library of Congress Cataloging-in-Publication Data

Nicolson, Ronald
    A Black future? Jesus and salvation in South Africa / Ronald
Nicolson.
       p.   cm.
    Includes bibliographical references.
    ISBN 0–334–00120–X
    1. Christianity—South Africa. 2. Jesus Christ—Person and
offices. 3. Salvation. 4. South Africa—History—Philosophy.
5. Race relations—Religious aspects—Christianity. 6. South
Africa—Race relations. 7. Black theology. 8. Liberation theology.
9. South Africa—Church history—20th century. I. Title.
BR1450.N53   1990   89–28180
276.8′0828—dc20

Typeset at The Spartan Press Ltd, Lymington, Hants
and printed in Great Britain by
Billing and Sons Ltd, Worcester .

Contents

For Lindiwe

Preface

Most of this book was written during a year's sabbatical leave from my teaching responsibilities, for which, and for their financial support, I am very grateful to the University of Natal.

The financial assistance of the Institute for Research Development of the Human Sciences Research Council towards this research is also hereby acknowledged. Opinions expressed in this book and conclusions arrived at are those of the author and do not necessarily represent the views of the Institute for Research Development or the Human Sciences Research Council.

I was privileged to spend much of my sabbatical time as an Honorary Research Fellow at King's College, London, and would like to express my warm thanks to Stuart Hall, who made it all possible, and also to Colin Gunton, Christoph Schwöbel and others there who welcomed me and permitted me to pick their brains in discussions and seminars. They will not necessarily agree with very much in this book, but I gained a great deal from listening to them, and the book is more balanced than it would otherwise have been.

I also spent a semester at Union Seminary, New York. My indebtedness to Tom Driver and the 'ST271' class will, I hope, be obvious. Less obvious but also greatly appreciated was the benefit of working in the elegant, comfortable and well-stocked library at Union. I am grateful, too, to Dean Fenhagen for making it possible to use the library resources at General Theological Seminary.

My stay at Union would have been impossible without the warm and loving hospitality extended by Hays Rockwell and the congregation at St James's Church, Madison Avenue, New York. Whatever small value this book may have to others, the value to me, who have benefitted from all these friendships, is incalculable.

I was greatly helped by research work done by the Revd Solomon Jacob which pointed me in the direction of much useful material.

My wife Gail read through the entire typescript several times to correct my grammar and to force me to write in comprehensible English. I thank her for this labour of love.

Introduction

This book is an attempt to build some sort of bridge between the theology of Europe and America and the theology of the Third World. The two seem to have little in common. They are aimed at different audiences, and answer different questions. Yet it may be that each has something to learn from the other. Certainly it is not right that First-World theology should continue to ignore the very different and perhaps more urgent theological issues faced in poor Third-World countries, and in so far as it does so it deserves all the scorn that Third-World theology sometimes directs towards it. But Third-World liberation theology, and more specifically Black South African theology, engaged as it is in the heat of the struggle, needs, I believe, the intellectual underpinning that First-World theology can provide if its answers are to be credible.

In the 1970s English theology was very concerned about christology. The fierce debate centring upon *The Myth of God Incarnate*[1] seems to have fizzled out, or to have moved on to even more controversial ground. The question now is not so much 'Is Jesus God?', but 'Does God as a personal entity exist?' The theological enterprise involves balancing up the fruits of biblical scholarship, the questions raised by 'cultured despisers' and the need to preserve some significance for Christian belief and identity in a modern secular world.

Third-World theology in its different forms – liberation, Black, Minjung, etc. – is also concerned with christology and with the existence of God. Unlike English theology it is not really interested in questions like 'Is Jesus God?' or 'Does God exist?' It assumes the truth of a divine-human Jesus, and of the presence of a loving God, and asks how that faith can be harnessed to help with the struggle to throw off the chains of colonial and capitalist exploitation. Many

Third-World theologians would regard the concerns of First-World theology as irrelevant and time-wasting.

Another book about christology seems *passé*; another book about contextual theology unnecessary in an already flooded market. The publication of *The Myth of God Incarnate* brought into the public eye issues which go back at least to the period of the Enlightenment and the Deists, perhaps back to the days before the Nicene Creed and the Chalcedonian Definition of orthodox Christian belief about who Jesus was. Can there be anything new to say?

My concern in this book, however, is not only 'Is traditional Christian belief about Jesus true?', but 'Is it helpful, does it make any effective difference?' Jesus, however he is understood, has been the pivot of Christian faith because people have believed that he made God real for them and available to them. He is seen to be the means through which God deals with the world. Believing in a god or gods who exist in some academic sense on some inaccessible Olympia, far from human concerns except for occasional forays into the created world, is not the same as believing in a God who is intimately, constantly, purposefully, transformingly, part of our being and existence. Christians believe that Jesus makes this kind of difference to our relationship with God. To put it crudely and provocatively, they believe that Jesus makes God 'useful' to us.

Of course from a theological point of view that last sentence is very wrong. 'The chief end of man is to glorify God', said the Westminster Shorter Catechism; not 'the chief end of God is to be useful to human beings'.[2] Of course (if there is a God) it has to be true that God is primary, that we are totally dependent on him, if God is what we mean by God. Nevertheless, if God is to be God, he must be the pivot or the foundation – or whatever other metaphor we may choose to use to indicate that it is God who gives life – who gives meaning to existence. He is not an irrelevant God, and if he were, our meaning of the word 'God' would have changed. Even the call to worship God is a call made for our sake. God does not need our worship – or he is not God. We need to worship him, to give meaning and centre to our lives.

Whatever meaning may in theory be ascribed to the word 'G-O-D', Christian belief is surely that the God of our faith does not remain isolated or irrelevant or an occasional *deus ex machina*, a sort of once-off bolt from the blue, but makes himself constantly available to us. He helps us. He saves us. It is also basic Christian belief that it is through Jesus that this availability of God is especially channelled. If all this is not true, then there is no point in

Christian faith. Jesus is the one who manifests and mediates the love and gracious help of God to us.

So it seems to me worthwhile to return to the christological debate, but from a somewhat different perspective from the form which some of the debate thus far has taken. In a post-Enlightenment Western world, there has been a concern to make Christian belief acceptable to a community which no longer accepts truth on other people's authority but wants personal and empirical evidence of that truth. We can, of course, argue about whether post-Enlightenment empiricists are really as independent from external authority as they think they are, and we will indeed touch on this argument later.[3] For the moment my point is only that, whether rightly or wrongly, post-Enlightenment Western philosophers, after centuries of authoritative church dogmatism culminating in the blood of the Reformation, have largely insisted that concepts must make logical sense, must be reasonable, must be consistent with empirical experience. Philosophers like Hume and Kant have been very influential in England. Much of the christological debate has been concerned with whether traditional belief in Jesus as being divine as well as human is in fact a rational, reasonable belief, and revisionary ideas about Jesus have been shaped in order to meet the rationalist challenge.

Section I of the book is an attempt to summarize some of the issues that have been raised in the christological debate to date. I will suggest that there are indeed quite serious historical and logical problems in traditional belief about Jesus. On the other hand I will suggest that because we know very little, if anything, of what it could mean to be God, and not even very much about what it means to be human, we cannot become modern dogmatists and rule out *a priori* the idea that Jesus is both divine and human. Is that perhaps why at present the debate has fizzled out? Perhaps there is no more to be said on either side. The logical problems are apparent, but the traditional rejoinders are equally weighty, given the mystery about divine and human nature, thus bringing the debate to a point of stalemate.

But since the belief in Jesus as being both divine and human arose as a logical entailment of belief in Jesus as Saviour, perhaps this is another starting point to the debate. Jon Sobrino[4] suggests that the post-Enlightenment challenge to traditional christological doctrine consisted not only in the logical challenge from Hume but also in the practical challenge of Marx. Faith in Jesus has to be shown to be effective in liberation. Does Jesus, or faith in Jesus, liberate people from their bondage? If so, how? We need to try to understand not only how Jesus was perceived as saviour through New Testament eyes and the eyes of subsequent tradition, but how he can be perceived as saviour in our own circumstances. Jesus was born to a particular place and people with their particular problems. Yet Christian faith believes him to be of universal significance to all places, times and people. We will have to see whether, and how, that is true.

Edward Schillebeeckx says that the crisis for modern Christians

> . . . lies in the fact that Jesus is still regularly explained to us as salvation and grace in terms which are no longer valid for our world of experience, i.e. in terms of earlier experiences; and on the other hand in the fact that we seem no longer capable in words or actions to 'make a defence for the hope that is in us'.[5]

Section II of the book examines some of the ways in which Jesus has been perceived as saviour in the past, and asks: does this perception still fit our own experience? We cannot ignore the tradition. Our present circumstances and our present faith grow out of the past. There are universal truths and universal human experiences which overarch the ages.

> Present and past are not 'two things' in juxtaposition. In reality, the message of the New Testament and our present experiences do not stand over against each other and alongside each other as two things. They already touch each other.[6]

Nevertheless we need to ask ourselves just what, in the common experience of past and present, is still real for us, and what constitutes a universal truth about the saving work of Jesus to which we can still say 'Amen'. To quote Schillebeeckx yet again,

> Christians who continue to experience decisive faith in Jesus will be able to invite others to renewed possibilities of experience, if they search from their own Christian self understanding for something in our present pattern of experience of salvation from God in Jesus.[7]

and,

> in my view this gulf between *faith* [Schillebeeckx means here the faith received from our fathers, the faith of the church] and *experience* is one of the fundamental reasons for the present day crisis among Christians who are faithful to the church.[8]

I wish to ask, then, whether the received understandings of faith are still true to our experience. And since 'our' is a widely encompassing word, I narrow it down to my own time and place, and to understandings of salvation for an oppressed people. I live and work in South Africa. I try to ask how salvation can work in the South African situation.

In section III of the book I look at theologies which claim to be theologies of the oppressed. I look at Latin American liberation theology, and at what can be learned from the still very new and yet-to-be-developed field of Black theology. I try to understand from the outside what these theologians are saying. It is true that I am neither oppressed (relatively speaking: none of us is ever entirely free of political and economic restraints) nor black. Yet until black people are free, I cannot be free. Their concerns are, or should be, my concerns. I make no attempt here to tell those who are oppressed how they should think, or to impose my own interpretations upon them. The reflections are purely my own as I try to discover how I can best interpret Jesus within the tragic circumstances of my own country.

To indulge in speculative theology while an intense struggle is raging, a struggle in which at present I do not bear more than a tiny part of the suffering that ordinary black families endure, may seem heartless and frivolous. The concerns of Third-World theology are of great importance to the concerns of Western theology outlined in section I. Third-World theology attempts to show just how it is that Jesus is relevant to the situation of the Third World, how he saves, what he does. Whether their answers are right is another matter: but their questions are the ones that First-World theology needs to be asking as well.

Yet the philosophical concerns of Western theology are surely not irrelevant to Third-World theology, either. Unless we can show that belief in Jesus as saviour is a reasonable belief, then he is not a saviour but a false crutch, a superstition which may comfort but has no solid basis in reality.

Thus in section IV I attempt to construct an understanding of Jesus and a model of salvation in Jesus which takes both experience and logic into account. I offer my reflections in the belief that philosophical and theological attempts to understand, to discover meaning, are an important part of any movement of social change, and as a humble contribution to that cause. In the South African agony, or all other agonies that surround us in our world, can Jesus still save us? How? Who is he for us? What must we do to be saved?

I do think these questions are relevant. Most South Africans, black and white, are Christian, or claim to be. If Jesus can save, then there is, after all, hope for the 'Beloved Country'.[9] To understand that hope might change the course of events. If we can find no meaning in or content to the notion of salvation in Jesus, then we must put our hope elsewhere, or surrender all hope and let the tragedy take its inevitable course. The answers, however speculative, however academic, however removed from the front line of battle, do matter.

In order to give real context to the questions which I ask, I have chosen to ask them with a real person in mind. Sipho Mkhize figures quite prominently in sections II and III. He is a real person, although Sipho is not his real name. The facts about him and his family are true, and fairly typical for many black people in South Africa today. Yet my thoughts, of course, are mine and not Sipho's. It is possible that Sipho would view the questions and the answers quite differently. I cannot think his thoughts. But in South Africa I cannot think theologically without having Sipho and others like him constantly in mind. Because of the structure of my argument, we do not actually meet Sipho until Chapter 2 of the second section; readers impatient with the theological discussions of the first section may want to turn to that chapter first, but they will understand the exploration of the burning problem it raises better if they have also read the first section.

I

Jesus

Human and Divine

1

The New Testament

If we are to talk about Jesus at all, our first question must surely be, what does the New Testament say? How did Jesus describe himself? How did the first Christians perceive him? The Chalcedonian fathers, says Bray,[1] certainly saw themselves as making explicit what was always implicit in the New Testament. For many Christians, this is the end of the argument. The New Testament teaches that Jesus was fully divine and fully human, therefore this definition cannot be doubted, and all that remains is perhaps to explore any further implications of this for faith. Thus Michael Green, referring to C. F. D. Moule's *The Origin of Christology*,[2] can say that 'it is probable that if his book had been available a year ago *The Myth of God Incarnate* would not have seen the light of day'.[3] Since Moule's book, at least in Green's view, shows that the New Testament view of Jesus is that he is divine and human, there is an end to the matter.

Would that it were so easy! Even if the New Testament does teach that Jesus is fully God and fully human, unless we are able to show that this definition makes some sense, the usefulness of the New Testament teaching is called into question, and the authority of the New Testament thus weakened. Whether the New Testament does teach this is a matter of considerable and ongoing debate. Modern biblical criticism has driven a wedge between the historical words and deeds of Jesus and the interpretation and retelling of these words and deeds in the Gospels. The Chalcedonian fathers may have thought that they were only building on the New Testament foundations, but they did not have the advantage and burden of

modern scholarship; they did not make so clearly the modern
distinction between history and interpretation, or between the
physical/historical realm and the realm of metaphysics and metaphor; they were unaware of the extent to which their interpretation of the New Testament was conditioned by their own non-
biblical philosophical assumptions.

The neat and tidy assumption of many modern traditionalists is
that the Chalcedonian Definition is the product of a long process –
although not necessarily the end-product, as we may have to build
further on the foundations which Chalcedon establishes. Their
view is that we have, as the raw facts, the deeds of Jesus and the
teaching of Jesus about himself: 'I and the Father are one', etc.[4]
Then we have the teaching of Paul about Jesus, based on the
tradition which he received about those deeds and teachings and
on his own experience of the presence and power of the risen Lord
on the Damascus road and subsequently. Paul, it is assumed,
taught clearly that Jesus was God yet human. Subsequently we
have the evangelists and other New Testament writers, who provide the written record of the tradition. They do not express the
philosophical implications of the tradition in any systematized
way, but the beginnings of what will become a systematized
doctrine are present.

In the ensuing three centuries, this view continues, we have a
progressive clarification of these implications, culminating in the
Chalcedonian Definition. No one pretends that Chalcedon is
without problems; everyone concedes that the definition does not
in itself explain how Jesus can be divine, yet possess a human soul
and live in a particular human culture as a particularized man (and
not a woman) of his own time, with all the ensuing limitations that
are inevitably part of this particularization. It is in trying to do
battle with this mystery and to reduce these problems that much
modern christology is concerned, as we shall see. But, so the
argument goes, the Chalcedonian Definition illuminates the inner
logic of the uncodified, unsystematized New Testament christology; it shows us where the New Testament teaching must inevitably lead. The Chalcedonian Definition may not be the whole
truth; since the whole truth is a divine truth it will in any case be
beyond human understanding or expression. But what the Chalcedonian Definition teaches is what the New Testament requires.
Jesus showed himself, and claimed, to be God. The New Testament writers believed this. Chalcedon put this into logical form.
We may try to extend Chalcedon with further elucidation. We

cannot, however, build on any set of foundations other than that provided by Chalcedon.

There are a number of problems with this tidy scheme.

1. The raw facts of Jesus' life and teaching are notoriously difficult to pin down. Even Moule concedes this, though Michael Green seems unaware of this.

> I hold no doctrine of the inerrancy of the New Testament, no brief for the view that every estimate of Christ within it is to be accepted uncritically, simply because it is within the canon.[5]

Modern biblical scholarship has shown us that, operating in all sincerity with a different concept of history from our own, the evangelists have certainly interpreted and recast Jesus' words. Even if we do not go all the way with Bultmann in his doubts about the historicity of the Gospel accounts, few would now argue that all the deeds of Jesus recorded in the Gospels are historically true. Even if they are, the deeds in themselves do not prove his divinity. Miracles, even the resurrection, do not prove that Jesus is God, only that he is an instrument of God. What we are presented with in the New Testament is secondary data. The writers, or at least some of them, thought that Jesus was divine. That is a fact. The primary data – what Jesus himself said or did or his own self-understanding – are not so clear.

We may, of course, still argue that the writers were under the guidance of the Holy Spirit and that their interpretation can therefore be trusted, but we must at least concede that we do not have the undoubted actual words of Jesus. Leslie Houlden says:

> The study of the gospels is far from yielding total scepticism about the Jesus of history, but it remains unclear where exactly accurate information is to be found, and we see that the information is always reflected through the evangelists.[6]

2. Let us grant the argument that Jesus did claim to be God. Does that mean he was necessarily right? The old 'mad, bad or God' argument really cannot hold water. The argument runs thus: to claim to be God, Jesus must have been either insane and possessed of wild delusions about himself; or a very evil person deliberately misleading gullible followers for his own ends; or he must have been right. Such evidence as we have does not in any way support the first two propositions, therefore he must indeed be divine, as he claimed.

Since he did not operate with the clinical preciseness of Greek philosophical terminology, what would Jesus have meant by such a claim? That he spoke with the authority of God, that he acted with the power of God, that he willed what the Father willed? In the Old Testament there are a number of texts which describe the King of Israel in almost divine terms (e.g. II Sam. 7.14a; II Sam. 21.17; Psalm 2.7, 8), but it is clear that the king was not actually regarded as metaphysically identical with God or in any terms approaching the Chalcedonian *homoousios*. Jesus could have envisaged for himself a similar 'Son of God' status without being mad or bad, and we can believe all this about him without agreeing with the Chalcedonian Definition. If Jesus had claimed the right to be worshipped as God that would be another thing. The one thing that as a pious Jew he could not have claimed without blasphemy would have been that. Certainly he is reflected as having been condemned as a blasphemer – see Mark 2.7 and parallels, where he is accused of blasphemy for forgiving sins, or Mark 14.61 and parallels where he is accused of blasphemy for claiming to be the Messiah. There is, however, no New Testament evidence that he invited people to worship him. Indeed he seems to have disclaimed any such right (Mark 10.18 and parallels): 'Why do you call me good? No one is good save God alone.'

3. Jesus, we may argue, may not have claimed the right to be worshipped, but the church in a very short time was indeed worshipping him. Matthew (2.11) says that the wise men 'fell down and worshipped' Jesus. When the word *proskynein* is used, says Heinrich Greeven in Kittel's *Theological Dictionary of the New Testament*, . . . the object is always something – truly or supposedly – divine.[7] Matthew also says that the disciples worshipped Jesus[8] when they recognized him to be the Son of God after a nature miracle. C. S. Lewis argued vigorously that these writers, being closer to Jesus in culture, language, imagery and unconscious assumptions than any modern writer, should have had a better understanding of his nature than is possible for us.[9] He argued further that our scepticism about the reliability of the Gospel records is misplaced, since we have even fewer reliable records about every other figure in ancient history.

Eric Mascall, like C. S. Lewis, argues that however sketchy our historical knowledge of Jesus, as an historical figure he is as well attested as any other figure from ancient history, and he quotes the classical scholar A. N. Sherwin-White to support his point.[10]

Even if this claim is true, it leaves aside the problem that the unconscious assumptions and world-view of people of antiquity may be quite unworkable in our modern culture. Don Cupitt points out that these other figures from ancient history are not the basis of faith, and that therefore the truth of their history is less important.

> Once having adjusted ourselves to the critical view of Jesus, we may realize that he is after all pretty solidly rooted in known history, and we do know something about him, even if not much. Nevertheless, the fact remains that our knowledge of Jesus is not great, and in principle no more than probable. How can something as serious as religious commitment be based on shaky foundations?[11]

Perhaps it is asking too much to insist on historical certainty as a basis for faith. All historical evidence requires selective interpretation, and the interpretation can never be certain. 'Faith' is not 'factual knowledge', but an attitude towards the facts which casts a different light upon them. Mascall's real point is that sceptical biblical scholars reject the divinity of Jesus on *a priori* grounds, and then use the paucity of historical evidence to back their assumptions. He argues that if (with Austin Farrer) we put historical evidence and faith together, then our judgment will be far more positive.

> Thus it is possible through faith and evidence together, and through neither alone, to believe that Christ really and corporeally rose from the dead.[12]

On what, however, is our faith in an historical figure like Jesus to be based, if faith is not derived from historical evidence but is itself a supportive factor to supplement historical evidence? It must be derived from our own experience, which then predisposes us to interpret the historical evidence of the experience of others.

4. Our real difficulty is that the views of the New Testament writers about Jesus are not all the same. They do not understand him to be divine in the same way. Moule does not think that belief in the divinity of Jesus evolved after the New Testament under the influence of Hellenism and Semitic saviour cults. He believes that the very earliest Palestinian church already had a high christology. He also thinks that people experienced Jesus from the beginning as divine, and that this fits the impact that Jesus made on his followers better than the idea that Jesus was initially perceived by his first followers as human, and as divine only as the church became Hellenized.[13] He does not think that belief in Jesus as divine

'evolved' as a result of subsequent extraneous influences, but that it 'developed' from the immediate experience of the disciples and Paul.[14] However, Moule agrees that Paul, with his idea of the corporate Christ into whom we are incorporated, sees Jesus differently from the non-Pauline writers. There is not one uniform New Testament christology; New Testament writers may have all attributed divinity to Jesus, but they did not mean exactly the same thing by that claim.

James Dunn makes the same point:

> . . . within acceptable Jewish Christianity there was diversity; even within the New Testament writings themselves we can see that they do not all represent a single uniform type of faith.[15]
>
> As with Jewish Christianity, so in the case of Hellenistic Christianity [Dunn is referring to Q, Paul and John], we are dealing with a diverse phenomenon.[16]

Thus Dunn concludes

> Christology should not be narrowly confined to one particular assessment of Christ, nor should it play one against another, nor should it insist on 'squeezing' all the different New Testament conceptualizations into one particular 'shape', but it should recognize from the first the significance of Christ could only be apprehended by a diversity of formulations which though not always strictly compatible with each other were not regarded as rendering each other invalid.[17]

If we are to believe these scholars, there is not just one single way of looking at Jesus in the New Testament, not just one way of understanding how it is that he is important for us. New Testament writers have a number of different perspectives, which cannot all be subsumed under one heading. There are a number of different themes or ways of looking at Jesus and at how he affects us. How do we choose the one that is best for us? How do we decide between 'orthodox' or 'liberal' christology?

Houlden suggests that the study of the New Testament reveals that it does not really match with either the Chalcedonian Definition or the looser, more liberal interpretation of Jesus being a special, but human, channel of the divine. In fact, he says, the New Testament writers have very diverse christologies. What they have in common is the conviction that Jesus is the centre of their world; Jesus makes 'all the difference' to them,[18] but since their world views differ, so the way in which Jesus makes 'all the difference' differs too, depending on their own outlook, circumstances, etc. Thus for Paul, the death of Jesus is a sacrifice which achieves reconciliation between humans and God. The resurrection of Jesus achieves a victory over the four tyrants of sin, flesh, law and powers. Christian baptism achieves an incorporation into the fruits of that sacrifice and that victory. The death and resurrection of Jesus are what matters to Paul, more than his life and teaching. For Mark, on the other hand, the life of Jesus is a life of obedience even unto death, a path which we are called to emulate. For Matthew, what makes all the difference is Jesus' teaching of the new Law which is the gateway to our heavenly reward. For John, Jesus makes it possible for us to share in the stable, unchanging, eternal relationship between Father and Son. For the writer of Hebrews, Jesus is the fulfilment of scriptural patterns, particularly the pattern of Yom Kippur.

There is, however, no single interpretation of Jesus and his saving significance in the New Testament. The Chalcedonian Definition is yet another attempt to say how Jesus makes all the difference in a world view shaped by Hellenistic philosophy. It is for us to work out how Jesus makes all the difference for us, in our very different world and circumstances.

Houlden argues that we are now more aware of the origins both of the Chalcedonian Definition and of the scriptural teaching on christology, and that no one can now merely invoke these as if that were the end of the matter.[19] Whereas in the past New Testament studies and patristics provided the agenda for christological study and modern human experience only the material for illustrating these timeless truths, we now need to start from our own experience, as did the New Testament writers, and interpret that experience.[20]

The interaction between New Testament studies and doctrinal theology for which Houlden asks is given monumental expression by Edward Schillebeeckx.[21] Schillebeeckx painstakingly summarizes the views both of biblical exegetes and of doctrinal theologians. In his conclusions he, too, says that, while exegetes differ, it is clear that the New Testament writers write about Jesus with their own presuppositions about human nature and about what it is from which we need salvation, and that the

> . . . original experience of salvation in Jesus gets filled out in the gospels with doctrinal and practical problems of the later Christian congregations.[22]

The Gospels, he says, have diverse christologies; there is no single kerygma, or message of good news, behind the Gospels.[23] During Jesus' lifetime he was probably understood as a prophetic figure calling people to obedience to God as part and parcel of his preaching of the kingdom of God.[24] After his death, however, because of what they believed to be ongoing experiences of his forgiveness and his presence, different understandings of Jesus emerge.

What we find is that each successive part of the church turns to Jesus with its different assumptions and needs and world-view, and finds salvation in him.[25] Schillebeeckx traces in the New Testament a number of different 'credal theories' about Jesus: Jesus is the One who will come to usher in the last age; Jesus is the embodiment of the Kingdom of God; Jesus is the suffering Son of Man; Jesus is a *theios aner*, a mighty miracle worker; Jesus is a pious embodiment of wisdom; Jesus is the resurrected Lord.[26] All of these are interpretations of the historical Jesus, the 'factual' Jesus, as each part of the church legitimately seeks to see the relevance of Jesus for their own needs.

This, however, means that in each new age the church can still rightly give new names to Jesus, from the current situation and needs.

> When we take into account the structure that characterizes the 'naming of Jesus' by Christians in the New Testament and the way that structure changes in the light of the continually shifting experience of God's gift of salvation in Jesus, it is clearly in full accord with the gospel for us, with a like experience of salvation, to give new names to Jesus.[27]

Part of the intention of Schillebeeckx's books, as we shall see later, is to build up a picture of Jesus which is compatible with the view of Jesus in the New Testament and in subsequent Christian tradition but is also relevant to the issues of our own period, and compatible with the understanding that we now have of human nature and human well-being. He does not feel himself bound merely to reproduce New Testament or Chalcedonian doctrine. Although he does not use the term, he is embarked on a demythologization programme, endeavouring to get to the heart of the New Testament experience of Jesus and to express an experience of Jesus in our own time which is consistent with that heart but not necessarily with its culturally conditioned expression. In this way Schillebeeckx tries to combine a historical-critical approach to the Bible with dogmatic theology.

5. We cannot follow through the New Testament evidence in detail here. We can only note that some scholars believe that from the beginning Jesus was perceived as divine, while others disagree. Almost everyone concedes that the historical facts about Jesus' life are difficult to reconstruct, although some believe that enough can be established about his life and teaching for this to be a foundation for subsequent interpretation.

Many scholars argue nevertheless that even if we do not know much about the historical Jesus, we do know how the early church perceived him; we have the fact of his impact on the people. Wolfhart Pannenberg argues that whatever our difficulties in expressing what the resurrection means and in reconstructing the historical facts of the appearances of the risen Jesus,

> . . . only the resurrection of Jesus, conceived of in the framework of the cultural situation of primitive Christianity, renders intelligible the early history of Christian faith up to the confessions of Jesus' true divinity.[28]

Pannenberg has his own rich theology about how God can be involved in time and space or in the outworking of human history, all of which has its problems which need not detain us now. Pannenberg is an influential representative, however, of the school which says that the resurrection is a historical event; that it is this that proves the divinity of Jesus; and that we know the resurrection is true because of the faith and courage of the early church, which are inexplicable if the resurrection is not true. Had Jesus not risen from the dead, his claims would have been no more than dreams; but he did rise, and thus is the ultimate revelation of God's purposes, and thus is God.

> . . . if the resurrection of Jesus is certain as an event which really happened, what would that mean? Would it be possible to recognize by this that Jesus was the Son of God, that he was the One who died on the cross for the sins of all men? This is precisely the case.[29]

In its basic form, the argument runs: We cannot be sure how Jesus regarded himself, or how his followers during his lifetime perceived him. We cannot even be sure of exactly what happened at the resurrection; but the transformation in the lives of the disciples, and the growth of the early church, are historical facts which make no sense unless Jesus did truly rise, and did impart his risen power to the early church; and this in turn makes no sense unless he is God. The basis of our faith is thus the experience of the risen Christ in the church from earliest times until now.

This is not to argue that the resurrection of Jesus in itself proves that he is God, though Pannenberg seems to suggest this. The resurrection, if true, only shows that God raised Jesus. Since Christian belief is that we too shall be raised, this proves no more than that Jesus was raised first as a kind of first fruits or proto-resurrection. Thus Pinchas Lapide as a Jew is able to say that he can accept the historicity of the resurrection of Jesus, indeed that he thinks the resurrection of Jesus is more probably true than not.[30] He claims that any Jew of the house of Hillel could say the same. This does not make Lapide think that Jesus is divine, or even the Messiah.

> Jesus therefore without doubt belongs to the *praeparatio messianica* of the full salvation which is still in the future. This does not mean that his resurrection makes him the Messiah of Israel for Jewish people.[31]

Although some Chalcedonian defendants may have used the resurrection of Jesus as proof of his divinity, the better argument is somewhat different. It is that even if the earthly life and miracles and power of Jesus are not directly accessible to us in history, the ongoing experience of the power and presence of Jesus in the church proves that he is God.

Thus Moule can say that there is congruity between the traditional account of Jesus' ministry and the post-resurrection experiences of Jesus in the church. How, he asks, could Jesus have triggered off such a response if he was not a person of appropriate magnitude? So Peter Hinchliff argues that the experience of the presence and power of Jesus long after his human death establishes the uniqueness of Jesus.

> The uniqueness of Jesus does not simply rest . . . upon the character of the historical person (which may not be fully recoverable) but upon the undoubted fact that all this 'mythology' grouped itself around the historical person. Moreover it appeared to be vindicated by the further fact that the claim that the faith was communicable seemed to be borne out in the experience of subsequent generations.[32]

Not all of those whom I have just quoted are necessarily defending the way that Chalcedon defines the divinity of Jesus; they are only arguing that the experience of the early Christians, and indeed of subsequent Christians, is a historical fact which is accessible to us, and which demands an explanation. Chalcedon is one way of explaining these facts. If we reject that explanation, another is required of us.

There is, however, a weakness in the argument. What these authors claim to be the ongoing power of the risen Jesus in the church could, it seems to me, with equal likelihood be called the ongoing power of God. That is to say, God worked through the human Jesus as far as we can historically establish. God continues to work through those who seek, like Jesus, to be obedient to him. This does not seem to require that Jesus himself be God.

There are many who argue for the historical facticity of the resurrection. Some have argued that the biblical evidence for that facticity is convincing. Others, like Pannenberg, concede that the biblical evidence is confusing and might in any case be *post facto* special pleading, but argue that the vibrant faith, courage, and new power in the early church are inexplicable unless Jesus truly rose. Francis Watson[33] has reviewed these arguments and finds them unconvincing. The Gospel accounts of the resurrection are contradictory; the emergence of the belief in the minds of the disciples is not miraculous nor even all that surprising, given the teaching of Jesus about the coming Kingdom of God in a soon-to-be-realized eschaton or Last Day. The evidence of the courage and new power in the early church depends upon accepting Acts as historical, which is not proven – and indeed there is much internal evidence in the Gospels, if form critics are to be believed, which suggests that the mission of the early church to the Palestinian Jews and the Greeks and Romans was not the success that Luke claims.

This is not to say that the resurrection is proved to be unhistorical either. There may be other reasons for believing in a historical resurrection. Schillebeeckx, for example, argues that only a historical resurrection of Jesus could show us that God is truly on the side of the sufferer.[34] Thus we may believe in the resurrection because '. . . the vision provides a solution to the riddle of the world',[35] and all that is required to permit such a belief is that the historical evidence, such that it is, should not be totally incompatible with such a belief.

If Watson is right – and I am convinced he is – then we are not required to believe that Jesus is God because he rose from the dead.

If we believe that he is God, and rose from the dead, there will be other, probably soteriological, reasons for these beliefs. Belief in the resurrection does not prove Jesus is divine; belief that Jesus is divine leads to a belief in the resurrection. This is not how the New Testament presents its case, of course, but it is arguably how the early church reached its beliefs.

A problem for those who wish to argue that the Christian experience of being filled with power is evidence that Jesus as God is the author of that power is that God seems to work through others also who, following other religions and other ways, do not consciously imitate the path of Jesus. It is common for Muslims to argue that the rapid spread of Islam is proof that Muhammad's message was true. Even if in the church today we share much of the experience of earlier Christians, with different perspectives we may place a different interpretation upon that experience.

6. We have reached the point of saying that ultimately claims for the divinity of Jesus arise out of soteriological factors. People found their lives transformed by Jesus. The only explanation for this, or at least the best explanation, seemed to be that for Jesus to have accomplished that transformation he must be divine, however we choose to express that divinity.

However, we have already had to muddle the tidy pattern of the development of the Chalcedonian Definition outlined above. The pattern is not as neat as we had hoped. We need to observe that even in the centuries leading up to Chalcedon not everyone agreed with its logic. Reading the same scriptures, observing the same phenomenon of lives transformed and of church growth, considerable numbers of pre-Chalcedonian Christians thought that the logical implications of this were different. The majority of Jewish people did not see Jesus as divine. As far as we can tell, the lives of the majority of those who met him in the flesh were not transformed – or at least, they did not become disciples. Of those who did, i.e. the early Christian community, there were many early 'heretics' who believed that logic and experience led them to a different conclusion – though the conclusion varied from adoptionism to docetism. Most of the heretics were probably minority opinions, until we reach the arch-heretic Arius. Although Arius was outvoted at Nicaea, the minority which supported him was a very large one, and it continued to support him even after being shown the 'error' of its ways.

Now of course we may still argue that Nicaea and Constantinople and Chalcedon were right; that their logic is better than that of

Arius, Apollinarius et al.; that they are more true to the New Testament and to church experience. What we cannot do is argue that the Chalcedonian interpretation is self-evidently true to all sincere enquirers.

2

The Chalcedonian Definition

We should examine in more detail the logic of Chalcedon. Despite the fact that the existence of two natures in one person is problematic, Chalcedon argued that however mysterious and difficult to understand, the combination was required. Once the interpretation of Jesus as agent of salvation, as source of power and new life, began to emerge, the early church had to explain both to itself and to outsiders how a human Jesus of Nazarath could be offered worship, *proskynesis*, without supporting a two-God theory. The development of trinitarian belief is not part of my study, beyond saying that the church had to develop this compli-cated doctrine because it believed that Jesus did have divine status; and it believed that Jesus had divine status because in no other way could its experience of his saving power be explained.[36] Since by this time the predominant thinking in the church was being done by those brought up in Greek culture, particularly that shaped by Platonic thought, it was inevitable that this philosophy would provide the framework.

Christian thinkers believed that our experience of truth in this world is fleeting and ephemeral, but that beyond mundane experi-ence there is a true nature of all things, which we in this life must try to imitate. Thus for Christians there is a true human nature which we must discover and emulate if we are to be saved and liberated. Jesus is therefore one who '. . . is simultaneously paradigm and imitation; he is the "primal image" in which the tarnished *imago Dei*, man, is at the same time restored'.[37]

But if Jesus is the one who shows us the true nature of humanness, and the one who recreates in us the image of God, he is clearly himself the Creator, or so closely associated with the Creator as to be identified with him. How could this be, without ditheism? The debate went on, becoming more and more sophisticated, for more than 200 years. The church was divided between those who believed that Jesus, the Logos or Word, was divine (Johannine christology had superseded the synoptic models of Jesus) and those who believed with the pre-Chalcedonian 'heretic' Arius that to avoid ditheism the Logos must be less than divine. However, it seemed to his opponents that if Arius was correct, their concept of salvation in Jesus lay ruined.

Chalcedon and the preceding councils did not argue that a full incarnational christology was necessary simply for soteriological reasons. Their members believed that the doctrine was required by scripture and by the traditional worship of Jesus in the church. Nevertheless, although the Chalcedonian fathers may not have been fully conscious of the fact, the scriptural and traditional ascriptions of divinity and 'worshipability' to Jesus themselves arose, as I have suggested, for soteriological reasons.

Athanasius, in his *de Incarnatione*,[38] argued thus:

(i) It is God's intention that his purposes in creation should be fulfilled, and fallen humanity saved.

(ii) Human repentance for sin is not enough to secure that salvation, since human nature has become corrupt and the corruption must be cured.

(iii) Athanasius also has the beginning of the theory that sin must be paid for, and that it is beyond human power to make that satisfaction, although in the context he may possibly mean that the payment has to be made to the devil.

> But since the debt paid by all men had still to be paid, for all . . . had to die, therefore after the proof of his divinity given by his works, he now on behalf of all men offered the sacrifice and surrendered his own temple on behalf of all in order to make them guiltless and free from that first transgression.[39]

(iv) Humanity needed to be shown again the true nature of God in whose image humans are made, since that image has become distorted.

(v) Only one who is truly God, and who also becomes truly human, can cure the corruption, pay the debt, and show us the true likeness of God. To be saved we must be recreated into a new being, have the debt due because of sin paid for us, and be taught what

humans are meant to be. Only one who is God himself can make a
new creation, pay the debt, and give us a true example. Only one
who is truly human can do this on our behalf.

(vi) To prove that Jesus is truly God, Athanasius points to the Old
Testament promise of a Messiah and Suffering Servant, and claims
that no other figure has fulfilled these promises, nor attracted the
worship of pagans. He alleges that no other religion, Greek or
Jewish, has produced any effective change in people. In Christianity, however, Christian virgins and martyrs prove that the grace of
Christ does produce change. Christ's unique healing miracles,[40] in
his earthly life and through the church subsequently, also prove his
divine power. The successful spread of the gospel; the high moral
standard, particularly in sexual matters, of Christian lives;[41] the fact
that fierce savages have been converted to ways of peace;[42] all this
proves that Jesus is God, and that the incarnation, death and
resurrection of Jesus have achieved the redemption of those who
turn to Christ.

With regard to the question of how a person can be both divine
and human, Athanasius as an Alexandrian bypassed the problem by
paying very little attention to the human soul or mind of Jesus. For
Athanasius the Incarnation meant that the Logos, the divine Word,
the second person of the Trinity, took on a human body rather than
human nature. In fact Athanasius did not think that Jesus had a
human mind, that he shared our ignorance, or felt our pains.

> Athanasius displays a general tendency to weaken the character
> of certain of Christ's inner experiences which might be attributed
> to a human soul.[43]
> Athanasius . . . has admitted the Logos . . . as it were in the
> place of the soul.[44]

Thus it was very easy for his friend and admirer Apollinarius to deny
that Jesus even possessed a human mind, and it was only in the
subsequent debate that this issue was grappled with.

What of Athanasius' proofs that Jesus is really God? Hardly any
of them could be advanced seriously even by a conservative
apologist today. Few scholars would suggest now that the Old
Testament authors themselves believed that the promised Messiah
or the Suffering Servant had to be divine. Even if Jesus is the
fulfilment of these promises, this does not therefore in itself require
divinity. So far as evidence for the sanctity of Christian life is
concerned, the moral standards of Christian lives are as mixed as
any other lives. Certainly there are Christian heroes of purity and

sanctity of life – but that is not an apt description of most Christians, and as many heroes could be found amongst followers of other religions. The miracles of Jesus, if historical, can also be matched in many other religions. Colin Brown, who certainly believes in the facticity of the New Testament miracles, is nevertheless clear that the miracles do not in themselves prove the divinity of Jesus, but are part of a 'package'. In Brown's view, the miracles illustrate the teaching of Jesus, and the nature of the God incarnate in Jesus. They are not proofs standing in their own right.[45] Brown, of course, does believe that Jesus was divine and taught of himself that he was divine, but that is another matter. Athanasius' argument from evangelistic success could at some stage or other in history have applied to most of the world religions, certainly Islam and Buddhism – and would be an embarrassment for the church now as it steadily shrinks in membership proportionate to the growth in population.

At the same time, the failure of these 'proofs' is a problem. Athanasius was surely right in expecting that there should be some evidence to which he could point to support his claim that Jesus brings salvation, and if there is little evidence of this kind, the relevance of Jesus is brought into question. This will be something to which we shall return in later chapters.

From Nicaea onwards, Christian consensus has been that Athanasius correctly insisted that an adequate redemption demands an adequate redeemer, and that Jesus is truly, literally, God. Maurice Wiles' questioning of this proposition seems absurdly simple. He makes two criticisms.[46] Athanasius believed that God's intention is for human beings to be restored to non-corruption and to a knowledge of God. They should have the image of God restored in them. Athanasius also assumed that the restorer must himself possess the qualities that he imparts to others. He must himself be incorrupt, perfect, and in full possession of the *imago Dei*. Athanasius assumed this because Plato assumed this. For Plato, something cannot bring into being that which is its opposite. As cold is the opposite of heat, snow cannot bring warmth. Mortality is the opposite of immortality. The soul, since it brings life to the person, cannot itself therefore be mortal; thus Plato believes he has proved the immortality of the soul.[47] By extension Jesus, since he is the bringer of new life, immortality, incorruptibility and divinization, cannot himself be mortal, corruptible, or less than divine.

Wiles points out that although in some contexts it is true that what bestows a quality must itself possess that quality, in many other familiar situations, particularly didactic ones, this is not the case. It is not necessary for ballet teachers to be themselves virtuoso performers. If this were so, no human advance in skill could be possible, since teachers could not impart that which is beyond their own achievements.

Perhaps we might counter this by referring to the indwelling Spirit of God which enables us to surpass ourselves. But Wiles' real *coup-de-grace* lies in his second observation. The restoration of human beings to the image of God, which is what is in Athanasius' mind when he says that Jesus must needs be divine in order to divinize us, does not mean that Athanasius thought we should ourselves become God, but only that we should become restored to innocence of life and by adoption becoming God's children in his image. If we are to be adopted as God's children (and if Plato is right about the qualities necessary in that which bestows), then in order to bestow adopted sonship upon us, Jesus need be only the adopted son of God. The saviour who is logically required in order for corruption in human nature to be cured and for the image of God to be shown forth once more, is a saviour who is truly human, and who through obedience and total commitment to God becomes, by God's grace, an adopted child, the first to be so adopted, one who becomes first what we hope to become later. A Saviour who is God by nature, equally divine with the Father, would seem to be precluded, since his divinity is of a different kind from ours, and therefore cannot be communicated to us.

Part of Athanasius' point is that if humans are restored to innocence, this is in effect a new creation, and only God can recreate. However, it seems equally logical to posit that while the restoration *is* a new creation, God does this new creating, and Jesus is the first in this new creation. In that case he would not be a God but a human being restored to the image of God, and as an obedient servant of God, a human agent of this recreation.

There is one other aspect of Athanasius' argument, not much stressed by Athanasius himself, but which in due course would become the major emphasis in the church's reasons for requiring belief in the divinity of Jesus: the need for a divine saviour who alone could pay off the debt of sin. This was to be given its classical expression in Anselm's *Cur Deus Homo?*[48] We shall examine this in more detail later. At this point, I will only remark that it is at least debatable whether a satisfaction theory is really necessary. If, through grace, true repentance and true amendment is possible, does God's justice still require the payment of an infinite debt of sin; is his justice not adequately protected by repentance and amendment?

Athanasius' insistence upon the divinity of Christ was brought sharply into focus during the debate in the church about Arius. Arius' concern was to defend the unity of God; hence his insistence that the Logos was not to be called 'God' except in a purely honorific sense. Since it is not our concern here to enter into the debate about the Trinity, we need only notice that part of the reason for insisting on a trinitarian doctrine arose out of the conviction of the early church that in order to bring salvation, Jesus must be the Logos, and the Logos must be God in the fullest sense. We, however, are beginning to question whether this conviction is necessary.

Having sided with Athanasius against Arius at Nicaea, the pre-Chalcedonian debate moved on to a concern about the unity of the person of Jesus. We have noted that Athanasius and the Alexandrian school generally paid minimal attention to the individual humanity of Jesus. In their eyes, he became Man (i.e. human) rather than 'a man'. Arius would have agreed with them. Whether Jesus had a human soul was not yet a question which had made itself felt.

> It is probably undeniable that in his [i.e. Athanasius'] picture of Christ, the soul of Christ retracts well into the background even if it doesn't disappear completely.[49]

The issue was soon to come to the foreground, however, with the controversy surrounding Apollinarius. Apollinarius said that Jesus did not possess a human soul. The Cappadocians countered that since the human soul was precisely that part of humanness which had become corrupt, unless the Saviour possessed a human soul no salvation could happen. The Council of Constantinople agreed.

Unless one shares with the Cappadocians the strong view of human solidarity which they inherited from Paul and the early church, the arguments both ways seem rather forced. Is there an eternal and unchanging human essence or nature? Were Neanderthals and Cro-Magnons human? This would not be a fair question to pose in retrospect to the early church, but with our more panoramic view of human evolution and development we cannot avoid posing it to ourselves. This is an example of the difficulty of retaining christological definitions framed in a different culture and world view. Can we still believe in an eternal human nature for the Logos to assume?

Why must the Logos as healer assume the nature of the unhealed? Wiles questions whether a doctor needs to become tuberculotic to heal tuberculosis, or a psychiatrist become psychotic to heal the mentally ill. Of course the Cappadocians were not arguing that Jesus became sinful to heal sinners, only that he became human; and their reason for insisting is again the same Platonic conviction that in order to impart a quality, the imparter must itself/himself possess that quality. Jesus imparted restored human nature to us, therefore he must himself possess perfect human nature.

But unless we can give some meaningful content to 'human nature' apart from particularized kind of humans, this belief is vacuous. And if Jesus became merely a *particularized* kind of human – a first-century Jew living in Palestine – and if the Platonic view outlined above is correct, then how is his incarnation relevant to other kinds of humans? Further, how can God become a particular kind of human being without being limited; how can Jesus be fully divine and fully yet 'particularizedly' human? We may argue that because in his humanity he was limited to a particular time and place, he must also be divine in order to be universally relevant to all humanity of all time. We may also argue that although humans differ from age to age, there is still a common thread running through all human life, and that Jesus' life on earth can still be relevant to us now in our different age without his having to be God. The truth is that our concept of human nature, and what would constitute 'perfect' human nature, is as fuzzy as our concept of God, and the problem of a particular person being a universal saviour lives with us still. Neither Chalcedon with its divine Jesus nor the Enlightenment with its Jesus as ideal human person have resolved the problem of what universal or ideal human characteristics are.

Apollinarius was aware of the problem of the particular and the universal, which was why he insisted that Jesus was not fully human but human only in body. Nestorius was aware of the problem, which is why he tried to keep the two natures of Jesus separate. The Council of Chalcedon, influenced by Cyril's fear of a 'two-sons' theory, rejected Nestorius' solution – and it is not clear that Nestorius himself really believed that a separation of the natures in Jesus made sense, or to what extent he shared the two-sons theory of Diodore. Chalcedon quite rightly said that one person, if he is a whole person and not schizophrenic, must have one will. Of course all of us have periods of inner conflict, with two opposing wills pulling us in different directions. But a whole, healthy person has to resolve this conflict.

Chalcedon, then, lays down the limits for the church of what is permissible doctrine. Jesus must be fully human, fully divine, the two natures united in one will. As to how this can be possible, Chalcedon has no answer. Nicaea had already decided that Jesus must be regarded as God. Consideration of the unity of Jesus seemed to demand, therefore, that although he dwelt in a human body he did not have a human soul, since then he would have had two wills, two driving forces in his personhood. However, soteriological considerations led Constantinople and Chalcedon to insist that he did have a human soul. How that soul operated, or what this combination of statements meant in fact, was a problem that Chalcedon shelved for later generations.

3

The Authority of Bible and Councils

In many ways the problem referred to above is more acute than ever for us now, but more of that a little later. If our view is that what general councils of the church have decided is unalterably true, then the problem is just one we have to live with. This is, of course, the situation for many Christians. 'Biblical' Christians argue that if it is in the Bible, it must be true, whatever the logical problems – and human logic is never the equal of God's logic, so one or two problems in comprehending need not worry us unduly. 'Catholic' Christians argue that if undivided councils of the church say it, it must be true, whatever the logical problems. (Of course, exactly which constituted the undivided councils is debated – Roman Catholics would say that Vatican II is an undivided council of the true church.) A cursory knowledge of the history of even those councils leading up to Chalcedon raises questions about how genuinely representative of the churches they were, in view of the jerrymandering and rigging of votes. The Council of Ephesus in 431 CE was an example of the conciliar process at its nadir, but even the Council of Chalcedon was a meeting where 'unholy passions mingled with political ambitions and intrigues were . . . at work'.[50]

There are all sorts of subtleties within these claims for biblical and conciliar authority. Almost everyone concedes a degree of cultural conditioning in their formulations. Because the evangelists believed in a 'three-decker universe' of underworld, world and heaven, that does not mean that even fundamentalist modern Christians share that view. Many traditional Christians would concede that the language of Chalcedon assumes Greek philosophical concepts which we no longer share, and that even the comparison of Greek terms such as *ousia* and *hypostasis* with their Latin equivalents of *substantia* and *persona* led to misunderstandings, as the terms were not exact equivalents. When not only the language but the concepts are translated into, for example, modern English language and culture, the problems are greater still. We may allow for this by insisting that only the essential kernel of the traditional teaching be preserved, and not the philosophical expression of that kernel, which will change from age to age and culture to culture; but whether a naked kernel exists without a philosophical framework is questionable, and determining what is the kernel and what the disposable philosophical husk makes the authority of the conciliar definitions seem at best somewhat unclear.

Nevertheless it would be an injustice and a mistake to regard traditionalists wishing to remain faithful to the Chalcedonian definition as obscurantist. Even though they may insist that the essentials of Chalcedonian christology must be preserved, they do not regard Chalcedon as the final word on the subject. Karl Rahner, for example, says of credal formulae:

> But these derive their life from the fact that they are not the end, but the beginning; not goals, but means, truths which open the way to the – ever greater – Truth.[51]

And Mascall:

> It will be my purpose to argue here that the Definition of Chalcedon is the truth and nothing but the truth, but also that it is not the whole truth.[52]

Mascall goes on to outline a number of questions which Chalcedon does not answer, and which require an answer: how a particular man in a particular set of historical events can be a universal saviour; how Jesus can be divine and yet humanly limited in knowledge; how the incarnation of God in Christ is relevant to other religions. Klaas Runia as a conservative Protestant concedes the ambiguity of the Chalcedonian Definition[53] and that the terms used, or their English equivalents, have changed in meaning over the years.

Nevertheless, traditional Christians still retain the belief that, however mysteriously, Jesus is fully God and fully man, and they believe that if this mystery is abandoned, the experience of Christ in the church over the centuries will be denied or at least truncated.

It is important to take tradition seriously. Every new age has its own insights and every age its own blindnesses. There is a real danger that if with twentieth-century arrogance we reject traditional formulations as being disproved by modern knowledge, we shall be slaves of this blindness. There is a suitable humility in conceding that, even though such formulations may seem to us to be more mystery than enlightenment, another and later age may perceive again truths that at present are impenetrable for us. The insights of the past need to be taken seriously as the ground and springboard of our own understanding. Wiles himself argues that in part the test of the truthfulness of our own reformulations will be the extent to which they preserve the genuine insights of the past.[54] There is always some similarity between present and past situations, a certain perennialness about human nature. John Macquarrie's formative factors in theology[55] include tradition along with experience, revelation, scripture, culture and reason, and 'theology must hold a nice balance or tension among the formative factors'.[56] Macquarrie does not say whether these are equal factors, nor what one does if they lead one to contradictory conclusions – that is, if tradition and reason seem to clash. Elsewhere[57] Macquarrie refuses to defend traditional Christian belief on fideistic grounds. Our doctrine of Christ must be true to what we know of his history and his historical effects, and to our experience of things as they actually are. Our experience of truth is an inward, subjective, intuitive apprehension, which we then with some inevitable clumsiness try to express verbally.

Wiles says that doctrine is the intuitive combination of scripture, tradition, prayer and liturgy with reason and common sense, but that in the final outcome doctrine must be coherent: it must make sense, and hold all these factors together in a logical way. He also pleads, sensibly, for economy or parsimony, seeking for what the evidence requires us to say in the most economic way, not for what the evidence will allow us to say.[58]

In our own reformulation of doctrine, then, we cannot disregard what scripture and tradition say about Jesus. What we find in fact is that both scripture and tradition say many things about Jesus. We need to ask ourselves why they say what they do, what their experience was that led them to say this, whether it matches our own experience and makes sense. Those things which seem to us to contain logical fallacies, or to be inconsistent with our own experience, we will not reject out of hand, for it might be our own limitation of knowledge and experience which make it impossible for us at present to understand – but we will put such things aside as not being useful at present. Stewart Sutherland says of his own revisionary approach that:

> There is much that has been central to that tradition which I shall either discard or leave on one side like an engine idling in neutral gear with apparently no role to play in the affairs of life.[59]

Perhaps on the other hand Schillebeeckx is right when he says that despite the great cultural changes between the time of the New Testament and Chalcedon, or between Chalcedon and us, there is always still some link or connection with what went before.

> Chalcedon . . . has something meaningful to say, while . . . it may irritate and alienate.[60]

Since Schillebeeckx sits somewhat lightly to the Chalcedonian Definition, however, he is interpreting 'meaningful' rather widely. Clearly the church of Chalcedon, like the church of the New Testament, bore witness to the truth that Jesus was, in their experience, the source of their own salvation. As I ask myself whether, and how, Jesus is the source of salvation now, I shall argue, with Wiles, that it is our own reason and experience which must be the final arbiter of what we choose from scripture and tradition as being useful at present, while we try to be open to and to understand the experience of those who have gone before us. It is our reason and our reasoned interpretation of our own experience that is normative, not scripture or tradition. Just because scripture or traditional formulations say something does not alone make that normative doctrine – and I defend this stand partly on the grounds that neither scripture nor tradition has a single doctrine of Jesus; rather, they present us with a number of different insights, from which we have to choose. However, those concepts which we find contrary to our own reason and experience we do not reject, but merely put aside. For the present, we need to work only with those insights which are consistent with a logical, economical interpretation of our own experience, building upon insights from the past.

Brian Hebblethwaite says of Wiles' concept of parsimony that while he does not disagree with it, the concept should not be used in a restrictive way.

> My objection is not to the criterion of economy as such . . . my objection rather is to stress an economy to the neglect of comprehensiveness.[61]

He concedes that we cannot hold a doctrine in the face of contradictory evidence, but that we should not limit ourselves to believe only what the evidence requires.

> . . . we need to beware of thinking that historical evidence alone must be seen to necessitate such an interpretation before we can allow ourselves to accept it. [62]

I think we need to go a little further than this. Much of the doctrine handed on to us from the past will not be contradictory to what can be proved by historical evidence, but will not be required by that evidence either. Does that mean we should continue to believe everything from the past, unless it is proved to be untrue? Hebblethwaite argues that since those arguing within the church live in a tradition, they cannot abandon that position unless it is proved false. [63] Alister McGrath argues the same point at greater length. [64]

I am not arguing for restriction of belief to that which is consistent with hard evidence; but traditional belief did not emerge in a vacuum. It arose out of the socially and culturally conditioned experience of our forebears. If our own socio-cultural environment no longer requires the same interpretation as that of our forebears, or if we no longer have that experience, the specific belief in question will not be usable by us. We may not be able to prove that it is not true. Indeed, we should keep an open mind lest a wider experience or a broader understanding shows us that there is a reason for the belief after all. Without some comparable experience, however, and without some shared understanding of the nature of that experience, the belief cannot really work for us.

Hebblethwaite points out that many traditional doctrines – the creation, the Fall – have had to be restated in a different way in the light of new knowledge and evidence, without abandonment of these doctrines, [65] and suggests that the doctrine of the Incarnation can likewise survive. This is only true, however, if by 'survive' we mean in a radically changed form. The doctrine of creation can fairly easily be restated in evolutionary terms without loss. The doctrine of the fall surely cannot. We can no longer easily believe in a literal fall. To say '. . . the doctrine of the Fall is more profoundly grasped when it is articulated in terms of the radical gap between human achievement and the divine purpose.'[66] is to say that 'fall' does not literally mean fall, but a falling short. The doctrine then is no longer about a state of human perfection once existent but now lost. We may still have a doctrine of human falling short, but it does not mean what it once did. To say 'the doctrine of the Incarnation is more profoundly grasped when it is articulated in terms of human kenosis' is surely to invite a similar response. It represents a considerable change from what the doctrine of Incarnation once meant. Liberal Christians may then put forward a concept of Incarnation suggesting that Jesus is a human agent of God rather than being himself ontologically divine, without being charged with disloyalty to inherited tradition. They surely have as much warrant to do this as has Hebblethwaite to put forward his radically revised fall or kenotic incarnational theories.

We need, then, to find the interpretation that fits our own experience, and that part of the experience of our forebears with which we can still identify, as logically and as economically as possible. Mascall, for example, quotes extensively from the works of modern French christologists to show that it is logically possible to believe that Jesus is divine without denying his true humanity, with sophisticated arguments about the nature of human consciousness.[67] His intention is to show that the mystery of christological doctrine does not mean that it is illogical or nonsense. Using Wiles' principle of economy or 'parsimony', I shall be suggesting that this effort is not really useful. Later in this book, I shall explore our own experience and interpretation of salvation, and I shall be suggesting, in the light of that exploration, how I can best understand what 'salvation' means. I will be suggesting further that for this concept of salvation to work, there is not the same logical necessity for Jesus to be 'consubstantial with the Father', equally divine with the Father. A humanly obedient Jesus makes more sense to us, is more true to our experience and our interpretation of the evidence, and still provides the salvation that we need. A principle of economy in explanation must lead us to choose the simpler explanation. The unresolved mystery of Chalcedon as to how in one person a fully divine and a fully human nature can be united is, on this argument, an unnecessary mystery.

There is, however, an inevitable degree of tentativeness about this judgment. Subsequent experience and reinterpretation may show that salvation does mean what Anselm or other traditional theorists have suggested, and that a logical *sequitur* is that Jesus is, after all, both divine and human. At that point, Mascall's arguments become useful again. For the present, I shall suggest[68] that the most coherent view of salvation does not require us to believe that Jesus is both divine and human, and that the belief is therefore an unnecessary complication which makes the practice of religion more difficult.

4

Modern Problems with Chalcedon

Our understanding of the world, of human nature, and of the history and place of humans in the world, even our understanding of the Bible and the New Testament, has changed since Chalcedon. Because inevitably our understanding of God is linked with our understanding of ourselves and of the world, the concept of God has changed too – if in no other respect than that events which in a prescientific era could only be explained by the direct agency of God are now seen to have their own causation within the natural laws of the universe. Christological doctrine is affected by our understanding of God, of human nature, and of the world. A number of ways in which our understanding has changed are set out below.

They amount to the implications for christology of modern science, modern psychology, modern biblical criticism, and modern (or at least post-Aristotelian) philosophy. The term 'the Enlightenment' is used in this book in a very generalized sense to refer to all those, from the Cambridge Platonists on, who claimed to prefer reason to dogma. Following the trauma of Reformation and Counter-Reformation, with the associated massacres, inquisitions, burnings, all in the name of religion, there was a fairly general tendency from the late seventeenth century onwards to stress the value of each individual's reason. Scientific advances from Newton through Darwin to Einstein made it seem as though the real key to discovering truth lay not in theology but in the empirical sciences. The supernatural, the miraculous, were all suspect. Hume and Kant had shown that the traditional proofs for God's existence from cosmology or teleology were shaky. The very existence of God was questioned – though not so much in public, for fear of reprisals. The traditional sources of revelation were seen to be the products of human rather than of divine agency. The human element in the authorship of the Bible was increasingly recognized. The human element in the formulation of church doctrine had become all too apparent, as Catholic spokesmen and the various rival reformers all made their differing claims to speak with the authentic Christian voice. Colonial expansionism brought Europe back in touch with the great world religions, so that the cultural relativity of particular religious doctrines became clearer, as well as the fact that wisdom and virtue were to be found outside as well as within the church. There was no one single philosophical outlook that dominated the scene, as Platonism and Aristotelianism had done successively in earlier generations. There was no longer one single Christian voice either; separated churches taught diverse and contradictory doctrines. But into this vacuum of uncertainty, a claimant for renewed optimism and certainty was offering its comforts. There was great optimism about the power of human reason, aided by human discovery about the world in which we live. The human conscience, too, could discern right from wrong without the necessity of imposed dogma. If all followed their reason and conscience, then the potential for the human race was boundless, provided that the merchants of obscurantism – church, monarchy, overweening state – were kept in check.

Within the Enlightenment as I have defined it there were different views. Not all Enlightenment or post-Enlightenment thinkers shared all these features. Nor would we necessarily agree with all of them ourselves. Modern scientific indeterminism – the conflicting wave/particle theories are usually offered as an example of this point – means that Newtonian positivism about the models of physics no longer hold. Some philosophers tentatively defend again the Thomist and even Anselmian views for God's existence. After two world wars, the holocaust and the threat of nuclear destruction, it is hard to maintain unmixed optimism about the advance of the human race.

It is true, as well, that the philosophers of the Enlightenment had their own unconscious cultural biases. Their rigid exclusion of all that they regarded as supernatural we suspect to be as arbitrary and doctrinaire as the views of those whom they opposed. After all, the validity of a decision to discount any evidence or experience but that derived from the empirical senses is notoriously unable to be proved on empirical grounds. Alvin Plantinga[69] with his notion of basic and properly basic beliefs has made a possible case for the equal, or even superior, validity of traditional theism. With regard to biblical authority, by no means all modern biblical scholars would share the extreme scepticism concerning the New Testament records of the nineteenth century reconstructers of the 'Lives of Jesus'.

Nevertheless for all this, biblical scholarship, even of a conservative nature, makes it virtually impossible for us to regard the Bible as a source of revelation in exactly the same way as before. Modern scientific knowledge may have its indeterminacies, but at a micro- rather than a macro-level. We can no longer revert to an earth-centred view of the universe, or to a naive creationism, or to belief in an unhistorical Garden of Eden, or to a pre-Freudian view of human nature. Between ourselves and the world of Archbishop Ussher[70] there is a great gulf fixed.

> Ours is the post-Enlightenment world, however fragmented and pluriform we find that world to be, and however critical of that world we may become. There have been changes of permanent significance since ancient and mediaeval times.[71]

So we set out to look at some of these changes.

1. Maurice Wiles[72] suggests that it is arguable that the Chalcedonian Definition arose as much out of the fathers' understanding of creation as out of soteriological considerations. Patristic belief generally, if we exclude Irenaeus, was that God created Adam and Eve, literally the forebears of the human race, in a state of perfection. Paradise was a brief golden age. Adam and Eve were perfect human beings, possessing superhuman powers, blessed with superhuman knowledge, and possessing immortality by nature. With the fall, all that was lost. Human power and knowledge became more limited; immortality was lost. In order to restore humans to their proper destiny, God had to recreate humanity through a new Man – and, since the divine Logos was the agent of God in the first creation, it was necessary that the Logos be the agent of the new. Thus, the Logos became the new Man.

There is already a problem in this scenario, implicit even in Paul. Belief in a literal Adam and Eve makes it possible to understand how humans are one with Adam and his fall. We would be Adam's descendents, we would share his genes, we would have, perhaps, a shared 'family' responsibility. But how do we explain the solidarity of Christians with Jesus as their new Adam? There is no genetic link. Paul uses the imagery of dying and rebirth in Christ, but exactly what that means is problematic, as even Moule concedes.

Biological solidarity with Adam was (for Paul) a fact; mystical solidarity with Christ is a metaphysical theory.

Few Christians now believe in paradisal humanity as a literal historical fact. We may explain the Fall as the cumulative effect of generations of human sin, but we no longer believe that there ever was an original man who was perfectly good, with all the super-human powers of the traditional Adam. We may want to argue that Neanderthal humanity had a certain naive moral innocence, but that is beside the point. Early Christian belief did not see Jesus as the new Neanderthal. It makes more sense for us to see in Jesus a prototype of future humanity than a recreation of a past Adamic figure. Thus salvation for us is not a reaching back into the past, a recreation of that which had become marred, but a reaching forward into the future. In that respect our understanding of salvation is of necessity radically different from that of Chalcedon.

It would be untrue to say that all the pre-Chalcedonian Fathers thought the same about Adam, although of course they all believed that Adam was literally the forefather of the human race. Irenaeus, although he believed that Jesus was a recapitulation of Adam, also believed that Adam himself was '. . . morally, spiritually and intellectually a child', who because of his '. . . very weakness and inexperience . . .' was almost bound to fall into sin.[73] Adam was not perfect Man.

Irenaeus could not be expected to understand fully the force of his own argument. In a post-Freudian age, however, we know that the human will is determined by more than the power of reason. Our understanding of things, and the decisions we take in the light of that understanding, are inevitably flawed not only because our rational and moral knowledge is imperfect, like Irenaeus' Adam, but by the unconscious effect upon us of environment, upbringing, childhood experiences and many other factors which we do not understand. This is what it means to be human. There never was a human being who could make perfectly rational decisions unaffected by these extra-rational factors.

If Jesus was fully human, the same must have applied to him. His knowledge and power must have been human, and therefore limited and imperfect. Scholastic theologians could talk about Jesus in his human knowledge possessing infused knowledge as well as experiential, learned knowledge. Rahner and some other contemporary theologians reinterpret this and talk of Jesus' prereflective, primordial consciousness of himself and his world. Nevertheless, as Gerald O'Collins concedes, there must have been real limitations in the knowledge of the human Jesus.[74] A pre-reflective knowledge is not the same as a fully reflective, fully interpreted knowledge, and is really, in Rahner's own terms, only an openness, a sort of vague hunch (a 'Vorgriff'), towards that full knowledge and understanding.

This is a particular problem for traditional theism with its belief in the omnipotence and omniscience of God. How can Jesus be omnipotent and all-knowing and yet truly human? The kenoticists[75] in varying degrees of sophistication from Thomasius of Erlangen to Vincent Taylor tried to suggest ways in which the incarnate God in Jesus divested himself of these 'omni-s'. Their critics pointed out that this implies change in God, which for traditional theism is out of the question. If, rather, we wish to say with Taylor that these 'omni-s' are latent but still present during the Incarnation, and that God has therefore not changed in his nature but only in his relationship with the world, this comes close to meaninglessness. If latent, how are the divine qualities in Jesus present in any meaningful way? What can latent omniscience mean? However, since clearly some kenosis is nevertheless absolutely necessary if the humanity of Jesus is to be any kind of true humanity, critics like Brunner have said that kenotic theory errs in trying to explain the human psychology of the God-man, which by its nature must be mysterious and impenetrable to us.

> We can only understand [the self-consciousness] of Jesus rightly if we understand it not psychologically but purely positively.[76]

In what way the divine consciousness of the Son functions while he is incarnate is not revealed to us.

Thus Mascall suggests,

> It is, I suggest, futile for us to try to guess what it feels like to be God incarnate.[77]

Brian Hebblethwaite believes that some kind of kenotic theory is necessary if Jesus is to be seen as truly human.

> In no way do we follow the 'docetic' tendencies of early Christianity, which found it hard to believe . . . that Jesus shared the limitations of human psychology and cognition.[78]

Hebblethwaite, while regarding himself as a defender of Chalcedonian orthodoxy, still says

It is highly implausible for us in the light of informed and critical study of the New Testament, as well as of philosophical and psychological realism about what it is to be a man, to suppose that Jesus knew himself to be or thought of himself as divine.[79]

Thus Hebblethwaite grants that our christology needs to be adapted, not only because of the assault of post-Enlightenment views about human nature, but also because of the findings of biblical criticism. However, he thinks that recognition that the human Jesus must have had limitations of psyche and knowledge does not rule out belief in Jesus as God and human, because we know so little about the nature of God or of human nature.[80] Also, since humans are made in the image of God, there is no alien incompatibility between divine and human nature.[81] Despite his human limitations, the divine authority, power, and effect upon people still shines through in Jesus.[82]

However, as soon as Hebblethwaite comes to consider how Jesus can have had a human consciousness and yet be God, we seem to revert, as with Mascall, to mystery once more.

It is at this point that we must remember that we are struggling to speak of the infinite, internally differentiated being of God, whose own eternal love, given and received within the Trinity, is mirrored in the love of Jesus for the Father.[83]

If Jesus is divine, then it must be true that his self-consciousness will be mysterious and largely unknowable to us. I agree with Mascall that our own self-knowledge is mysterious enough, so that the addition of additional mystery is not in itself unacceptable. I agree with Hebblethwaite's observations that many liberal theologians have a concept of God which is just as paradoxical and problematic as the divine/human concept concerning Jesus,[84] so that Chalcedonian refuge into mystery is not a closed-shop activity. Thomas Morris shows that a kenotic concept could be defended as not being illogical. He prefers a different approach by means of which to show that Jesus can be omnipotent and yet operate with a human mind.[85] A kenotic approach, for Morris, has too weak a concept of the immutability of God, and deals unsatisfactorily with the modalities of divine attributes. Nevertheless, for Morris, if his own two-minds theory should be shown to be untenable, the kenotic approach would not be illogical. The question is whether it is in fact necessary. The mystery certainly makes an understanding of Jesus less attainable for us. If we stay with Wiles' principle of economy – that we do not bring into our explanation extra complications which are not required – then the struggles of the kenotic school are beside the point, unless we are shown that a less than fully divine Jesus has no soteriological significance for us. We shall give our attention to this later.

The problem is compounded for us once we take into account the environmental and developmental factors raised by modern psychology. Jesus, as a human person, must have been influenced by unconscious cultural factors. He must have shared not only the limitations of knowledge of his time but also the prejudices and moral blindnesses. Not to have done so would mean that he did not have a human personality, since this is at least partly how personality is formed. Human personality does not exist in a vacuum, but exists in relationship to other persons, who affect and change the person that I am.

Indeed there is possible scriptural evidence that Jesus did have moral blindnesses and cultural prejudices. His reported vituperative attitude to the Pharisees[86] was, in the light of our understanding of Pharisaic teaching, unjustified. If Vermes is to be believed, much of Jesus' teaching is what the Pharisees themselves taught. The Pharisees were not the hypocritical 'whited sepulchres' of the Gospels, and though 'there is little doubt that the Pharisees disliked his non-conformity and would have preferred him to abstain from healing on the sabbath where life was not in danger',[87] the Pharisees themselves approved of suspending sabbath rules in order to save life. For them every part of life was invested with religious significance, so that the minutiae of religious observance were important as they seem not to have been for Jesus. Jesus' lack of empathy with the reasons for Pharisaic attention to detail may be seen to be understandable in the light of his human attempts to reform Judaism, but is lacking in the balance and fairness we would expect of a divine being.

Jesus seems also to have shared the Jewish xenophobia of the time. His interchange with the Syro-Phoenician woman,[88] his initial reluctance to help her, his rudeness in addressing her as a dog, is an embarrassment. He seems as a teenager to have shown a typical self-centredness in his absorption with his own affairs and his own dignity to the exclusion of any understanding and concern for his parents in their natural worry when he went missing for three days.[89] He seems to have shared the male chauvinist prejudices of his time in his manner of address to his mother.[90] He even seems to have made a human error of judgment in including Judas amongst his twelve closest companions.

Looked at from a human perspective, none of this need worry us. He seems to have learned from his mistakes. He did, after all, befriend a Pharisee in Nicodemus. He was impressed by the Syro-Phoenician woman's persistence and courage and changed his attitude to her. He made provision for his mother's welfare from the cross. None of these initial limitations in his attitude are culpable – all are fully explained by factors such as immaturity, upbringing and cultural conditioning. For humans, not only cognitive knowledge but morality and values have to be learned through experience. Any moral immaturity in Jesus, however, makes it more difficult to understand what is meant by saying that Jesus is God, though if Morris' two-minds theory is accepted, the problem is not logically insuperable. Nevertheless, the necessary logical argument becomes more and more complex, and less parsimonious.

Of course, since we have raised caveats about the historicity of some of the Gospel stories, and since certainly some of these stories come from what the form critics would regard as legendary material, perhaps these accounts are not historically accurate. Perhaps Jesus' prejudices against the Pharisees are really the prejudices of Matthew's church community. But if Jesus was truly human, some such blindnesses and errors must have happened, or else he did not develop in a truly human way. Thus whether or not the scriptural accounts are historical is not material to the point.

Perhaps it is a mistake to think that Jesus' humanity, his growth in knowledge and consciousness and moral values, was like our own? Stephen Sykes suggests that liberal Christians are illogical. They want Jesus to be fully human like us for soteriological reasons – for if his life is not human, how can his life be of relevance to those of us who are human? – and they think that a human Jesus who is also divine is not like us. But unless Jesus is unique, is different from us, Sykes asks how he can save us anyway.

> But this is the exact point of the greatest difficulty. If we deny that there is anything remarkable about Jesus, if Jesus really was an ordinary fallible human being and no more, then our Christology has no basis in fact . . . Can Jesus both be ordinary *and* a climacteric?[91]

Mascall makes much the same point.[92] If these critics are right, liberal Christians are in a cul-de-sac. They cannot have a purely human Jesus who is also a saviour. Hebblethwaite develops the point further: liberal Christians cannot easily have a Jesus who is humanly conditioned and who is not divine, but who is still of universal human significance.[93]

Sykes does not underestimate the contrary problem of understanding a Jesus who is both divine and human. In fact he adds further dimensions to it. He asks whether Jesus was ever childishly selfish and harsh – and if not, was he a truly human child? Was his consciousness a masculine self-consciousness? And if not, how was he a true man? And yet, if his consciousness was that of a man rather than that of a woman, how is his incarnation of relevance to women? Nevertheless, in Sykes' view, for soteriological reasons we must, in faith if not in full knowledge, claim that Jesus was at every stage of his life perfect with a perfection that befits that stage; he was not merely like us, or else his life is irrelevant to us, and he is not a Saviour. We are back with the same issue: it is difficult to understand how Jesus can be God and man, but we must accept the mystery as a concomitant of salvation.

Schillebeeckx points out that from Lessing and the Enlightenment on, people have assumed that Jesus' relevance to us is that he enables us to reach a truer humanity or 'humanum' – but that the nature of the humanum is not necessarily clear to us.

> Our age has come to see that mankind does not have at its beck and call this humanum; what is truly worthy of man is not something we all know and have within our power.[94]

The nineteenth-century liberals perhaps deserve Sykes' rebuttal. It is always dangerous to decide what the truth is on *a priori* grounds and then interpret the evidence to suit the truth. Like the deists before them, the many Life of Jesus authors in the nineteenth-century had already decided that miracles were impossible, the virgin birth out of the question; that to be human meant to be just like themselves – and then had to face the challenge as to why they bothered with such a Jesus at all.

Our view of what it is to be human now is not quite the same as it was in the nineteenth century. The factors which we are discussing in this chapter were beginning to make themselves felt then but are now much clearer. I shall suggest that in view of these factors it is more difficult for us to make sense of Jesus as fully divine. I am not, like the nineteenth-century liberals, ruling this out *a priori*. If it can be shown, as Chalcedon and Christians throughout the ensuing centuries believed, that unless Jesus is divine no salvation is conceivable, then I will concede that Mascall's pointers to the work of the French christologists, and their efforts to show how Jesus could conceivably have been God and yet possess a properly human consciousness, and Sykes' suggestion (with many others) that it is possible in faith to make some sense of the mystery of the human/ divine nature of Jesus, would all be helpful. I shall be suggesting later in this book, however, that traditional views of salvation are not the most useful or relevant ways of understanding salvation in view of the problems which face humans today, and that with a different concept of salvation, we no longer need the same emphasis on the divinity of Jesus. If this is indeed the case, then the factors to be discussed in the following paragraphs become more decisive.

2. Cupitt makes the point [95] that we cannot be as human-centred in our view of the cosmos as was once the case, nor as grandiose in our concept of human importance. In the cosmos, the earth is a tiny and transient entity, with a very brief history in cosmic terms. The period over which humans have been present in that brief history is infinitesimal. To believe that the incarnation of God as a man is of cosmic significance is harder to accept than it was. Paul's 'whole creation groaning and travailing' until Jesus sets it free (Rom. 8.22) seems a somewhat aggrandized notion. We shall see below that even the much reduced concept of Jesus as being of universal human significance is not without difficulty. To say he is of cosmic significance is harder still.

Thomas Morris says that the cosmic insignificance of humanity is not such a new concept. He quotes Psalm 83.4 to make his point:

> They [the enemies of God] say, 'Come, let us wipe them out as a nation; let the name of Israel be remembered no more!'

He says that it is not necessarily true that smallness, or newness, implies insignificance. [96] Cupitt is following Thomas Paine or Ralph Waldo Emerson in concluding that the vastness of the cosmos renders Christian claims arrogant or anthropocentric; but in fact the significance of humanity lies, for the theist, purely in the fact that God has chosen humans for his purposes. The existence of other worlds or other aeons of time before humanity appeared on the scene is no argument for denying the centrality of human destiny in God's plans.

The possibility of other rational beings in other worlds raises the problem of human incarnation again. Paul and Linda Badham argue that it is statistically likely that there are countless millions of planets where there is, has been, and will be, rational life. Either such beings have not sinned, in which case humans are surely of less importance and value than they are, or more likely (since, for the

Badhams, like Schleiermacher, sin is a virtually inevitable result of living in a physical world), they have sinned, in which case God must have been redemptively incarnate in all these millions of planets. Since the planets exist in time, even if God does not, there is no time for God to be successively incarnated in them all. Thus, say the Badhams, the received ideas about both incarnation and atonement need to be substantially revised.[97]

This may seem a very speculative, pernickety argument, since we do not know for certain that any such rationally inhabited planets occur. Also, traditional theology has always believed in the existence of sinless angels without that cutting across belief in the specialness of humans. The matter is easily resolved by saying that God simply chose to love humans specially. Morris shows that multiple, even simultaneous, incarnations, if shown to be theologically necessary, are not logically impossible. To put it rather roughly, if Morris is right and Jesus possessed simultaneously and distinctly a divine and a human mind[98] and this constitutes the Incarnation, there is no logical reason why he cannot possess simultaneously a divine + human + Martian + Venusian (or whatever) mind, incarnate on earth and Mars and Venus and however many more planets are required, all at the same time.

Nevertheless, while an anthropocentric view of the world may be logically possible, and while a full incarnational christology is thus not ruled out, it must surely be conceded that these views are made somewhat more problematic, somewhat less self-evidently true, than was earlier the case. Pre-Copernican anthropology fits more easily with the idea of God becoming uniquely incarnate in human form. Even if we may claim no more than this, it makes it more important to show why traditional incarnational views are still the best way to explain our present combination of knowledge and experience.

3. Biblical criticism has brought about two rather contradictory results. On the one hand we are more keenly aware that there are a number of different theologies operating in the New Testament and not one single overriding view. We have also become aware that the theological interests of the New Testament authors and of the early church which was the cradle of the New Testament have coloured and shaped their account of the historical Jesus. What seemed in the past to be the teaching of Jesus himself turns out in many cases to be the reflective teaching of the post-resurrection church. The authority of the New Testament has been weakened, or at least been shown to have a greater human element than was earlier realized.

On the other hand, careful use of the tools of biblical criticism has enabled us to build up something of a more reliable picture of the historical Jesus. Although most scholars would concede that these results are tenuous, the picture of Jesus which emerges is, while attractive, a very human picture: a prophetic figure, affected by the cultural and historical viewpoint of his own people, shaped by the rabbinic tradition, with a deep love of God and a sense of the closest personal intimacy with him.

He seems to have been subject to many of the same failings that any growing human person experiences – childhood self-centred-ness, male chauvinism, ethnic closedness. He made mistakes. He predicted, it seems, an early parousia, that is, that he would return along with the general resurrection of humankind in the very near future. When the Epistle to the Hebrews says that he was tempted as we are,[99] we can understand that to mean not only external temptation, but the inevitable limitation and conditioning that is part of being a human person of a particular age and stage of development. This is not to say that Jesus sinned in any culpable way; of that we have no knowledge. It does, however, imply an imperfection, not culpable, that is part of being human. When the Cappadocians said that what is unassumed is unhealed, they necessarily implied a sharing in these imperfections which are part of the human lot.

This does not seem to be reading back into the synoptic Gospels a modern humanistic understanding. These elements are present in all these Gospels, alongside other strands. Some of them are present even in the Gospel of John with its far more explicit Logos Christology. And certainly Hebrews says that Jesus 'learned' obedience and 'was made' perfect.[100]

4. The point was made earlier that we no longer believe in a literal Eden and a literal pair of human forebears. The idea of Jesus as the New Adam, so important to Athanasius, has therefore to be seen as a mythical concept, having a certain evocative or poetic truth but not as the basis of a factual statement. To the extent that Athanasian doctrine builds on this mythology as fact, it can no longer hold water. This has some consequences.

I have argued that the human nature of Jesus must have involved him in cultural conditioning, contingency, the limitation of know-ledge and of moral maturity. I shall be arguing below that to understand Jesus as human, we would need to understand him as being able to make autonomous decisions, and to be able even to choose sin. We shall also be exploring the implications of the human suffering of Jesus. For us, to be limited and conditioned and subject to error and uncertainty and pain is part of the human situation.

Because of their belief in paradisal Adam, for the early church these conditions of the human situation were seen as part of sharing in a *fallen* human nature. Jesus, for them, could be truly human, truly Adam-like though even more perfect, without any of these limitations, because he was not fallen, since the first Adam was without these limitations. The option of this understanding is not open to us. We may still argue that Jesus was 'human-as-humanity-will-be', that he was the living example of a perfected man; but, if he was truly human, he must have reached that point of perfection through sharing in and overcoming all the limitations, for human knowledge and human values are learned knowledge and learned values. Thus if we wish to say that he is and always was God (that is, not that he became perfect but that he was perfect from the beginning), we shall have to show how divine perfection can subsist together with contingency, pain, emotional immaturity, the possibility of error and of sin.

Morris points out that to say that all human beings in our experience are culturally conditioned, limited in knowledge, liable to sin, etc., does not necessarily entail that these qualities are essential to human nature. The fact that they are common, or even universal, except for Jesus only means that 'mere' humanity includes these limitations. 'Full' humanity need not. He refuses to accept that there is anything indefensibly illogical about the traditional docrine of the Incarnation. He believes that with his 'two-minds' approach we can show how divine perfection can subsist together with contingency, limitation in knowledge, openness to sin, and the other limitations of 'mere' humanity.

I discuss below[101] some possible problems with Morris's approach. Even if he is right, it must be clear that our modern understanding of what it is to be human is in important ways different from that of Chalcedon.

5. When Christians believed in Adam as a literal forefather of the human race, it was logical to see Jesus as the New Adam, and all those who were not incorporated into Jesus as still being lost and banished from Eden along with the old Adam. Since we no longer share the old belief about a literal single ancestor, the logic no longer works. The heart of New Testament belief in the solidarity of the human race has been excised.

Christians have come now to have moral qualms about excluding other religions from salvation. Sutherland[102] has said that we cannot accept as religiously true anything which runs counter to our moral convictions. Orthodox Christianity used to teach – and many still believe it to be true – that since forgiveness of sin was possible only because Jesus had died for our sins, and since the effect of Jesus' vicarious sacrifice had to be accepted by faith to be efficacious, then only those who had accepted Jesus as Lord and Saviour (however that acceptance was understood) could be saved. But it is surely morally outrageous to believe that God will condemn over half the present population of the world to eternal damnation because they are not Christian. Few would now feel able to argue with Hugh of St Victor that the damnation of the majority of the human race is part of God's loving providence to make the fortunate saved ones appreciate their blessedness the more. Perhaps in an earlier age, when most of those with whom Christians came into contact were either fellow-Christians or were the sworn enemies of Christianity, such views were easier to accept. In modern South Africa, with the need to break down barriers between the races, where significant numbers of South Africans of Indian descent are Hindus or Moslems, and a proportion of South African black people are followers of primal religion, such views are part of the problem, not part of the solution.

South Africa is not the only country in the world where religious differences are part of the reason for oppression and violence. We cannot fail to take into account that it was Christians who carried out, or who at least condoned, the Holocaust, and that the inhumanity of Auschwitz was but the climax of many centuries of persecution of Jews by Christians. Rosemary Radford Ruether[103] suggests that antisemitism is built into the New Testament itself and into subsequent Christian tradition. It did not arise as an unfortunate deviation from true Christian ethics and teaching, but was an intrinsic part of the tradition, the almost inevitable result of Christian–Jewish rivalry. Christians believed that Jesus was the Messiah, Jews did not. Christians believed that Jesus was the revelation of all truth. The Jewish prophets, in Christian eyes, had not really been Jews but proto-Christians pointing to the truth of Jesus' claims. Jews who refused to recognize this or to acknowledge Jesus' messiahship were therefore believed to have been wilfully blind, setting up a deliberate falsehood in the place of Christian truth. It was therefore possible for Christians to marginalize them, see them as evil, and even liquidate them. The only way to avoid Christian antisemitism, in Ruether's view, is to excise from the New Testament and from Christian teaching all references to Jesus as

being the only truth, or the only Saviour. Hyam Maccoby makes
this point even more strongly:

> The remedy to antisemitism does not lie in cosmetic excisions of
> 'rejectionist' passages in the New Testament, nor in exhortations
> to recognize Judaism as an independent religion, much as these
> measures are to be welcomed. It lies in radical criticism of the
> central Christian myth of salvation, as a means of shifting guilt
> and responsibility.[104]

Religious arrogance is part of that from which we need to be
saved. This is more keenly part of our consciousness now. With
easier communication leading to a shrinking of the world, with the
post-colonial growth of religions other than Christianity in the
West, and with the rise of religious studies as a discipline distinct
from theology, we are more conscious of the richness and beauty of
other traditions, and the fact that saintly and heroic lives are not
confined to the Christian tradition. Orthodox christology has to be
able to show that it has taken this into account.

By no means all of those who defend the Chalcedonian definition
believe that non-Christians are damned or are without saving grace.
They certainly do not all, or even mostly, condone antisemitism or
intolerance towards other religions. It is arguable that Paul himself
with his reference to natural conscience in his letter to the Romans
was implying that the Hellenistic world had access before Christianity to God's grace – though Paul seems to have meant that natural
conscience was an agent of damnation, along with the Jewish law,
rather than of salvation, since no one, in Paul's view, is able to obey
conscience and all have sinned.[105]

Karl Rahner with his concept of anonymous Christianity[106]
argues that all religions contain 'elements of supernatural influence
by grace'. Their members are therefore already on the road to
salvation and can be regarded as anonymous Christians. Rahner has
been criticized for the tactlessness and arrogance of implying that,
for example, Moslems really worship Jesus without knowing it; but
of course this is going further than Rahner intended. He does not
say that such persons worship Christ. He is only extending the
Logos concept to say that the Word of God is already operative in
all creation outside the confines of official institutional Christianity.
Nevertheless I suspect that Rahner's argument carries within it
powerful criticism of orthodox christology if followed through
logically. For if the saving grace of God is operative in other
religions before the full Christian gospel is learnt; if members of

such religions can be *saved* by this grace, which Rahner seems to mean,[107] then there is no soteriological necessity for an incarnation. We may still argue that an incarnation is a fitting climax to this process of God's self-revelation, or an apt finishing touch, but it is not soteriologically necessary. Thus the cornerstone of Chalcedonian christology is removed.

Perhaps we may wish to cover our tracks and say that, although other religions have some saving power, Christianity has more; or perhaps we may say that although God's Word is inevitably present in all human life, only in Christianity is it possible to respond to God's word, since only in Christianity is sin forgiven. Other religions then prepare the way for Christianity but ultimately Christian conversion is still necessary for salvation. Then, however, we are still left with a morally questionable God who neglects to give some persons full grace or as good a chance as Christians for salvation for no other reason than that they have had the misfortune to be born into a non-Christian culture.

Amongst the defenders of a full incarnational christology, Hebblethwaite is commendably frank about this point. He concedes that:

> The most powerful argument against traditional incarnational Christology comes out of the encounter of religions; for it is very hard to do justice to the spirituality and religious worth of the great world religions and at the same time to maintain the divinity and hence finality of Christ.[108]

If Jesus is uniquely divine, then other religions are not of equal truth with Christianity, though Hebblethwaite regards himself as an inclusivist (i.e. the whole truth which the doctrine of incarnation represents includes some of the truths grasped in other religions) and not an exclusivist (i.e. there is no truth in other religions). He recognizes the moral problem of his position, but believes it to be necessary if the essential truth unique to Christianity is to be preserved.

Hebblethwaite may be right. If belief in the divinity of Jesus is necessary for salvation, then the moral problem of non-universalism just has to be accepted as mystery; but it is, nevertheless, a moral problem, and one of growing significance, particularly in South Africa.[109]

Rahner's anonymous Christianity has more to do with a kind of extended Logos doctrine than with the idea that the human Jesus, his life and his death, is of universal significance – though Rahner, of course, is not denying the latter. But how is the human Jesus significant for those who have never heard of him? Unless we have a very strong concept of human solidarity, so strong that we believe with some of the Eastern fathers that in some mystical way Jesus' life and death does recreate and change the whole human race, even though this does not know about him, or unless we argue for a vicarious atonement, that in his death Jesus paid for the sins of the whole world whether the world knows it or not, it is hard to see how he is of universal significance. Moule argues that in the eyes of the New Testament writers the death of Jesus has significance for all persons and for all time.[110] But without belief in a historical Adam and Eve and in Jesus as the new Adam, is a consequent strong belief in a corporate human personality possible? We may still believe in a weaker way in human solidarity, that is, in the influence that each person has upon others around. We may concede that in a shrinking world of instant news and television satellite pictures the interdependence of each human culture with others is stronger than before. But can we still believe that Jesus influenced even those who went before him, or whose culture is entirely removed from his historical influence? Surely we can believe this only in such an attenuated way as to make the concept of universal salvation in Jesus devoid of serious meaning. I believe we simply cannot share New Testament theology in this respect.

The issue here is not that of whether a Cantwell Smith-type of world theology is possible,[111] or whether Christianity and other world religions are all partial accounts of an overall truth that is greater than any of them. It would be difficult today to make the case that all religions are really saying the same thing in different ways or aiming at the same goal – that 'all roads lead to heaven'. It is a simpler issue. Traditional Christianity has claimed that we must believe that Jesus is God, for only then can his saving power be accounted for. If that is the case, then other religions which operate on lines quite different from Christianity are excluded from the fullness of salvation, which is morally unpalatable. We may say that those who do not know Christ, or are not able, through no fault of their own, to respond to Christ in this life, may still come to know him and be saved by him in the next life. This may be true – but removes the main concern of soteriological theory from this life to the next, and means that God still leaves most people unsaved in this life, which is the same moral problem. If other religions do have saving power distinct from a relationship with the person of Jesus, then we are let off the moral hook but caught on a new one.

Salvation in this view is possible without reference to the person of Jesus. In that case the basic Chalcedonian reason for claiming the two natures of Jesus is substantially weakened.

6. The concept of personality is a particularly perplexing one in modern times. What exactly is it about Jesus which is divine? It would be nonsense to say that Jesus had a divine yet physical body, for a physical body is a steadily changing agglomeration of cells which individually die and are replaced. To be ridiculous, what could it possibly mean to say that Jesus had a divine leg, or a divine oesophagus? The concept of incarnation is that the divine person *enters* a human body; the body is a vehicle for, a vessel of, divinity rather than divine in itself. The Apollinarian debate was about whether, in addition to entering a human body (which Apollinarius believed), the Logos also became incarnated in a human personality or soul (which Apollinarius did not believe).

Of course we may say with the Chalcedonian fathers that the person of Jesus cannot be divided up into parts, some parts human and some divine; but unless we have some concept of soul, or mind, or personality, which is distinct from the body, how can we talk about the divinity of Jesus at all? Austin Farrer comments:

> But the flesh is not the point of union; the divine action does not fuse with the throbbing of Jesus' pulses; it fuses with the movement of his mind.[112]

If those who hold that the mind is no more than the brain are right, if there is nothing other than the physical body, then a concept of incarnation will be very difficult, if not impossible, to defend. Morris argues that belief in a monistic human nature does not make belief in incarnation logically impossible, but nevertheless he does seem to think that a dualistic view is more congruous with that belief.[113]

We do not yet know that the mind-brain identity theorists are right. Theologians themselves are very divided. The respective articles on Soul in the *Dictionary of Christian Theology* and the *New Dictionary of Christian Theology*[114] illustrate this division very neatly. In the former volume, Alan Richardson prefers to say that belief in a soul is speculative and not required by the Bible. In the latter, Paul Badham argues strongly that the concept of a soul is very important for Christian belief. Whichever side we choose, the concept of soul is extremely difficult to pin down in any philosophically meaningful way, and is thus a problem for traditional views.

In fact, with Constantinople II and the doctrine of *enhypostasia*, the early church abandoned any idea that Jesus had a human personality, and taught that his human personality was the Logos. Thus O'Collins denies that Jesus was a human person at all:

Jesus Christ was (and is) then a man, a human being, and a human individual, *but not* (his italics) a human person.[115]

Nevertheless he asserts that '. . . through his humanity Jesus Christ enjoyed his own rationality and freedom'.[116] There are considerable problems for me in understanding how *enhypostasia* differs from Apollinarianism, or how, if Jesus' human personality is the Logos, he can be humanly rational and free.

O'Collins insists that the person of the Logos entered human form. Jesus is not a human person, but the divine second person of the Trinity. This opens up the very complicated area of defining what is meant, in trinitarian doctrine, by God being three persons and one God. Tertullian's Latin *una substantia*, *tres personae* was translated by the Greek church, especially the Cappadocians, with great wariness. Basil was at pains to show that in his Greek terminology of one *ousia* and three *hypostases*, *hypostasis* did not denote a 'person' as a human individual. That need not concern us now. The point is that if the doctrine of *enhypostasia* is held, then Jesus' personality means something very different from a human personality. Human personality, as we have already remarked, grows from experience, from contact with others, from exercising free choice where there is a real possibility of choosing incorrectly and having to overcome the consequences of that. If none of this is true for Jesus (which it cannot be if his personality means the same thing as the Logos), then it is very difficult to see how Jesus' humanity consists of any more than being temporarily encased in a human body. Since our bodies and our personality or soul (or whatever we believe makes us a human person) are in any case interdependent and form a psychosomatic whole, so that a bodily illness affects our personality, personality for us has a constantly changing quality, even though there may be a certain basic consistency. Can we say that the Logos is constantly changing? None of these are new issues, as the debate over Apollinarianism shows; but modern behaviourist psychology sharpens the issue for us considerably.

7. Traditional christology requires us to say that God acted in Jesus in a unique way: that the actions of Jesus were the actions of God. Liberal Christians sometimes want to state this less strongly,

and to say that Jesus was human rather than divine, but was uniquely obedient to God, so that God was able to act through him uniquely.[117] Yet the whole concept of God acting through humans is in itself an extremely problematic one which has not yet really been resolved. A debate in *Religious Studies* and *Theology*[118] between Maurice Wiles, Brian Hebblethwaite and David Galilee highlighted the problem, and although Austin Farrer is invoked as an answer, I am not convinced that Farrer takes us much further. The problem lies in differentiating between God's actions and human actions. How can there be two agencies responsible for a single action? Where does human action stop and God's action begin? It is true that Farrer makes a valuable contribution to this debate about double agency in one of his typical arguments between himself and an imaginary partner where (again typically), he shows his inventive genius by arriving, apparently independently, at much the same point as process theology. It is never easy, as Wiles remarks, to pin down exactly what Farrer means: but in essence it appears to be that God does not act in this world except as the mind of the world: he enters the world's constituents '. . . by prior causality, willing them into existence and the activity they exercise'.[119] Having created them, he leaves them to make their own actions.

> His concern for his creatures is for them to be themselves, or more than themselves; not for them to act as pawns in some specifically supernatural game which any divine hand is bound to play.[120]

'Double agency' is therefore meant by Farrer only in a very reduced sense. God initiates by constantly willing the world's constituents into being. God does not act in the world. 'The world is so made as to run itself.'[121] God's actions are to create, and constantly to confront the world with his will and purposes. Farrer is no pantheist. The fact that the voice of God is met with only in what he has made does not mean that everything we meet is the voice of God. Concerning the story of Saul consulting the Witch of Endor, Farrer says:

> If God is a living will and a heart of love directly concerned for us, why should we look for him, or why listen for him, in the remote and dubious margins of our experience. It is folly . . . to look away from the point where God's will touches us in our present

existence . . . The will of God is everywhere present: it is experienced by being obeyed.[122]

Farrer means that what God does is to call us to act in obedience to his will: and that the evidence of God's act of willing and calling can best be seen in the lives of Jesus and of the saints. Even in the life of Jesus, however, what we perceive is his obedience to God's call. God does not, on this account, so it seems to me, act in Jesus in any way differently from how he acts in us. I suspect that Farrer and Wiles are saying very much the same thing.

Wiles gives extended attention to the problem of God's action in the world.[123] He argues that for a number of reasons – the regularity and growing explicability of the physical world where God as *deus ex machina* is less and less needed; more importantly the fact that blessing and disaster are both found in that world so that if God is seen to be directly involved in blessing it is hard to deny his action in bane – it makes more sense to say that God does not actively intervene in the world.

This is not, Wiles believes, the same as Deism. God is not withdrawn from the world. Nor is Wiles returning to a neo-Platonic view of an immutable God who is removed from the universe. Much as Farrer argued, Wiles believes that God is present at every level in every action in the world, in the sense that he has created all things and holds them in being; he is the ongoing source of their energy and life. Each creature in the universe is nevertheless free, within its own created nature, to make its own choices. If this applies at a sub-human level, it applies even more at a human level. Wiles puts a '. . . strong emphasis on the radical degree of freedom with which I believe the human creation to have been endowed'.[124]

God's action in the world is constant. It is one of creation and of establishing the overall purpose for creation. Wiles rejects the idea of any *special* action of God, either in miracles of nature, healing miracles, or special grace to certain individuals. I would argue that he is right. God's purposes are surely stable and constant, and his love equally disposed. Why would he intervene with special miracles in some cases and not in all? And if he intervened in all cases, they would no longer be miracles, exceptions to the rule. If God is active in some historical acts, for example in leading the people of Israel out of Egypt, he must be equally active in all historical events, in which case the exile is his work too. Old Testament Jews were able to say of the exile that it was indeed God's action, the consequence of their own sin, and rationalize it in that way; but what then of God's involvement in the Holocaust, surely beyond rationalization. We may explain that the Holocaust is the result of human free will, and thus indirectly attributable to God who made us with that freedom. We surely cannot say, as the Old Testament Jews were able of the exile, that God wished or intended the Holocaust or was directly involved in bringing it about. If God is seen to have taken what we might call direct action in some cases, he must either act equally in all, or be held accountable for his lack of action. God then becomes morally blameworthy, unless we take refuge in mystery and say that his apparent immorality is only attributable to our imperfect understanding, which must blunt our own moral sensibility. Otherwise we must say, with Wiles, that God's actions are those of creation and calling, but that beyond that he does not intervene or overthrow the free choices of his creatures.

In what way, then, can God be said to have acted in Jesus differently from how he acts in all humans? The New Testament understands Jesus as the culmination of God's actions both in history and in personal individuals. The virgin birth and the resurrection certainly suggest the special action of God. However, Wiles makes the familiar but true observation that the New Testament narrative about Jesus is best understood as retrospective perception of Jesus' significance for the church community rather than as an historical account in the way modern history would be written. It seems to me that the objections raised above about the special action of God in history also apply to special action of God in Jesus, although this is going beyond Wiles' point. If God acted in a unique and special way in Jesus, why did he wait so long? And why did he not act in other histories and cultures?

It is not clear to me in what sense Wiles believes in the resurrection, whether as objective physical event or an event in the subjective awareness of the disciples. Nor in *God's Action in the World* does Wiles trace out the implications of that book for a doctrine of incarnation. However the logical problems of believing in God's special, one-off action in the world seem to me to apply as strongly to belief in the Incarnation as a distinctive, different action by God in Jesus which God does not will to do in every other person. That does not mean that Jesus is not unique. We may well argue that in his response and whole-hearted obedience to God Jesus is unique, that he is thus a unique saviour who makes it possible for God to act uniquely in him as God would *like* to act in every person.

Wiles goes on to show how a reduced belief in God's action in the world is not incompatible with a continuing practice of prayer, worship and sacraments. Indeed one could make a case for saying that it strengthens these practices, as channels to the underlying and constant creation and calling of God rather than as semi-magical purveyors of special miracles. However, that is beside our present point.

By way of contrast with Wiles, Brian Hebblethwaite suggests that:

> Most theologians would now affirm that, at least in his relation to the world, God is a God who acts, and that the story of God's dealings with his people constitutes an unfolding and indeed unfinished history . . . The influence of Platonism is on the wane.[125]

This is an important point, and one to which I shall return in later chapters. It helps to clarify what Wiles is *not* saying. Hebblethwaite is surely right; in a world which is increasingly aware of suffering it is intolerable to believe in the old classic way in an immutable, impassible God who is not involved except as distant transcendent first cause and prime mover in his world. Wiles is not arguing that God is not active and present in the world, but that God does not act in special, different ways at some points or in some persons in history. Wiles's case rests not on Platonic concepts of the immutability of God, but on the more telling grounds of divine consistency of justice, fairness and constancy of love. I think it is hard to refute.

The question, then, for a traditional view of the Incarnation is how the actions of Jesus can be spoken of as divine actions. If Jesus is both God and man, how far are his actions divine and how far human? Does it add anything to our understanding of Jesus to say that when he spoke words of forgiveness he spoke not just on God's behalf, just as God's spokesman, but with the voice of God himself? When he urged his followers to enter the Kingdom of God, did he invite them as spokesman for God, or as God himself? When he stilled the winds and waters (granting the truth of the nature miracles for the moment) did he still them as the Creator of his universe, or as the servant of God speaking with the confidence that the Creator would hear and heed? Whatever traditional Christianity may say about the *communicatio idiomatum* (the interrelation of human and divine in Jesus, so that his actions can be described as being both divine and human in one breath), does such language really add very much to our interpretation and understanding of the events? Is there a significant difference between speaking as one who himself loves and serves God and assuring the woman taken in adultery that she is not condemned by the God who is her 'Abba', and speaking as God to the woman with the same assurance?

Perhaps we shall have recourse to the idea of God confronting the world with his will and purposes through a human Jesus acting as God's spokesman or representative. Perhaps Jesus' unique obedience made it possible for God to speak to the world as never before. This might be the liberal answer. For liberal Christians who want to say that Jesus is human rather than divine, but a human person who is a vehicle for God's actions, there is another problem. How can God be thought of as acting through the human person Jesus? If special divine action is ruled out, as I have supported Wiles in saying, then all that is meant by such language about Jesus is that, as a human person, he responded in a unique way to the underlying grace of God and the ever-present call of God, equally available to us but to which we respond and obey to a much lesser degree. The actions of Jesus would be his own actions, in obedience to God, certainly, made possible by the ever-present grace of God and in this sense the actions of a son of God, but nonetheless his actions and not God's. This is much less than liberal Christians usually wish to say. Sympathetic Jews, Moslems, and Hindus could probably accept such a formulation without much of a problem. But if special divine action is ruled out, what other formulation would be possible? And if special divine action is not ruled out, we are left with the problems which Wiles has raised.

There is, of course, the refuge of mystery, a refuge to which we might still need to have recourse if the basic Chalcedonian assumption – no full incarnation, no salvation – is found to be true.

8. Cupitt insists that the ideal modern view of humanness is of autonomous persons, choosing for ourselves what in the light of our reason seems to us to be the most appropriate values and actions, and not forced by outside persons, human or divine. He argues that Jesus himself, if he is truly human, must have had the same freedom: freedom to err and indeed freedom even to sin.[126] Not to have this freedom is to be less than fully human. For Jesus to avoid sin because he is by divine nature unable to sin is to reduce the human praiseworthiness of his goodness: but then, if he is free to sin, how can we talk in the traditional way of his being God?

To return for a moment to the pre-Chalcedonian debate, we have seen that for the Alexandrians the humanness of Jesus was of a very reduced kind. Following the Platonic tendency to stress genus or class more than the individual, they had little idea of Jesus as an individual, decision-making human being. The Antiochenes laid more stress on the individual humanness of Jesus – but with the two-sons theory of Diodore lurking in the background. Like Cyril, we cannot accept Diodore's thesis; but with a modern understanding of the value and importance of the individual we cannot follow the Alexandrian route either. Our concept of humanness is fuller than, or at least different from, the Alexandrian one. We see individuality, individual choice and responsibility as being a strength and a virtue. To be fully and ideally human Jesus must possess these qualities, with the consequent difficulty in calling him divine also. His actions must be human actions, not God's actions through him – but then how can he be divine?

When faced with the question 'Can God will what is evil or illogical, and if not, is this then a limitation on God's freedom and power?', Thomas Aquinas replied that for God to do what is less than morally or logically perfect would itself be a limitation of his nature, so that the problem is a false problem; if God did what is evil, that would constitute a limitation of God.

We might argue, then, that Jesus, divine and human, might humanly have chosen sin but in his divinity could not do so since this would again imply imperfection. For the Chalcedonians this did not entail a serious problem, for a true, perfect human being equally would not sin, so that there was no logical problem involved in saying that Jesus, God and man, was fully and perfectly human and could not sin. He could endure temptation; he could know the drives of hunger, thirst and fear; but it was impossible for him to have succumbed to that temptation.

The issue is not so easy for us. To be human, to know humanly, is to know by the exercise of choice and by learning from experience. We have no eternal Platonic 'ideal' of humanness. There was no past human perfection. The experience on which we base our knowledge will certainly stretch beyond our own experience to include the experience of our predecessors and our community, but this will not give us a sufficient basis to make a perfect choice. We do not know what is sinful until we learn it from the community and from our own experience. The community's view of what is sinful will always be less than perfect. Perfect moral choice is not a meaningful human possibility. The exercise of autonomous moral choice, and the obligation to live through the consequence, is what constitutes the human challenge; but how can this be ascribed to a divine person if we wish 'divine' to retain any meaning? The process theology concept of a limited, growing deity might provide some refuge, but this would be much less than Chalcedon meant, and would consequently have been seen by Chalcedon as soteriologic-ally inadequate – a criticism which is levelled against the process concept of God anyway.

In a subsequent chapter I shall refer to Morris, who believes that his two-minds approach allows for this problem. In his human mind Jesus may have had to learn, cognitively, what constitutes 'good-ness'. He may have faced temptation and in his human mind not have known that he was incapable of sin. Thus sin would have been an 'epistemic' but not an ontological, actual possibility for him. The battle against sin would have been just as real, for he would not have known, humanly, that he would win the battle. Morris offers some analogies to illustrate the point.[127] In his divine mind, we may say, Jesus knew perfectly and ominisciently. In his human mind his knowledge is humanly limited, including knowledge of his own sinlessness.

The problem with Morris' approach is that it drives a wedge between Jesus' divine and human minds, which surely makes the Incarnation a much lesser identification of God and human in Jesus. I discuss the point below.[128] When all these problems are consid-ered along with the problems of understanding God as acting in the world in any special way at all, as discussed in the previous section, we see that Cupitt has raised a fairly weighty objection.

9. Although we shall deal with it fully below, I mention another modern issue here, which is that of suffering. We feel keenly aware of the existence of suffering, hunger, oppression, in our world, or if we do not feel keenly aware we know that we ought to. Modern media keep the world's tragedies before us. The rise of liberation theology is a recognition that the issue is of theological importance. The majority of Christians (if not the majority of theologians) in the world today are in the suffering, Third-World part of humanity.

Suffering is not new. Many of the early Christians were as poor and as vulnerable as Third-World Christians now. The Old Testament is full of assurance that God cares for the oppressed and the suffering, and intervenes in history on their behalf. The intervention of God is itself a problematical concept, as we have already seen, a matter to which we will give more attention later. Yet if God does not intervene to end the suffering, it becomes increasingly difficult to believe in him. Theodicy, that is, reconciling belief in a God of love with the existence and extent of suffering, has never been more difficult than in our post-Holocaust world. Since the mediaeval and Reformation church, the problem for theology has shifted from justifying humans before an accusing God to justifying God before an accusing humanity. Is it conceivable that a loving God could have permitted Auschwitz? Nowhere is this problem more acute than in South Africa.

> Just as the contemporary theological debate on suffering has been sparked off by events such as the Holocaust and Hiroshima, so within our own context [i.e. the South African one], theological reflection on suffering is called for by the reality of apartheid, and should be grounded in it.[129]

God seems to have no power to stop or prevent evil which is on a scale too great to be endured. In any discussion of the saving work of Jesus, we cannot overlook the stark experience of black South African people. John de Gruchy reports the words of a forlorn black woman taken by force to live in a barren 'homeland'.

> My man has gone and died, as have my daughters. They took my land away. The Lord has also gone, yes, I suppose he has also gone.[130]

Part of the message of the New Testament is that Jesus himself suffered. It seems to have been a particularly strong stress in Mark's Gospel. Not for nothing has that Gospel been called a passion story with a long introduction. In a situation where Christianity had begun to be persecuted, it was important to know that Jesus himself had been persecuted.

In one way a full incarnational view of Jesus strengthens the message that God cares about suffering, for in this view the Son of God himself suffered. In due course, however, the church would have to address the problem of how God can be said to suffer. The problem became more acute once the classic concept of theism had become entrenched, with its stress on the incorporeality and the aseity, the utter independence of God. If God is perfect, God cannot be vulnerable. Patripassianism was rejected, i.e. the idea that if Jesus was identical with the Father, then in Jesus' sufferings on the cross the Father suffers. In that case we must say that not the Father, but the Son, the Logos, who is God, suffers. But if the Father cannot suffer because he is God, then how can the Son, who is equally God, suffer? Thus the early church had to say that Jesus suffers in his human, not his divine, capacity – driving a wedge between the two natures of Jesus in a somewhat Nestorian manner.

It is true that for this reason some more modern concepts of God, for example process theology, argue that God can suffer, and is vulnerable. Bonhoeffer said that God becomes weak and powerless in the world, and thus is the only true help.[131] Others, for example Jürgen Moltmann and the South African theologian John de Gruchy, have also argued from other perspectives for a God who suffers. Karl Rahner has suggested that God, while immutable in himself, becomes mutable in another, and that what happens to Jesus is also God's history.[132] We may take it that mutability implies vulnerability. Whether a vulnerable God is a very satisfactory concept of God is a whole debate in itself. I am only arguing that if we take human Third-World suffering seriously, then the sufferings of Jesus are an important link between Jesus and the suffering world, but the question of *how* Jesus' human sufferings also link God with the suffering world has not yet been satisfactorily answered. Here again we are faced with a mystery which we must show to be a necessary mystery if we are to be properly 'economic' in our christology. The concept of a vulnerable God, a God who becomes mutable *in alio*, is perhaps an unnecessarily complicated concept unless we can show that if Jesus be not divine, there is no salvation.

These, then, are some of the factors of our modern consciousness which make it imperative that the Chalcedonian Definition be at least re-evaluated, as we ask how it can make sense to us in our modern culture. Chalcedon conceded the difficulty, but insisted that unless Jesus is fully divine and fully human, we cannot be saved. We are more acutely aware, given our modern understanding, of the difficulty. Although we have touched upon the concept of salvation, we shall have to examine it more fully in the following pages. We shall discover that in our modern situation even the concept of salvation has changed. To add to our difficulties, we do not have a *philosophia perennis* as in earlier times. There is no agreed single philosophical world-view which holds sway. Rahner makes it clear that we live in a world of philosophical pluralism.[133]

This is not a new situation for the christological debate. I have suggested that the New Testament church itself had many different philosophies and christological views. H. E. W. Turner suggests that the use of Greek philosophy meant the loss of some of the biblical flexibility of outlook, but the gain of a more stable and coherent framework.[134] In our own time, the Greek framework no longer fits the whole spectrum of our experience, and we are pushed into flexibility again. Whether this is a forward or a backward push is a matter of perspective. Rahner welcomes modern pluralism as a stage of necessary confusion and uncertainty on the way towards a fuller apprehension of the whole reality in a better, more adequate world view.[135] However, the emergence of that comprehensive philosophy lies in the future, and is not presently to hand. The same applies, as Sutherland says, to an emergence of an agreed reconstruction of the historical Jesus. Biblical scholars as well as philosophical theologians are subject to uncertainties and confusions as well. Nonetheless, Sutherland asks, 'Can and need the eternal significance of faith wait on the results of historical enquiry which can at best be approximate and revisable in principle?'[136]

We have to try to develop an understanding of Jesus and his salvation in a way that fits our present incomplete and unsatisfactory philosophical and biblical understanding. Our revised christology may in the end prove to need substantial revision itself. We may discover that the traditional views which we have left on the back burner, which we have temporarily put aside as being currently unhelpful, are in fact true and relevant after all. In the meantime, we have to reconstruct a christology which is as coherent and as consistent with our current experience as possible.

5

Problems with Abandoning Chalcedon

I have suggested above that all the problems posed for modern people in believing the full Chalcedonian Definition of the nature of Jesus do not mean that we have proved that the traditional doctrine is wrong, but only that it is possibly not the best way of interpreting our own experience. If it can be shown that our experience demands such a belief, then it is not logically incoherent to say that the belief, although it transcends our present understanding and is mysterious to us, is true.

Alister McGrath remarks that the liberal theologians who turn away from belief in the literal divinity of Jesus do so because they are conditioned by post-Enlightenment philosophy into assuming that traditional belief is incoherent.

> Modern Christian theology has been oppressed by the spirit of the eighteenth-century Enlightenment, on occasion even giving the impression of being a willing prisoner.[137]

McGrath regrets that the old idea of *fides quaerens intellectum*, 'I believe so that I may understand', has given way to a spirit of 'unless I understand I will not believe'.

McGrath is one amongst a number of theologians who argue that all rational systems have certain foundations, or what Polanyi calls a 'fiduciary framework'.[138] The logical system is then built on that framework, and as a system must satisfy the demands of logic; but the foundations themselves are not provable or disprovable on rational grounds.

One could therefore argue that the sort of logical problems with

the traditional doctrine of the Incarnation which were outlined in
the previous section are only problems if one takes the sort of stance
which post-Enlightenment critics of traditional doctrine adopt; i.e.
that knowledge is limited to that for which we have empirical evidence, etc. One could then go on to argue, as McGrath does, that
this post-Enlightenment stance is itself a fiduciary framework, not a
self-evident or necessary truth. One could argue that belief in the
Incarnation is something like Plantinga's belief in God: a 'properly
basic' belief which does not require rational proof or demonstration.[139]

However, I believe that to argue in this way is to miss the point of
the problems in the last section. I do not suggest that the traditional
doctrine of the Incarnation is impossible to reconcile with logic, but
only that it does not provide as close a fit with modern experience,
as good an interpretation of contemporary knowledge, as previously. It is not as useful as it once was. Now of course 'useful' does
not mean 'true', nor 'non-useful' mean 'untrue'. But the Christian
claim is surely not only that Christian faith is true, or consistent with
a sufficiently sophisticated logic (it is not merely a metaphysic), but
that it is true *and* useful. If traditional doctrines no longer prove
helpful, that does not mean in strict logic that they are no longer
true, but it may mean that they are no longer salvific. Such a
situation must surely mean that we need to re-examine both the
truth and the necessity of the old doctrinal formulations.

I think the same objections can be raised about the very
sophisticated work of T. V. Morris, collected together in his *The
Logic of God Incarnate*. He deals with three possible attacks on the
doctrine of the Incarnation: that the doctrine is incoherent in
making the identity statement 'Jesus is identical with the Son of
God'; that the vastness of the cosmos makes the doctrine cosmically
incongruent; and that if Jesus is truly human and fully human there
can then be no evidence of incarnation since if Jesus is different
from us he would not be fully human. Morris also deals with how the
doctrine relates to the traditional doctrine of the Trinity. He
believes that the doctrine of the Incarnation along Chalcedonian
lines can be shown to be logical and coherent and meaningful.

Morris does not compromise by taking any easy ways out in
considering whether the doctrine of the Incarnation is incoherent.
He refuses to take a Kierkegaardian line that theology need not
meet logical requirements, that human philosophy is irrelevant to
our knowledge of God. He refuses to say that the strict requirements for identity-statements (the principle of indiscernibility of

identicals) do not apply to Jesus Christ because he is *sui generis*. He chooses not to take a kenotic line or to water down the apparently irreconcilable divine qualities, so far as incarnation in human nature is concerned, as immutability, omniscience or omnipotence.

> So it seems clear that a defender of the orthodox doctrine of the Incarnation ought not to respond to the contemporary challenge based on the indiscernibility principle by either devaluing the status of human logic, rejecting the problem outright, or revising it in such a way as to square with what seem to be essential divine-human property differences. The best response to the challenge will consist in meeting it head on in acknowledging the governance of the traditional indiscernibility principle over identity statements and arguing that, contrary to what has been alleged, the incarnational identity [i.e. Jesus is God the Son] satisfies the requirements.[140]

By the 'principles of the indiscernibility of the identicals' Morris means that if object 'x' is identical with object 'y', then every property possessed by 'x' is possessed by 'y' and vice versa. On the face of it, this principle means that it should be extremely difficult to show how Jesus of Nazareth, possessing human properties, can be identical with God the Son. Again, Morris uncompromisingly says that the doctrine of the Incarnation

> . . . is not true unless Jesus had all and only the properties of . . . the individual referred to in Christian theology as God the Son.[141]

He claims that a 'significant number' of contemporary theologians have held this identity-statement to be not only false, i.e. untrue in fact, but impossible, incoherent, unintelligible; and he sets out to show that the doctrine is no such thing. He does this by making some simple, perfectly legitimate, distinctions between such things as common properties and essential properties. For example, it is common for humans to have lived at some time on the earth, but not necessarily essential to their humanity if space travel becomes a reality. It is common to humans to have a beginning in time, and to die, and thus to be what would classically be known as 'contingent', but it is not logically imperative to say that contingency is then essential to what it means to be human. Jesus then could be said to be human and yet not contingent. Morris draws a distinction, too, between 'merely human' and 'fully human'. A mere human is sinful, but must a full human then be sinful too? Mere humanity may be

common, may in fact apply to everybody except Jesus, but
'mereness', because common, is not therefore essential to being
human.

Morris takes what he calls an Anselmian view of God. God is
therefore in his view omniscient and omnipotent. God is also
essentially immutable. How then can Jesus be God the Son, and
therefore omnipotent, etc., and yet also possess a truly human
mind, without any change in the qualities of omniscience? Although
Morris believes that logical coherence *could* be shown for a kenotic
approach, that is to say, an approach which says that in the
Incarnation God the Son voluntarily divested himself of his
omniscience and omnipotence, he does not favour this, since it
would weaken too far what he regards as another essential quality of
God, i.e. his immutability. Thus in his view God (and therefore
God the Son) unchangeably possesses all the kind-essential attributes of his deity, which include all the 'omni-' qualities. God can
add further attributes, provided these are not contradictory to the
existing attributes (thus Morris is not an absolute immutabilist), but
God cannot *lose* them.

In the Incarnation, therefore, Jesus did not lose any of his divine
attributes, according to Morris, but he added to them a human
mind. In Jesus there are two ranges of consciousness: eternal,
omniscient, intuitive; and temporal, limited and developing. The
first set of qualities includes the second. Thus in his human mind
Jesus grows, learns, needs teaching, is limited to his historical and
cultural viewpoint. But all of what he knows in his human mind is
included in his divine mind. There is no logical contradiction.

Morris offers various analogies to show that his two-minds theory
is not inconceivable.

> But can we really understand what it is to attribute two minds, or
> two ranges of consciousness, to one person?[142]

He reminds us that we cannot know what it is to be God, or for God
to possess two minds – a retreat into mystery, but not illogical for all
that. He offers the analogy of dream consciousness in which I am a
participant in the action of a dream story but simultaneously know
that I am the dreamer. He reminds us that modern psychology
claims that there are various strata of the mind, e.g. subconscious
and conscious, operating simultaneously. He refers to occasional
instances of multiple personality. All analogies, of course, have
their weaknesses: we might object to Morris that a dream world is
not a real world, while incarnation requires that Jesus be really

human; that psychologists regard states of divided consciousness as pathological rather than ideal.

Morris says:

> If it is defensible, which I think it is, the two minds view along with the distinctions [between common and essential qualities, between mere and full humanity] . . . gives us all we need for philosophically explicating the orthodox doctrine of the Incarnation and defending it against all forms of the contemporary incoherence challenge.[143]

Morris's two-minds theory as I have suggested in the previous subsection, also enables him to deal with the problems of cosmological insignificance and of how Jesus can be really tempted.

This summary of Morris' closely packed arguments does not do justice to the detail and care of his work. I think that in fact he does show that the traditional doctrine of the Incarnation is neither anti-logical nor entirely incoherent. The Chalcedonian fathers would not easily have recognized his version of the doctrine. His two-minds theory sounds a little like the two-sons theory which Cyril hated – though of course it is nothing of the kind, since Morris is clear that the human mind of Jesus is subsumed within the divine mind. But then the two consciousnesses of Jesus (the divine consciousness including the human so that he simultaneously knows all and does not know, simultaneously is able to do all things, knows that he is so able, and yet is humanly unaware of his divine omnipotence) makes of Jesus a person very different from ourselves. It is true that I may have a subconscious awareness of abilities in myself of which I am not consciously aware; but then I am not able to harness those abilities except vestigially. They are potential rather than actual. Jesus' divine attributes must surely be known to his divine consciousness, which cannot be a mere subconscious. His divine attributes cannot be potential and not actual – unless we go back to Vincent Taylor's version of kenoticism. Morris can argue in logic that this does not mean that Jesus is not human; he is fully human where we are merely human. If, however, Jesus does not share our 'mere' humanity, if in his human helplessness and weakness he is simultaneously and (divinely speaking) consciously, all powerful and all mighty, then does he share our condition? 'What is unassumed is unhealed', said the Cappadocians.

This is the chief difference between Morris and the theologians whom he criticizes. Morris, as a philosopher, is concerned with issues of coherence, meaning and logic. Theologians have to take that into account, but are also concerned, perhaps primarily concerned, with issues of helpfulness and relevance. I do not think that Morris is correct in saying that most contemporary theologians who are critical of the traditional doctrine of the Incarnation claim that the doctrine is 'impossible, self-contradictory, incoherent, absurd, and even unintelligible', although Don Cupitt does so. The real issue is not that the doctrine cannot be rendered coherent or logical, but that it is not relevant to the human situation.

From a philosophical point of view, relevance is no guarantee of truth. I am aware of the danger that a socially relevant religion is relevant only to its own time and has a built-in obsolescence. I have argued above that truths which once seemed very helpful and relevant may return to be helpful and relevant once more.[144] Christianity claims, however, to be not only true, but to be of saving truth, and saving truth does require a high degree of social relevance, to humans both individually and collectively. That is not to deny that we may be blind to what is truly of relevance to us. Social relevance does not mean merely what is commonly perceived to be socially relevant. Nor does it mean we are not concerned with what is universally and always true. It is a question, for Christianity, of trying to do both; to look for eternal verities, but also to say how these truths are evidence of God's love for us now.

There may be a certain irony in the spectacle of theologians trying to reinterpret the person and work of Jesus in ways which do not offend post-Enlightenment susceptibilities while some philosophers like Gadamer and Polanyi are saying that Enlightenment views are themselves outdated. It might seem that the church is, as so often, adapting too late to issues that are already *passé*. This criticism is not, however, entirely true. Modern critics of the doctrine of the Incarnation, those who wish to reinterpret it, are not always motivated by outdated philosophical demands for verifiability and for empiricism so much as by the conviction that the doctrine is no longer of *saving* truth. This is particularly evident in the work of Maurice Wiles.

In *The Logic of God Incarnate* Morris evidences no interest in issues of salvation. As a philosopher he is justified in that omission. He shows that the traditional doctrine can be defended against charges of incoherence or nonsense. If the doctrine is still needed to make sense of Christian claims that the person and work of Jesus are of saving significance, then Morris' work would be of great importance. However, since the doctrine grew out of soteriology, the soteriology must be prior and we must ask not only 'Is the doctrine logical?' but 'Is it the best explanation for what we experience as salvation in Jesus?' This is the question I shall try to address in a later part of this book.

It is not, then, true that all liberal christology is influenced only by sceptical rationalism, though that may sometimes be the case. It is concerned to discover and communicate the meaning not only of the Incarnation but of salvation. It is also influenced by modern biblical criticism – itself to some extent the product of sceptical rationalism, to be sure, but not entirely so. Some of the fruits of the labours of biblical critics are now widely accepted. McGrath and Hebblethwaite are not urging us to return to precritical fundamentalism. The distance between the historical Jesus and the Jesus of the evangelists is also a reason, quite apart from philosophy, for needing to reconsider a pre-critical christology.

There is little mileage to be gained by restricting religious belief to what can be proved on rational grounds to be unquestionably true. Since with religion we are dealing with ultimate 'metatruths', we must grant that the foundations for our theology may be metalogical. Our belief-systems need to be consistent with experience as well as with historical evidence and logic, and experience may transcend these latter criteria.

Hebblethwaite must therefore be taken seriously when he says that a liberal christology, while it may appear more logical, will cause us to lose much that is of real value in our Christian experience. He lists a number of these losses.

If Jesus is not truly God, then our knowledge of God is greatly lessened and our relationship with God made more distant.

> The moral and religious value of the Incarnation lies in the greatly increased potential for human knowledge of God and personal union with God introduced by God's own presence and acts in human form [i.e. in Jesus], this side of the gap between Creator and creature.[145]

Hebblethwaite concedes that in other religions people may come to know God, and to be in a close personal relationship with God through mysticism, but to a lesser degree than a much more direct, face-to-face way of personal encounter with God in Jesus.

If Jesus is not God, we cannot have a belief in a Trinity, a belief which enables us to see God in 'richer relational terms',[146] perceiving God as love in himself. If God is love, there must be a Trinity, or at least Binity, within the Godhead – unless we say that

God is love because he loves his creation which makes the creation eternally necessary to God, which is a denial of Godhead.

It can be seen that Hebblethwaite is quite influenced here by Leonard Hodgson[147] and his relational analogy of the Trinity, and perhaps by the Greek fathers, rather than by the more monistic trinitology of Augustine. Hebblethwaite acknowledges that belief in the Trinity did not historically come about because people recognized the necessity of love within the Godhead. Trinitology was a consequence of believing that Jesus was divine, rather than a cause. In retrospect, however, he believes, we can now see that without trinitarian belief, which requires that Jesus be divine, our concept of love within the Godhead would be damaged.

As an extension of belief in the Trinity, Christians are enabled to see themselves in their worship and sacraments as being caught up into the trinitarian love-relationship themselves, so that they become part of the Son's self-offering to the Father.[148] They are enabled to see themselves as part of Christ's body in a Pauline way,[149] enabled with Jesus to call God 'Abba', Father. If Jesus is not God, 'we no longer have a living saviour, by incorporation into whose body we too can say Abba, Father'.[150] A full trinitarian belief enables us to see that our response to God was not purely our response, but is God's own response in us to his own initiative.[151]

Unless Jesus is God, we can only say that God suffers with us in our sufferings in a very reduced way:

> This whole dimension of the Christian doctrine of the Incarnation, its recognition of the costly nature of God's forgiving love, and its perception that only a suffering God is morally credible, is lost if God's involvement is reduced to a matter of 'awareness' and 'sympathy'.[152]

This concept of God sharing our suffering and our humiliation with us is carried further by Hebblethwaite in his embracing of kenoticism, which I have already touched on.[153] It is central to the soteriology of Jürgen Moltmann, and will be considered under that heading later in this book.[154]

The traditional doctrine of the Incarnation has considerable ethical implications. That God became human gives a value and importance to human life that makes a great difference in an often impersonal world. It may have considerable political implications in struggles against capitalism, or régimes like South Africa that devalue human life. That God took on himself a human body means that the physical and material universe is given its proper, positive, non-Manichean place in the scheme of things. That God emptied himself and suffered with us on the cross underlines the central values of self-sacrifice and of service.[155]

We have already noted that Hebblethwaite joins others in pointing out that if Jesus is not divine it is more difficult to see why or how Jesus is central to human salvation, and that liberal assumptions that a human Jesus is still of universal human significance are difficult to sustain.[156] If liberals are right in ascribing to Jesus a unique closeness to God or harmony with God, then surely, says Hebblethwaite, a more consistent conclusion would be that Jesus is not only human but that 'his human life was lived out of a centre in God',[157] and that within his humanity God himself lives in a unique way.

Keith Ward[158] offers some criticism of these points, and although Hebblethwaite responds to these criticisms,[159] I do not think he meets Ward's objections. I incorporate some of Ward's criticisms in my own remarks.

There seems to be validity in Hebblethwaite's observations that much richness would be lost if traditional incarnational theology were to be abandoned, and that the concept of Jesus and of salvation offered by the liberal christologists is thin by comparison. However, we have to ask ourselves whether Hebblethwaite's construction of the rich concept of God about to be lost, is based on sufficiently firm foundations. As Ward points out, we do not in fact have a face-to-face relationship with the human Jesus upon which to build our understanding of an otherwise shadowy and transcendent God. The first disciples may have had this relationship: we do not. We may be said to have a relationship with the risen Jesus, or with Jesus-in-the-church, but this Jesus is as far removed from our immediate perception as is God himself. This Jesus is also transcendent, and not part of our concrete sense-experience. If it be said that although we do not ourselves have a face-to-face relationship with Jesus, we read about and thus share in that relationship as described in the New Testament, we come up against the problem of the reconstruction of the historical Jesus. This is not to say that no such reconstruction is possible in even the smallest degree, but the knowledge which we gain from this encounter at second hand with Jesus is not as direct as Hebblethwaite would have us believe.

What is more, our concept of God is not very different from that of other monotheistic religions. Islam, and particularly Judaism, also believes in a personal God who is a God of love and compassion, without this knowledge of God being mediated to them through Jesus (or only very indirectly, perhaps, in the case of Islam). In fact, therefore, Hebblethwaite's construction of a knowledge of God based on a face-to-face relationship with Jesus and leading to a concept of God much deeper and more intimate than in any other religions, proves not to mean so much in reality.

Again, Hebblethwaite's point that if Jesus is not God we cannot say that God is at one with us in our sufferings is not as powerful as it might at first seem. Ward comments that God being somehow involved in Jesus' sufferings is of no great help to the rest of us. God, if he loves us, must equally be involved in all of our suffering. We might say that although God does suffer with Jesus' sufferings, he suffers too with ours, so that the uniqueness of Jesus is not in the degree to which God identifies with him, but in the degree to which Jesus in obedience identifies with God. The other problem with this aspect of Hebblethwaite's construction of the necessity for full incarnational belief is that it is difficult to see in what sense God suffers in Jesus. Moltmann's idea[160] that God suffers in sending and abandoning his beloved Son on the cross for our salvation, in the separation or distancing himself from Jesus for our sake, is susceptible to the same criticism from Ward: surely God suffers in the sufferings of all his beloved children who die unjustly. They too are 'abandoned' in their suffering – we may assume, because of the place of free will in God's universe. Why must he send Jesus as a sign of his solidarity in suffering with us? Does Jesus' suffering hurt God more than ours? However important modern theologians may think it is to drop the classic idea of God's impassibility, the concept of the suffering of God is extremely difficult. The patristic problem with patripassianism has not been answered. We shall have to return to this elsewhere.

Finally, a real problem with Hebblethwaite's list of what would be lost if we do not have an incarnational christology is that he seems to commit the ought/is fallacy familiar to philosophers of ethics. He argues that the logical problems of the God-man concept are not insuperable; God could (and therefore by implication should) have become man, therefore he did.

> If God might have become man, but did not, then the reduced claim [in liberal Christology] for what God has done in Christ fails to satisfy us.[161]

We might argue in reply that if a doctrine of incarnation is logically conceivable but not the most apparently consistent, economic and appropriate conclusion to draw from the evidence, then the enhanced claim in conservative Christianity for what God has done in Christ also fails to satisfy and is not the best answer.

II

Salvation

1

Preliminary Thoughts

I have argued already that a religious faith worth following has a soteriological power; that certainly Christianity claims such saving power; and that for Christians salvation is held to have been achieved in some way through Jesus. I have also argued that belief in the divine and human nature of Jesus arose because people believed and experienced themselves saved through Jesus, and that on reflection it appeared that the only way to explain how Jesus saved was to ascribe to him both full humanity and full divinity. We have noted that it is not easy to comprehend or make sense of this notion, but we are told by traditionalist theologians that we must accept the mystery, as without it we can make no sense of the saving power in Christianity. Thus: christology is largely an attempt to meet the demands of soteriology.

As Schillebeeckx says,

> The patristic and indeed the whole Christian tradition has always attempted to define the actual person of Jesus in terms of the purport of the salvation brought by him. Because the salvation is 'imparted by God', the one who brought it was himself called divine, and thence it was concluded that Jesus was a divine person.[1]

We must be careful not to push this point too far. It is also true that 'we cannot make of Christianity just what we fancy'.[2] 'Faith utterances [about Jesus] must have a basis in the history of Jesus.'[3]

I shall be taking account of liberation theology later, and its emphasis on the practical results of Christian belief; but we might note now that Jon Sobrino, for example, warns that christology and soteriology are not identical. I do not agree with Sobrino's point that 'christology cannot begin with soteriology',[4] since I have already played my hand and said that this is precisely how christology begins. But Sobrino's real point here is true enough. We cannot begin with human problems, then diagnose what we need to solve those problems, and then invent a Jesus or an interpretation of Jesus who provides that solution. In that case, as Sobrino says, 'Christ would become a symbol, a value cipher, to be filled with whatever set of interests one might wish'.[5] There must be some evidence that the historical Jesus of Nazareth provides the solution, and even that our knowledge of the life and teaching of the historical Jesus affects our perception of the needs and the solution, or there is really no point in choosing Christianity at all.

However, as we shall note later, the confidence of liberation theologians as to how much of the historical Jesus can be recovered is perhaps over-optimistic, and the degree of interpretation of the history of Jesus by liberation theologians in the light of their own perception of the needs and necessary solution is more marked than Sobrino allows. In due course we shall have to examine the problem of a prior commitment to an ideology in much liberation theology.

Granting for the moment, however, that there is a connection between the work of the historical Jesus and the salvation for which we long, liberation theology arose because Latin American Christians were discovering that traditional Christian teaching about the person and work of Jesus was not helping them find salvation from the sociological circumstances of oppression and bondage.

European theologians like Moltmann and Metz had already begun to make a similar point. Christianity, like any religion, faces changing circumstances and changing needs. What constituted salvation for Jewish Christians or Reformation Christians was, perhaps, freedom from the consequences of religious or ritual law. Other Christians, living in fear of the power of hostile external enemies – devils, evil spirits, pagan emperors – might look for victory over these forces. But this might no longer constitute the kind of salvation needed by people oppressed under colonialism, or oppressed by the impersonality and loneliness of life in an urban jungle, or by the loss of clear purpose and ethical guidelines in a new and confusing age, or by powerlessness in the face of little-understood forces of world economy.

William James, at the turn of the century, suggested that the truth of any logical proposition is determined in two ways: the origin and history of the idea, and the present significance of the idea now that it is here. Ultimately, for James, the value of an idea depended upon its usefulness. 'In the end it had to come to our empiricist criterion: By their fruits ye shall know them, not by their roots.'[6] This does not pose such sweeping demands for religious concepts as for those of the Vienna Circle or English analytic philosophy. James was not demanding that there be an empirical basis for any non-tautological concept to be meaningful in any way but only that without any empirical effect the concept is not useful.

He raised sceptical questions about the value of 'conversions' which did not lead to any discernible difference in the quality of life of the convert.[7] Of course we may counter this with G. K. Chesterton's well-known aphorism that Christianity has not been tried and found wanting, but has never been tried. However, the answer will not entirely do. Christian belief is that there is an objective reality about the power of salvation through Jesus. If Christianity has not been tried by most Christians, who presumably at least intend sincerely to want to try it, then what price the objective power of God in Jesus? And if, as James remarks, 'some natural men even excel such committed men in their fruits',[8] then in what way is Jesus the key to salvation?

Thus James suggests that people choose a God for his saving power, and that when the saving power is no longer evident or credible, their religious views change.

> They chose him for the value of the fruits he seemed to them to yield. So soon as the fruits began to seem quite worthless, so soon as they conflicted with indispensable human ideals, or thwarted too extensively other values; so soon as they appeared childish, contemptible or immoral when reflected on, the deity grew discredited and was erelong neglected or forgotten.[9]

There are dangers in James' pragmatism. He himself was not unconscious of them. It may be asked, he said, how a religion like Christianity which is concerned with two worlds can be judged by usefulness in this world alone. It may be claimed that truth, not utility, is what matters.[10] Until recently, American pragmatism had little appeal in European theology. Neo-orthodox theologians like Barth had bitter experience of theologians and churchmen before and during two world wars bowing down before the Kaiser and the Führer. Barth was thus all too aware that worldly utilitarianism may subvert Christian faith to make it the servant of what are in fact sinful, selfish and temporal human demands. This may be what Sobrino had in mind when he said that christology cannot begin with soteriology.

We may claim, too, that there is a constancy about human nature and that human needs do not basically change from age to age. It would be arrogant, therefore, to reject traditional christology and soteriology out of hand as irrelevant. The truth of what seem to us to be outdated notions may be hidden from us in our contemporary blindness.

These are powerful caveats, and history abounds with examples of ideas being thrown out on the grounds of contemporary expediency or narrow-mindedness, only to prove in the end to be right after all. Nevertheless, in integrity (even if with due humility) we can only operate on the basis of concepts and ideas which we do believe to be true and workable and which do not seem to us to fly in the face of evidence or moral justice. The future may prove us wrong, but for the present we must go where reason and conscience take us. Perhaps the failure of the German intellectuals who supported the Kaiser and whose apostasy so appalled Karl Barth, or of churchmen who joined the German National Church, was not that they tried to be aware of modern challenges to faith. Rather, they followed neither reason nor conscience but fear and selfishness to guide their choices.

I am going to suggest that many of the traditional concepts of salvation, while they may ultimately turn out to be true after all, are not currently useful and must in integrity be left in the background. Christianity may be concerned with two worlds, but it claims to be more than merely an other-worldly religion. The whole thrust of incarnational theology is that the saving power of God in Jesus is made available to us in this world; that salvation does have this-worldly implications even if not exclusively so: 'Thy kingdom come, they will be done, *on earth* as it is in heaven.'

We have to ask what are the present evils that afflict mankind, and how, if at all, Jesus saves us from them. What evidence do we have that such salvation is real and not merely a shibboleth? Given our present understanding of what Jesus does and how he affects us, does that require him to be, as Chalcedon claimed, fully God and fully human?

Schillebeeckx remarks that the crisis of faith for modern Christians

lies in the fact that Jesus is still regularly explained to us as salvation and grace in terms which are no longer valid for our world of experience . . . and on the other hand in the fact that we seem no longer capable in words or actions to 'make a defence' for the hope that is in us.[11]

Theology is a second-order activity. It is talk about religious experience. The first-order activity is what happens within the religious community. Theology seeks to rationalize and categorize and generally make logical sense out of this. It develops certain rules for the game. It is possible that sometimes the theological talk may continue after the experiences have stopped, or changed. The rules-discussion goes on when the game is over.

Ecumenical discussion between the different Christian religious traditions is an example of this. Because different religious vocabularies have developed within the separated traditions, ecumenical dialogue is concerned to try to understand and interpret these different vocabularies, hoping to discover that we may in fact be using different words to describe common experiences and thus be not so divided after all.

We sometimes discover that our different approaches can be harmonized, and that our different ways of theological expression mean in essence much the same thing, or have come to mean the same thing under changing circumstances. So we are able to build up an impressive doctrinal edifice such as the Lima Statement of some years ago and speak of 'significant theological convergence'.[12]

However, the significance of 'significant' can be seen in various ways! It is remarkable and significant that so diverse a cross-section of church traditions as shared in the Lima document, from Baptists to Pentecostals to Catholics and to Orthodox, should have been able to find such a measure of common ground. But whether that common ground represents ideas that are significant for the Christian life is another matter. Paul Badham devastatingly questions whether much of the language used in the Lima document is really significant at all. The document is filled with familiar Christian jargon; Badham's questions point up the fact that much of that jargon covers over some very empty experience.

Badham comments, for example, on the Lima agreement about the significance of baptism.

> If . . . Lima is intended to describe what baptism actually means today, one can only say that it is engaging in massive self-deception and bad faith.[13]

Where the Lima document claims that baptism means a 'participation in Christ's death and resurrection', 'an enlightenment by

Christ', 'a liberation to a new humanity where class and sex are transcended', the reality of church life, Badham claims, is not at all like that. In church life, says Badham, race, sex and class distinctions flourish; participation in Christ's death and resurrection is meaningless in terms of any difference in quality between the lives of the baptized and the unbaptized. We cannot comprehend baptism as delivering us from bondage to the ways of sin if the life of the church is still sinful, or if there is no discernible difference between the lives of the baptized and the unbaptized. Thus,

> The problem with all the statements made about baptism in the Lima declaration is that they are too vacuous to contain any testable meaning, or they make claims on behalf of the Christian community which are falsified by the church's behaviour, or they display an arrogant ignorance concerning the non-Christian religious experience of the human race.[14]

This surely matters. We may argue along Wittgensteinian lines that religious language and 'God-talk' has its own inner logic and game-rules, and cannot be judged by external criteria such as empirical verification. I do not wish to enter here into the argument as to whether the existence of God or talk about God can be or needs to be empirically verifiable, although it seems to me that Kai Nielsen[15] makes the point powerfully that Wittgensteinian fideism really leads to a pointless and powerless concept of God that is not worth defending. Talk about whether and what God is may or may not need to have an empirical base. Talk about what God *does* surely cannot possibly make sense without such a base.

To quote John Macquarrie,

> It is the business of the theologian . . . to show in what way God-talk, in spite of its admitted obscurities, does have a meaning, and perhaps a very important one.[16]

We have noted already the need for christology to be grounded at least to some degree upon the historical life of Jesus, with all the attendant difficulties of establishing that life on the basis of modern historical enquiry. Soteriology must surely also be grounded in part on the experience – which must include empirically verifiable elements – of the person who claims to be saved. Salvation-talk is even less amenable to Wittgensteinian fideism than God-talk.

Schillebeeckx seems to have something of this in mind when he says:

A religious utterance always entails both anthropological and theological discourse; it is a way of speaking about man and about God all at once. This automatically implies that a religious utterance can only have a universal significance with a bearing on all human beings, if it can be at any rate to a degree sensibly verified.[17]

That need not necessarily mean that it is empirically verifiable that God, or Jesus, is the saviour. In analysing a faith-healing 'miracle', it may be argued that it is God who lengthened the short leg to match its partner. It may equally be argued that there is a purely natural explanation, such as the power of positive thinking, the relaxation of tense muscles, etc. Wittgensteinian language games would permit either explanation. Choosing between them is a matter of faith, or 'blik', or of existential choice. But what does need to be verified is that the leg has indeed been lengthened, or we shall have been having a very impassioned and no doubt logically elegant argument about nothing.

The argument that salvation-talk needs to be grounded in empirical reality is thus stronger than the argument in this regard about God-talk. A good deal of salvation-talk looks very well rounded and neatly finished off in logic, but bears no relation to any observable reality. This is essentially Badham's criticism of the Lima statement. We may continue to defend the logic of such salvation talk, but from a this-worldly perspective it has become an empty shibboleth. It may still be logically defensible. It does not help us, or convince us that we are in fact saved. Christianity claims that the salvation which it offers is at least in part a here-and-now salvation, though the fullness of the salvation may lie in an eschatological future.

> In the Bible, in both the OT and the NT, salvation is real, achieved and active, but is not yet fully realized, made visible to all, or finally consummated.[18]

and yet,

> The Biblical doctrine of salvation is an assertion of something that actually happened.[19]

Whatever our concept of salvation (and we shall see that there are a number of concepts), if we wish to show that salvation is 'real, achieved and active' we shall have to show the fruits of that reality. We shall also have to show that our concept of salvation does not 'conflict with indispensable human needs, or thwart too extensively other values'.[20] Or else, like James's discredited deities of old, Christian concepts of salvation will be quite rightly neglected or forgotten.

Liberation theology in particular has emphasized this point. Much of European theology had come to seem to Latin American Christians, as they reflected on their own situation, to be irrelevant, to be an exercise in logic which had no practical relevance to the needs experienced by people living under oppressive regimes in poverty, powerlessness and degradation.

Thus Juan Luis Segundo speaks of a hermeneutic circle. The word of God needs to be interpreted according to our own experience; and the reality of our experience needs to be transformed (or saved) by the word of God.

> Each new reality obliges us to interpret the word of God afresh, to change reality accordingly, and then to go back and re-interpret the word of God again, and so on.[21]

Rosemary Radford Ruether says that liberation theology seeks to overcome any dualism between faith and life, prayer and action. The concept in liberation theology of the sin from which we need to be saved includes war, racism and economic exploitation;[22] salvation includes a commitment to the struggle for a transformed social order.[23] In some way our salvation should facilitate such commitment, and help us become more committed.

For liberation theologians, then, the starting point for theology is our own situation and our own needs and those of our community or class. These needs are the 'quarry for theological building material'.[24] We will become more sharply and accurately aware of these needs by means of the tools of sociological analysis.[25] There are, of course, problems for liberation theology. Many liberation theologians will concede that salvation from economic and other exploitation is never fully achieved or completed in this life.[26] There is the problem of how, if the normative events which give rise to our theology are to be interpreted by praxis, their normativeness is to be retained.

This is why some would like a *cordon sanitaire* between secular and sacred interpretation. Barth emphasizes *Heilsgeschichte*, the interpretation in faith of the events of saving history taking place in a realm known only to faith and not susceptible to empirical verification of any kind. However, even Barth's teaching on salvation certainly has a very strong social dimension. Since

Christians know they are saved, Barth believes, they must love and serve their fellows in gratitude to God.[27] This does not mean that Barth agrees that the truth of salvation claims must rest upon any empirical verification, but does mean that even the neo-orthodox school with their *Heilsgeschichte* must be embarrassed if the social implications of salvation are not seen to work in fact. If there is no evidence that the love of Christians for their fellows is any stronger than that of non-Christians, and if Barth is right about the social implications of salvation, then we must ask whether those Christians are truly saved.

Bonhoeffer made the same point from a different perspective. Bonhoeffer certainly believed that salvation is a matter of justification by faith alone, that this is ultimately what life and salvation are about. He was very much a reformation Christian. Yet he says that alongside of the 'ultimate' – grace, salvation – there is a 'penultimate'.

> For the sake of the ultimate, the penultimate must be preserved . . . if for example a human life is deprived of the conditions which are proper to it, then the justification of such a life by grace and faith, if not rendered impossible, is at least seriously impeded.[28]

Bonhoeffer is careful to say that it is not impossible for Jesus to come to one who is still a slave, still hungry, without first freeing and feeding him, but that it is more difficult for such a one to hear the word. We need therefore to prepare the way, and to see that in doing this, in taking care of the physical and social needs of people, we are not dealing with a purely physical realm. For the penultimate concerns overlap with the ultimate; they are for the sake of the ultimate.[29]

I think we need to go beyond Bonhoeffer's position. We shall see in the next section that in the Bible salvation is not only to do with healing the alienation which sin causes between God and humanity. Justification by faith is not, by itself, the ultimate. It is only part of the ultimate. If God is a loving, caring God, then the salvation which God offers will have physical, this-worldly, here-and-now aspects which are not just penultimate to salvation but are part of what salvation means.

At this stage I am not endorsing the understanding of salvation in liberation theology, but only making the point that it raises an important challenge. Salvation must include here-and-now realities; it must include the social dimension. Structures and forces in society which lead to oppression, to the limitation of the development of human potential, to degradation, to the spoiling and wasting of lives, are a very important part of what is meant by sin. Unless we can show that in Jesus there is some here-and-now salvation from this sin, some answer to these problems, then our salvation-talk is severely limited in meaning; and unless we can show that the concept of salvation by which we are interpreting the significance of Jesus' life has some connection with the historical Jesus, our salvation-talk is surely not Christian salvation-talk.

If this is true in Latin America, it is perhaps even more true in my own South Africa, as we shall now see.

2

The South African Experience

Some eighty per cent of people in South Africa claim to be Christian.[30] Virtually all the members of the present white government not only claim to be Christian but are regularly worshipping members of a Christian church. How can it be that sincere and devout Christians have spawned the evil practice of apartheid? Does this not raise real questions about the credibility of Christian claims to provide salvation? These men and their supporters have not been delivered by their faith from fear or slavery to racial ideology. I shall be suggesting later[31] that in some ways their Christian beliefs have contributed to an apartheid mentality; but even if this is not true, it is manifest that these beliefs have not prevented the emergence of that mentality. Might this not be a case where the understanding of salvation held by such Christians is an empty shibboleth?

Furthermore, nearly all the older black leaders of resistance to apartheid, both in South Africa and in exile, are products of a Christian mission education. Many of them are still practising Christians. They include prominent ordained ministers. Why has their resistance been of no avail? Their Christian faith has not given them victory over evil enemies. It might be argued, with some validity, that their current resistance is inspired by their Christian belief, and that any victory they may achieve in the future will be the fruits of that belief. But colonial oppression by Christians predates the present Nationalist government and is more than 150 years old in South Africa; and the full force of apartheid government has reigned since 1948, that is, for nearly half a century. Even if victory comes in the near future (for which pious hope there is little supportive evidence), generations of black Christians have been degraded already. How have these lost generations been saved by Christian faith? Is our salvation-talk, again, not something of an empty shibboleth?

At the time of writing, South Africa is governed under a state of emergency which allows for unlimited periods of detention without access to a court, and several thousands have been in jail under these laws. Of the conditions of their detention we know very little, since it is illegal to print any criticism of the police or armed forces without permission; but there is very strong evidence of the use of torture, even of children.

Although this now happens much less often, black people are still being forcibly removed from where they have their present homes, however humble, to new areas where they do not wish to live. It is estimated that over the past twenty years some three million people have been forcibly removed in this way.[32] Many of the new areas are miles away from any employment. It is common, therefore, for a working person to leave home at 4 a.m. and only reach home again at 8 p.m. Others, living in 'homelands' many miles from any work, must offer themselves as migrant labourers, living in single-sex hostels, able to spend perhaps three weeks a year with their families. How can stable family life possibly exist under such conditions? How can children be brought up with adequate role models?

Although more money is being spent than previously on black education, there is still an enormous discrepancy between white and black education. More than five times as much is spent per capita on the education of a white child than on that of a black.[33] Thus few black children ever go beyond primary school. Only sixteen per cent finish high school. For most there can be no prospect of being anything other than an unskilled labourer.

There is little prospect of blacks being able to change any of this soon. Although undeniable reforms have taken place, none of these, except possibly the legislation permitting black workers to belong to trade unions, have in any way increased the political power of blacks. While petty apartheid in shops, hotels, offices and places of entertainment has largely disappeared, and the Immorality Act forbidding interracial marriage has been withdrawn, none of these changes diminishes the powerlessness of blacks even to influence the political dispensation, far less actually to control it.

Add to this the general poverty endemic in any Third-World population. Add to this again the destruction of traditional African values, family structures, sense of community and community destiny, and the failure to create anything new in its place. Add to this the fact that because of the disintegration of black family life, many black children are born to single parents, and are brought up by ageing grandmothers. Violence has become so rooted in township life that rival political groups among blacks, especially younger black people, frequently kill one another; children grow up in an atmosphere of violence, distrust, and lack of respect for their bewildered elders.

White South Africans are in a quite different situation. Adequate employment, income, education and housing are for the most part readily available, as well as access to political leverage to demand change if necessary (though for non-members of the government party this leverage is certainly limited). But in different ways they, too, are trapped. Many live in fear of the black violence emptying into their peaceful world. Firearms are commonly carried. In more remote areas, landmines are a constant hazard. In subtle ways, many white people are filled with fear and guilt about the situation. The suicide rate is amongst the highest in the world. Increasingly stories appear in the press of men under pressure, unable to cope with stress, killing their wives and children before committing suicide themselves. Alcoholism is common. All of these are surely signs of a society under great stress.

Unable to bear the constant demands, the consciences of even good-willed South African whites inevitably harden. All young white men have to serve for two years in the armed forces. Many are inevitably brutalized in the process. Those serving in the police force also become brutalized in their dealings with other races. Although they do not recognize it, they also are victims of apartheid, their humanity sacrificed for the sake of preserving white control. They are used by the old men who govern South Africa to perpetuate the power base of a government that rarely faces up to the ugliness and violence needed to enforce the system. Cabinet ministers have probably never lifted a *sjambok* (a quirt) in their lives, but depend upon others who must do this work for them.

Yet most of these whites are nominally Christian. Many (a higher proportion than in Western Europe) are regular churchgoers. Why has their Christian faith not saved them from this process? Why has their Christian faith not prevented them from imposing an apart-heid state? It is of course impossible to say it has made no difference at all. It is easy to argue and difficult to disprove that their lives and characters would be much worse without Christian belief to comfort and strengthen them. Nevertheless, the fact that it is Christians who oppress black people in South Africa raises questions about the saving power of Christianity.

A very great deal could be written about the hardships, inhumanity and injustices in South Africa. It is not my purpose here to provide a detailed study of this kind, but only to provide a foundation for my suggestion that a concept of salvation which has nothing to say to this situation is not, in South Africa, a helpful concept. Unless Christian salvation deals with issues of this kind, it is not relevant or useful in the here-and-now, and its claims are significantly weakened.

It might help to give flesh and bones to the reality of the situation if we personalize it by concentrating on a particular individual. I know a young black boy called Sipho. He lives with his mother and his older brothers and sisters in a township on the edges of Pietermaritzburg in Natal, the fairly small capital city of the province. He is at present three years old. He is the fifth child. His father sometimes lives with his mother and his brothers and sisters, but sometimes, when he is working elsewhere, lives with another 'wife' in the Transvaal – a fairly typical situation in South Africa. Sipho's mother Claudia loves him dearly. She is a most respectable, hard-working person who earns her living in domestic service, doing cleaning, washing and ironing. Her income is very small, and is not supplemented by help from her man when he is not living at home. Since she is middle-aged and has little education, it is unlikely that she will ever aspire to any better job.

Sipho's elder sister, aged fifteen, had to leave school last year as she was pregnant. There are now seven in the family. In addition, six others live with them: Sipho's mother's unemployed sisters and dependents. Sipho's mother is the only breadwinner. They all live in a four-roomed shack, with no electricity, and the nearest water is a stream some half a mile distant. Again, Sipho's and Claudia's circumstances are very typical, and certainly many others would be worse off still.

Sometimes Sipho goes to work with his mother, but as that is expensive and tiring, usually he must be left at home with one of Claudia's unemployed sisters. Unfortunately they are drunk for much of the day, and who can blame them in their depressing circumstances? Sipho's mother only sees him awake at weekends, as she leaves for work before he is awake and returns after he is asleep.

In two years' time Sipho will be old enough to attend the school which his brothers attend. Unfortunately the brothers are not always able to attend school every year, as Claudia finds it difficult to pay for fees, books and uniforms. Also, because some of the older children in the black townships have become convinced that a second-class education into a second-class status is a waste of time, they often mount school strikes. Police guard the entrance to the school to ensure that children who attend are not intimidated; but the strikers know the identity of those who continue to attend school, and beat them or kill them later. Thus it has become somewhat rare for any black school actually to complete a school year, making examinations and promotion to higher classes something of a mockery.

To add to Sipho's future problems, the townships around Pietermaritzburg where he lives have been deeply divided since 1987 between rival black political groups. Although the fight was originally between the United Democratic Front and the Azanian People's Organization, it has now developed into a battle between the UDF and Inkatha. The two organizations are both concerned for black liberation, but have different philosophies and ideologies, Inkatha being in favour of limited co-operation with the white government as a means to an end and in favour of a capitalist, sanctions-free economy, while the UDF is more socialist in its views. It is very difficult to sort out the rights and wrongs of the battle, and outside my purposes here. The actual political organizations have taken second place to gang warfare which uses the political labels.

How the warfare affects Sipho is that different areas, and the schools and other institutions in them, become identified, regardless of the views of individual who live there, with one or other group. Persons wander into the 'wrong' area at peril of their lives. It is common for hooligans to enter an enemy area and set fire to a house containing an 'enemy' leader or his family, and to kill the fleeing occupants as they scramble for safety. The death toll around Pietermaritzburg is difficult to establish but numbered more than a thousand from 1987 to mid-1989: more than in Lebanon and Ulster combined.

Sipho will probably attend the same school as his brothers in due course, but in some years will not gain admittance because of overcrowding, or because his mother cannot afford books and uniform that year. When he is admitted, his life will at times be in danger. His mother's life and brothers' lives are in danger now. By the time he is sixteen, he will probably have completed no more than seven years of schooling. He will not be eligible for anything other than a labourer's job. However brilliant or talented Sipho may potentially be, none of his talents will be realized, nor will those of virtually all his contemporaries. Although at present he is full of smiles and baby-talk, by sixteen he will have become an embittered, hate-filled young man, old before his years, with no hope of his situation ever improving. He will certainly have been a witness to, and possibly a participant in, violence and killing. In subsequent chapters, as I look at various models of salvation, and ask how Christian salvation can actually be of saving power for Sipho, I shall describe more of Sipho's circumstances where they are relevant.

Sipho's mother is a Christian, and she belongs to one of the Zionist churches. These are independent African churches with a strong emphasis on faith healing and community spirit. At weekends she finds some relief from her worries by going to church. She is comforted there because she is supported by others who are in the same circumstances. Those who are ill in body or spirit will be prayed over; hands will be laid upon them. In the excitement, with drums beating and music all around them, they may fall to the ground, filled with *Umoya Ncwele*, the Holy Spirit. Claudia is greatly helped by this. She is comforted, too, because in the singing and rituals of her church she is transported briefly to Zion, to the heavenly city where there is no more weeping, sorrow or death. For an hour or two she forgets her troubles; she is with God in his Zion. But her troubles are still there, ready to envelop her on Monday. Is that all that Christian salvation can mean for her? What could be closer to Marx's view of religion as the opiate of the people?

A brief moment of respite and peace may make a bad situation more bearable, but is not a very satisfactory concept of salvation, nor one which more orthodox Christianity would ever have wished to put forward, despite Marx's criticisms. Most commonly, orthodox Christianity has been concerned with salvation from the consequences of sin. It could be argued that the situation of Sipho and his family is marred not only by the effect of intransigent and unjust social structures but by the effects of their own personal sin – irresponsible sexual activity, selfishness, anger, and the rest – and that therefore the traditional Christian message of salvation through forgiveness of sins and consequent repentance and amendment is not irrelevant to them.

This may all be true, although it is difficult to know whether such things as sexual irresponsibility are really culpable in situations of misery, overcrowding and family breakdown. What is surely equally true, however, is that the concept and experience of salvation which is being offered to both black and white South Africa in much traditional Christian teaching is only marginal to the real problem of an evil social system which damages everyone involved in it. Traditional Christian teaching may have helped lessen the evil. It has not conquered it. The evil social system has grown up in a Christian society. Perhaps we need to change radically our concept of what is meant by salvation.

I am not arguing that the meaning of salvation is to be determined exclusively by our own situation and context, or by the needs of which we are aware. Sometimes we may become so accustomed to our problems or failings that we no longer notice them. Christian tradition may make us aware again of issues which are real for us, but to which we have become immune and blind. On the other hand, the issues which concern us at present may be ones which the tradition does not address. I propose, therefore, to examine the traditional concepts of salvation which have been offered at various times in Christian thought and to ask: Does this concept really help in the South African situation, or is there a better model? Does the concept really show what God is doing to help, or how Jesus is our saviour? I shall use Sipho as a test case in each enquiry. If it be argued that I am being unfair in singling out South African society as being particularly evil, I reply that this is not my intention. Similarly tragic scenarios exist in many parts of the world. But they are not my scenario. Christians elsewhere need to work out their own understanding of salvation. Perhaps we may find some common ground between us.

3

Views of Salvation in the Bible

Salvation is certainly a central theme of the Bible, and it is God who does the saving, but there are diverse views as to what we are saved from. However, it is, of course, of crucial importance to identify what we are saved from if we are to see whether the concept of salvation in the Old and New Testaments still fits our own needs, and whether our own needs correspond in any way to what is offered as salvation in the Christian faith. I make no attempt here at a detailed biblical exposition. What follows is a summary of the more commonly held scholarly views about what salvation in the Bible means.

Jesus is seen in the New Testament as the fulfilment of promises made in the Old. Thus salvation has its foundations in past history and promises, as well as being a present reality and a future hope; past, present and future are all combined in the concept.

> The Bible is concerned with the fact that God actually has in concrete historical fact saved his people from destruction, and it proclaims that the historical salvation thus attested is but the foreshadowing or 'type' of salvation that is yet to come.[34]

Salvation is not just a future promise, then. It is based on what God has already done, particularly in the Exodus; and for Christians, on what God has already done in raising Jesus from the dead. Salvation is also to be experienced here and now, while the fullness of salvation not only for humans but for the whole cosmos lies in the future.

What has God done, and what will God do? In the Old

Testament, God is understood to have delivered his people from slavery and oppression in Egypt. He can therefore be trusted to continue to deliver his people from present disasters. Many textbooks[35] suggest that the Hebrew word usually translated as salvation, *yasha*, has at its root the idea of broadness and of liberation from that which constrains and imprisons. Thus what God saves us from is anything that prevents us from freedom in growing or developing. This may be an incorrect reading,[36] but still at a less specialist level we can at least agree that salvation in the Old Testament is seen in basically practical terms: salvation from external enemies, salvation from oppression, salvation from natural disasters like drought or barrenness. It is a matter of God defending the helpless from the powerful. This may mean God's aid in war, or God's aid in justifying the innocent against the legal but unjust accusations of the powerful (Job 13.18).[37] God may well use human agents, especially the king, to achieve this victory or justification, but the power comes from God, and human efforts at self-salvation will be doomed to failure (Psalm 34.16; Psalm 44.67). God alone is saviour.

To a lesser extent salvation in the Old Testament can also mean deliverance from more impersonal afflictions, such as drought or illness,[38] though since these were often seen as punishments for sin, it could be said that they are extensions of the idea that God saves by rescuing the just from unjust legal accusations. It only rarely means salvation from a deserved judgment. Usually in the Old Testament God denies salvation to the sinner.[39] It is those who are faithful who will be saved. 'Redemption is conceived of as deliverance from adversity, oppression, death and captivity.'[40]

In the Old Testament redemption or salvation does not usually mean deliverance from sin. 'Salvation from sin . . . is not the ruling concept in the Old Testament doctrine of salvation.'[41] Salvation is rather a matter of practical rescue. Belief about salvation in the Old Testament is not based primarily on logic, nor on meditation about the nature of God, nor even on personal or mystical experience of alienation from and reconciliation with God, but on the historical fact that God did rescue his people in the past, and the confident hope that he will do so in the future.

God rescues his people not only because he loves them, but because he has a special purpose for them. Here sin does enter the picture, for God's people consistently fail to carry out his purposes. So although the promise that God would make his people great was still believed, by the eighth century BCE the prophets were saying that when God came to establish his kingdom in its fullness, that day of the Lord would involve judgment as well as vindication, and before salvation could be received there would have to be repentance. Salvation goes hand in hand with penitence and reform (e.g. Ezek. 36.26, 27; Jer. 17.9.10). Alan Richardson suggests[42] that the idea of justification by faith which Paul recovered in the New Testament was first preached by the prophets: the people of Israel have been faithless to God; however, God in his righteousness will not abandon them but will cover, blot out, justify their sins (Isa. 43.25).

As generations went by without the promised restoration of Israel coming to pass, the expectation of present deliverance merged into a hope for a more distant future and eschatological deliverance. There was an expectation that God would restore and recreate Israel as the centre of the nations (e.g. Isa. 49.5–13). In the later prophets there was an idea of a new creation of the whole world and cosmos, with a new social and political order, a new Garden of Eden where peace would reign (Isa. 65.17–25). The expectation of a future rather than an immediate salvation became the dominant theme in the exilic and post-exilic prophets. Yet still,

> . . . in the Old Testament, with scarcely an exception . . . salvation is in this world order, and even the restored paradisal righteousness of Isaiah 11.1–9 will belong to this age.[43]

With the intertestamental period, of course, when the promised vindication and restoration failed to appear despite the obedience and the martyrdom of the Maccabaean period, the idea grew (although the seeds were present in earlier times) of an eschatological vindication and deliverance in an after-life rather than in this world. The distinction between a this-worldly and an other-worldly view of salvation should not, however, be drawn too sharply.[44] Nor was there a sharp distinction between what we might call 'religious' and 'ordinary', everyday salvation. Both prophets and apocalyptists took history seriously, and expected God to act in history and in the everyday lives and pursuits of his people as part and parcel of his eternal plan of salvation for his people.[45] All their history was seen as salvation history.

The concept of salvation was a communal rather than a personal one. Even the future eschatological salvation was seen in societal rather than individual terms. The emphasis was on the establishment of peace and harmony between God and humanity, between humans themselves, and between all the parts of God's creation.

Although the prophets would not have denied that God loved each individual, they thought of salvation in terms of the saving of a community rather than of individuals. While at times the expectation was that the whole world would be saved, in the later literature there is certainly a narrowing down of the group which will be saved, and an abandonment of the expectation that the world or the whole nation will be saved (II Esdras 7.60, 61), but salvation is still group salvation, the salvation of the righteous remnant. Little is said about the concept of individual forgiveness of sins and individual reconciliation with God which would so dominate later Christian thought.

There was also neither expectation nor awareness of the need for a divine mediator. God uses human agents to save his people; he sends messengers to his people, but the work of salvation is his work. With Deutero-Isaiah in the songs of the Suffering Servant we get the idea of the faithful, innocent servant (whether individual or group is debated) who through living a life of obedience and love suffers so that others may be saved. But the suffering servant is not God, nor a mediator between humans and God. We also get an idea of the new Moses who will come to usher in the new kingdom, to proclaim and secure release for the captives (e.g. Isa. 42.1); however, the Mosaic figure, and even the mysterious Son of Man figure in the Similitudes of Enoch, is not a redeemer of sinners, nor a mediator between humans and God. He is an agent of God to humans rather than a mediator from humans to the divine.

The Old Testament speaks of God as *go'el*, and this concept, of the one who redeems, who recovers that which had fallen into alien hands, who brings back those who have become enslaved, is an important complementary one. A *go'el* is a next-of-kin who has a duty to recover the forfeited property of his relation, or bring him back if he falls into slavery. God who has adopted Israel is thus 'obliged' to redeem Israel from Egypt or from Babylon. E. M. B. Green suggests that there is an implication of costliness to God in the metaphor.[46] Certainly a human *go'el* had to pay a price. But the idea cannot be pushed too far. Isaiah 52.3, for instance, specifically excludes the idea of God paying a price for our redemption. Now there may be a sense in which the term implies that our redemption has a cost. Green quotes B. F. Westcott in his support, and says of *go'el*, *padah* and *kopher*, all Hebrew words parallel to 'redemption', that 'the use of these words does most forcibly suggest . . . that God's salvation is a very costly matter to him'.[47] However, this is not by any means a doctrine of vicarious atonement, nor is the redemption seen as being redemption from sin. 'The concept of redemption from sin appears nowhere [in the Old Testament] except possibly in Psalm 133.8.'[48]

These embryonic concepts of justification by faith did not imply that God cannot simply forgive sins when his people are penitent and ready to reform, or even as a prelude to penitence. There is no mediator, no in-between, no redeemer, no saviour other than God himself. If there is a cost, it is a cost to God.

In summary, then, in the Old Testament the concept of salvation is seen in very practical terms: the restoration of political freedom, the establishment of God's reign of peace, prosperity and harmony, and protection from all that would harm us or limit God's reign. With this salvation goes a correlated human responsibility: to repent of all we do to harm that reign, and to live in obedience. Salvation thus includes judgment, but it is not really salvation from judgment unless we push the idea of justification by faith beyond what Isaiah really says. In order to be saved, we must face God's judgment, repent, be forgiven and amend; only then will God save us. There is an individual response to salvation, but salvation itself is seen in social, corporate and practical terms. Though God may work through human agents, he himself is the saviour and restorer. Since he has done it in the past, the restoration of his reign can to a degree be expected here and now; but the culmination will happen in the end times, possibly (though this is really an intertestamental concept) in an after-life.

In the period immediately before Christianity, the Jewish people were under a new vassalage, this time to Rome. The expectations of redemption and rescue were still present, though there were a number of different understandings as to how God would accomplish this, and the expectation arose of another figure, distinct from (though closely associated with) God, who would usher in the day of salvation. The Sadducees had no immediate expectation of change, and believed that wise Jews should co-operate with the Romans as the best way of actualizing (at least partially) the hope for a limited freedom and prosperity. The Pharisees were adamant that God would intervene to establish his kingdom, and would raise a Messiah to lead his people into the kingdom, but in his own time: God's hand should not be forced. Faithful Jews should in the meantime observe the Law scrupulously and wait in patience. The Essene community seems to have expected that God would raise up a new king, a new prophet and a new high priest in the Aaronic line to establish his reign, but had no expectation that all Israel would be saved. Only the Essenes would be part of the restored kingdom. The Zealots believed that faithful Jews should work actively to throw off the Roman yoke, and that God would bless their efforts and their heroism with success. In each group, however, salvation was still seen in a corporate way, and as being concerned with the establishment of God's kingdom on earth.

It could be argued that John the Baptist was influenced by Essene ideas, though the evidence is sketchy, and though he seems not to have been exclusivist like the Essenes but to have had a concern for the whole people of Israel. What is important is that with his preaching comes the idea that the day of salvation is imminent. Like the old prophets, he too stresses that salvation and judgment go hand in hand; but salvation and the accompanying day of reckoning are very near. John therefore preaches a message of repentance before a looming day of judgment.

Then comes Jesus, who is sent to seek and save the lost (Luke 19.10). The New Testament is clear that, with his coming, the promised future day of salvation and of judgment has arrived, and the expected Messiah has come (Luke 4.14–21), culminating in 'Today this scripture has been fulfilled in your hearing'. The passage from Luke puts salvation into as social and practical a context as the Old Testament does. Jesus also preaches the kingdom of God. It is notoriously difficult to establish exactly what Jesus himself taught and how much of his reported teachings are really church teaching rather than that of Jesus in his human life, but it is commonly agreed that the kingdom of God is a central part of Jesus' message.

> With this theme [the Kingdom of God] Jesus began his preaching; it is the theme of his parables; it is the theme on his lips at the Last Supper. In the thought of the Kingdom of God he lives, and works, and dies.[49]

There are some differences, however, between the concept of salvation in the Old Testament and that in the New. For one thing, although the present-and-yet-future aspect is still there, the promised reign of God has already, in the New Testament, emphatically come with Jesus, and the ultimate culmination of the kingdom can be expected in the fairly near future.

> In the synoptics, *soteria* [salvation] is a future event, denoting entry into the future Kingdom of God, and yet is also a present event in the sayings about that which *was* lost and *is* found.[50]

G. B. Caird says that the expectation of an early culmination of the kingdom is suggested by Luke 9.2: 'But I tell you truly, there are some standing here who will not taste of death before they see the kingdom of God.'[51] Many of Jesus' parables were probably also aimed at securing the conversion of his listeners to the kingdom before it was too late.

Although the kingdom has come, it does not have overtly political overtones. The idea of salvation from sin, and from the power of evil spirits and the devil, is much more prominent than the idea of salvation from external political enemies. The name of Jesus, meaning 'saviour', is interpreted by Matthew as the one who will save from sin (Matt. 1.21). In Paul's letters, salvation is very largely seen as salvation from wrath and the consequences of sin.

That does not mean that Paul is not concerned with salvation from the principalities and powers of this world. As we shall see, this is an extremely important element in Paul's teaching about that which tyrannizes and enslaves us. But there is no open identification of the 'powers' which enslave with the Roman authorities, and in any case, while powers themselves are sinful, they enslave us because we, too, are sinful. Sin is the tyrant above all tyrants.

Nor was Jesus uninterested in the problems of everyday life. It is not true that Jesus' preaching of the kingdom had no socio-political elements. The evangelists, except for Matthew, were writing to a non-Jewish audience in a time when relationships between the tiny church and the Roman empire were beginning to turn sour. They therefore chose to portray Jesus as being in no way a threat to the Romans. Probably, however, the historical Jesus had a stronger anti-Roman profile than the Gospels suggest. The *Tendenzkritik* of the Tübingen school takes this view, though C. F. D. Moule[52] says that we should apply this technique with reserve and only when there is some evidence that the evangelists have made some distortions. There does, however, seem to be such evidence. Jesus' entry into Jerusalem on a donkey in fulfilment of Zech. 9.9 was surely a very public and political claim to kingship of a sort, which he must have known could hardly be ignored by the Roman authorities. Despite the evangelistic concern to show that it was Jewish leaders who sought his death, his death at Roman hands must have meant that the Roman authorities saw him as a threat to public peace. It is not really credible that Pilate, who according to Josephus had so ruthlessly offended the Jews' deepest sensibilities in others ways,[53] would have been browbeaten into crucifying Jesus against his will.

John Howard Yoder[54] makes a convincing argument that Jesus and Paul and the early church did have a very important social dimension to their teaching, and we shall return to this later. There *is* a strong social dimension to the kingdom of God for both Jesus and Paul. But there is no strong evidence that Jesus was interested in establishing political control for himself, for his followers, or for Israel. There is no emphasis on political liberation from the Romans, though it is possible, as Yoder implies, that the liberation which Jesus offers envisages freedom for Romans, Greeks and Jews together. While such a notion is indubitably political, this is not the same, however, as the Zealot hope for Jewish self-determination, nor is there any evidence that Jesus shared any such hopes. There is no promise of earthly prosperity – indeed, quite the opposite: 'Foxes have holes, and the birds of the air have nests; but the Son of Man has nowhere to lay his head' (Matt. 8.20).

The view expressed by Reimarus through to Brandon and some liberation theologians that Jesus was a Zealot or political messiah, or that he had primarily political or economic aims in his idea of mission, can be discounted, as the contributors to *Jesus and the Politics of His Day* make clear.

> The popularity of the Zealot or revolutionary interpretation of Jesus in the last decade witnesses to men's perennial propensity to look to him for support for their own ideals and aims. But it provokes the wry reflection that one can find support from Jesus for violent political action only by discounting those aspects of the traditional picture of him which gave most reason for seeking his support.[55]

Jesus does seem to have had a real concern for the poor. Luke's 'Sermon on the Plain' is probably nearer to the original words of Jesus than Matthew's 'Sermon on the Mount', and Luke makes it clear that it is the 'poor' and the 'hungry' who are blessed, not the 'poor in spirit' or those who 'hunger after righteousness' (Matt. 5.3, 6; Luke 6.20–21; compare). The poor are closer to the kingdom of God than the rich (Matt. 19.24).

However, even if Luke 1.53, 'He has filled the hungry with good things and the rich he has sent empty away', represents an intention of Jesus, there is no evidence that he ever achieved this aim, nor that he released any political captives, nor that he set free those who were politically oppressed in any literal way (Luke 4.18 notwithstanding!). If salvation has already come in Jesus, as the passage

asserts (Luke 4.21), then salvation clearly does not primarily mean
these things.

There is still concern with material and physical ills: the healing
miracles, the commandments to care for the oppressed, imprisoned,
hungry and poor (Matt. 25.31–46), the promise that nothing escapes
God's notice (Matt. 10.29). However, despite all these important
qualifications, the emphasis as far as salvation is concerned changes
from the primarily practical, political and corporate salvation envisaged in the Old Testament. In the view of the New Testament the
primary evil from which we are saved is a condition of personal
sinfulness – which has social and political consequences. The good
into which we shall be saved is a condition of personal obedience –
which will have social and political consequences, too, both in our
concern for the oppressed and in our continuing love for those who
oppress us. In the New Testament, the content of salvation becomes
one of personal liberation from sin, from the consequences of the
wrath of God against sin, from helplessness against the power of sin
to dominate and corrupt us – and, of course, from death as one of the
major consequences of sin. 'The mission of Jesus, whose object is
salvation, is closely bound up with the forgiveness of sins.'[56] Even the
healing miracles show that it is often sin which lies behind the illness,
so that healing and forgiveness go hand in hand. Sin is also personified in the evil spirits, and the exorcism miracles show that Jesus is
master over this personified sin.

Salvation is thus a personal liberation, even though once
liberated we become part of a new community, because each
individual person has to respond to the challenge which Jesus, and
following him the church, issues in his teaching. This again is a
change in emphasis from the Old Testament where Israel as a whole
is to be judged, and called back to obedience. The New Testament
directs its appeal at individuals, who then become the community of
the saved and as a community continue to reach out to other
individuals.

I do not think that we should push these differences too far. Both
Old and New Testaments talk to some degree of salvation as
liberation from political bondage and from the consequences of sin.
Both Old and New Testaments have corporate and individual
aspects. The New Testament is not purely individualistic, nor does
it draw a sharp distinction between the individual and the institutio-
nal/communal. There is continuity between Old and New. The
emphasis, however, changes. Individual destiny, and individual
decision-making, become more marked than before.

The basis for the belief that God can save in Jesus is, as in the Old Testament, a historical rather than a philosophical or ethical one. The historical basis in the New Testament for faith in God's saving power is not, however, just the Exodus, but pre-eminently the cross and resurrection of Jesus.

However, this again means a change in emphasis. The fact that the resurrection is offered as the proof that God saves means that however important salvation in this life and this world may be for the New Testament, the focus of the new life is not in this world but in heaven. The ultimate dimensions of salvation reach beyond history. The fact that resurrection lies on the far side of the cross means that for Christians there can be no salvation which excludes suffering. There is a paradoxical tension here. God cares about our sufferings, and wants to relieve us of them; and God calls us to suffer. The disciples of Jesus are to take up their cross. To be saved means not to escape from pain or death, but to triumph over them.

This attempt to summarize the meaning which the New Testament attaches to salvation makes the New Testament sound more homogeneous than it really is. Many different metaphors for salvation are used in the synoptic Gospels, in John, in Paul and in the other documents. How Jesus saves is perceived in different ways. Is it his life, his teaching, his death or his resurrection which achieves our salvation? All are emphasized by one author or another. As I have remarked before, the authors are all convinced that humans are saved in Jesus, and saved in Jesus alone, and there are some generally common features to their thought; but what salvation means, and how it is accomplished, is perceived by each author (and his group) differently, depending on needs, culture and world-view, and experience. Jesus is seen as the one in whom is experienced '. . . decisive, final and eschatological salvation, both by virtue of his life and also by virtue of his death and God's merciful attitude towards his death',[57] but all of this is expressed in terms conditioned by the culture of the time. Our problem, as Edward Schillebeeckx observes in making this point, is that the modern church seems to be unable to express the meaning of salvation in terms of our own culture in a way that brings joy and salvation.

What hope do the views which I have been describing offer to Sipho, mentioned in the previous section? Do they offer help to him in any way?

One might summarize what I have suggested are the distinctive features of salvation in the New Testament like this. Salvation, although still to come in fullness, has already come in Jesus; it is

primarily concerned with sin; although it has socio-political implications it does not offer a transfer of political power; nor does it offer
release from poverty, although the poor are especially loved; it is
offered to individual persons rather than to the whole community *en
bloc*, and its ultimate focus is heavenly and other-worldly.

We may ask in what meaningful sense a black person in South
Africa could say that salvation has already come for him or her in
Jesus. For very many, the only conceivable sense would be a
spiritual one. For most (admittedly not all), living conditions and
the hope of improving those living conditions remain quite unchan-
ged. Indeed in the case of this poorer majority it might well be
argued that living conditions have changed for the worse: there is
more humiliation, more fear, more hunger than there was before
their parents ever heard of Christianity.

The New Testament emphasis on sin and salvation from the
effects of sin needs some reinterpretation if it is to fit Sipho's
circumstances. For while Sipho and his family are the slaves of sin, it
is not so much their own culpable sin and guilt which is at issue.
Others have sinned against Sipho, making him the victim of their
own greed and desire to retain power. Certainly Sipho and his
family, because of their circumstances, are likely to be heavily
involved in what might superficially be called sin. Deprived social
circumstances mean that sexual promiscuity, casual theft, violence,
even murder, is likely to be part and parcel of their lives to a degree
unimaginable to cushioned Western society. Sometimes Sipho will
be the victim, sometimes the perpetrator. He will be vulnerable to
evil influences. There will be overwhelming cause for him to
become guilt-ridden himself, or alternatively to become a hardened
bully and a township thug; to become resentful and bitter. A gospel
offering forgiveness of sins, release from guilt, reconciliation or
acceptance with God and power to overcome guilt, temptation and
bitterness is certainly not totally irrelevant to him. Indeed there are
those in South Africa who believe that precisely because Christians
have a gospel which offers this, they are the only key to any possible
re-creation of a better social order in South Africa, for only
Christians will be able to approach the rebuilding with forgiveness
and lack of resentment, without demanding an eye for an eye,
without carrying over into the new order a destructive anger and
vindictiveness.[58]

We shall come back to some of these issues again in due course. I
will only say now that if people live in a situation that makes sin
virtually inevitable, then a concept of salvation which deals

primarily with sin and with release from guilt is dealing only with the symptoms, not the cause, of the problem. It is a marginal concept. A Christian life-style is impossible in conditions of gross overcrowding, poverty and brutalization. No doubt there will be heroic exceptions to this generalization, but exceptions do not help ordinary people. Sipho's problem is caused not by his own sin but by those who sinfully imprison him in an unjust and discriminatory system. Indeed we might well argue that his oppressors are to a large extent also victims of the system. It is clear that Afrikaner nationalism is the product of Afrikaner history, which in turn is the product, at least to a very large extent, of English imperialism and colonial exploitation. Until the system is changed, Sipho's position cannot really change.

Although there are individual moral heroes who live in squalidness and triumph over their circumstances, living a life of luminescent love and gentleness,[59] intolerable living conditions produce moral evil. Living conditions for Sipho will not change until political power is distributed differently. A gospel which is not primarily concerned with the transfer of political power cannot help Sipho with what is really the crux of his issues. As long as Sipho and his family live in such poverty as they do – we are not talking about a genteel poverty of mended clothes and simple meals, but a poverty where there is sometimes no food for several days by the end of the month, no money for basic medicine, no money to rebuild when heavy rains cause their mud-plastered wattle-and-daub shack to collapse – a gospel which makes no promise of material prosperity does not seem to offer a salvation of much power.

Perhaps, though, if it is the sin of his oppressors which cause Sipho's situation, a Christian faith which broke the power of sin in the lives of his oppressors could save Sipho too? But to add to our perplexities, those who have engineered and who still impose the injustices upon him are themselves Christians, who do *not* appear to have been delivered from fear, from self-justification, from resentment, from violence. It could be argued that those who do such things, despite any Christian claims they may make, are not true Christians; but what would that mean? They are baptized; they have (many of them) sincerely given their lives to Jesus in personal conversion; they hear the Word and receive the sacraments. If they have not been transformed, if their moral blind spots have not been removed by this exposure to grace, why should Sipho believe that Christian faith can transform him or his peers?

The call to individual repentance and conversion is also likely to involve Sipho in some tension. There is always a problem if the church is seen to evangelize people out of their original community, the unsaved community of the world, into the new community of the saved. In this case, how far does the convert still have loyalties to the old community? This is not an insuperable problem. The convert can hold dual citizenship. Indeed, for Christians to refuse to become swallowed up in a secular programme of political liberation but rather to insist on having dual loyalties, to the gospel as well as to the 'party' or cause, may well be of great significance. In South Africa, however, there is an increasing call for the church not to be a kind of third force in the clash between white and black, or rich and poor, lest this blunt the force of the black resistance.

> The Church must avoid becoming a 'third force', a force between the oppressor and the oppressed . . . the Church must not confuse the issue by having programmes that run counter to the struggles of those political organizations that truly represent the grievances and demands of the people.[60]

Where there are already two communities in conflict, it is difficult for Christians to hold back from total commitment to one side or the other, and indeed for them to do so may well weaken the political impact of the resistance. A Christian Sipho will feel pulled to identify wholly with his struggling black community and whatever methods that community decides to use as part of the struggle. If he should say that as a Christian he must hold back from violence or from the rejection of all white persons, he may be seen to be a traitor to his people's cause. It may be that as a Christian he will *need* to hold back from identifying totally with one side or the other, and that this is precisely the one contribution that Christianity can make, but the point still remains: conversion of individuals out of the oppressed community may weaken the power of that community to resist.

Certainly the emphasis on heaven as the only state where God's kingdom can be fully attained, and the focus on life after death, has been another way in which in the past the anger of the oppressed classes has been defused. The New Testament view of salvation is not exclusively heavenly, but in so far as it says that our real treasure lies there (Matt. 6.20) it can and in fact sometimes does act as the opiate that Marx said would be the case.

Perhaps, to do the opposite from Marcion, we should put our emphasis on the Old Testament instead. The Old Testament concept of salvation here on earth as the overthrowing of enemies and the restoration of peace and prosperity appears to be much more relevant to Sipho's situation. In this view God will deliver his chosen people from oppression, poverty and enslavement, and will establish a new deal for the righteous chosen group, if not for the whole world. Not surprisingly, black and liberation theology find much affinity with the Old Testament. It can easily be interpreted as saying that God will intervene on behalf of the poor, or the workers, or the black people, or whoever we conceive the current chosen group to be, and God will put their troubles right. The problem is that God did not ever establish this kingdom for the Jews of old. The exodus was never repeated. The restoration of the kingdom after the Babylonian exile did not prove to be the promised kingdom of freedom and righteousness. That kingdom has never come. We may answer that this is because of the sins of God's people, but it is still the fact that the Old Testament promises have never been fulfilled.[61] There are no grounds for Sipho to believe that the promises, if they apply to him, will be fulfilled in his lifetime.

But perhaps we have interpreted the Bible, especially the New Testament, too narrowly. Perhaps there are elements in the life and teaching of Jesus relevant to Sipho which have been developed in subsequent Christian tradition – or which could potentially emerge but have not been developed as yet: the value which Jesus placed on individuals; the sense of dignity and self-worth which comes from knowing that God loves us even if we are poor (or especially if we are poor); the example of courage and commitment which Jesus gives; the ideal of radical obedience transforming the world. We shall give our attention to these possibilities later.

The work of the biblical critics may show us that the evangelists, in the course of their own theologizing, have obscured some of the significance of Jesus for our salvation. They wrote for a largely Gentile church. Gentile Christians were not all at that stage the victims of political oppression, although some would presumably have been slaves and poor people. Nor, in the earlier New Testament documents, were they yet victims of a very serious religious oppression. The people to whom Jesus spoke in Palestine lived in quite different circumstances from those whom Mark's Gospel addressed in Italy. The people whom Jesus addressed were oppressed and humiliated. Some of Jesus' teaching may take on a new significance for those who at present share that situation in a way that the early Gentile church did not, and which Mark consequently did not emphasize.

We need, then, to discover a model of salvation which answers our problems, and which nevertheless fits the facts of Jesus' life and words.

> Our starting point, then, is the unjust reality of our present historical situation . . . [we cannot] assume that Jesus has all the answers to *our* problems. There is no point in trying to *make* him relevant. All we can do is look at him from the perspective of our time with an open mind.[62]

In its history the church has developed a number of such models, each from the perspective of its current historical circumstances. Each of them claims a scriptural basis; each is an attempt to interpret the New Testament in the light of these different circumstances. This is a very necessary process. Without a theory, the fact of Jesus' life has no significance for us. It is the theory which bridges his life and ours.

> It is all too simple to affirm that we are only concerned with the *fact* of the atonement and that theories are an optional extra.[63]

We turn, then, to examine how successive periods of Christian thought have interpreted the salvation which Jesus brings.

4

Traditional Models of Salvation in Christianity

Traditional models of salvation can be classified in a number of ways. While each has its own emphasis, they are often seen as complementary rather than each being an exclusively correct way to understand salvation. F. W. Dillistone, for example, speaks of two main types of theory: theories which develop patterns of corporate experience, and theories which develop examples of individual achievement,[64] though his subdivision of theories runs to nine! O. C. Quick perceives four types of 'atonement theories'.[65] Already we notice in that terminology a narrowing down of the concept of salvation, and perhaps an unconscious emphasis on certain types of theories, for at least the classic or victory theory which Quick includes in his list deals with more than the restoration of the relationship between humans and God, which is all that 'atonement' seems to imply. Ritschl lists eleven types of theory, though perhaps not all of his theories would be recognized by everybody as Christian.[66] Thus there are many different ways in which salvation can be perceived.

For my purposes, since the exact categories do not matter, I intend to deal with the material under four headings in this chapter, not in the chronological order in which they gain emphasis in the history of Christian thought, but in an order convenient for my theme:

> (*a*) The idea of substitutionary atonement;
>
> (*b*) The classic or victory theory;

(c)   The subjective or moral influence theory;

(d)   The idea of sacrifice.

Then in the next chapter I turn to some contemporary themes in the understanding of salvation. Throughout, my questions will be: Does this help us in any significant way in the situation in which we find *ourselves*? Will it answer to the needs of Sipho? We may find some elements in all these theories which are helpful, and other elements which are not. Quick suggests not only that all the theories are in fact complementary, but also that each is defective on its own and is not intended by its proponents to be exclusive.

> We can reach a reconciling point of view from which each type of theory is seen to make its essential contribution to the truth, although no one theory . . . can be sufficient to express its fullness.[67]

Quick's eirenicism is not echoed by everybody. John Macquarrie, for example, certainly does not agree that the substitutionary theory makes an essential contribution to the truth.

> Even if it could claim support from the Bible or the history of theology, [it] would still have to be rejected because of the affront which it offers to reason and conscience.[68]

Perhaps some theories, or some aspects of them, will have to be discarded, or, as I argued earlier, at least put on the 'back burner' as not currently credible or helpful.

(a)   *The idea of substitutionary (or penal) atonement*
In the words of Mrs Alexander's hymn,

> There was no other good enough
> To pay the price of sin.
> He only could unlock the gate
> of heaven and let us in.[69]

The idea has a long history in Christian thought, and is expressed in a number of different ways. At its most crude level, it means that God is righteously angry with sinful humans and must punish sin in his righteousness, but Jesus, although himself innocent, has borne the due penalty for our sins. Thus God is now able to forgive and be reconciled with us. To be fair, the theory within Christianity (whatever may be true of sacrificial theories in primal religion) is not intended to suggest that God changes his attitude towards us because of Jesus' death on the cross. God's attitude is always seen to be one of both righteousness and love. By sending his Son as an extension of himself into the world to bear the punishment due for sin, God changed, not his attitude towards us, but his relationship with us. He made it possible for love to win out, by himself paying the demands of righteousness. Nevertheless, the principle contained in this idea is that forgiveness requires that justice or honour must first be satisfied. Hence it is sometimes also called the 'satisfaction' theory.

All Christians believe that Jesus Christ, his life, death and resurrection (in some form), is the key to salvation from this world's ills. However, the nature of those ills and how Jesus saves us from them is perceived in different ways. The understanding with which we are now concerned is that the primary ill is the curse under which all humans stand because of human disobedience towards God. Because God is God, he cannot allow himself to be dishonoured; the honour due to him must be paid – or, to put it in a later form, because God is just, he cannot allow his justice to be undermined, therefore sin must be punished and paid for. Were God to fail to demand this, he would be less than God; he would be condoning injustice, and the moral fabric of the universe would be destroyed. Humans therefore stand under damnation; they must die, and not only die but be raised again in order to be punished eternally, since the affront to God's honour and justice is infinite in its seriousness.

But God is also a God of love; he therefore sent his Son, Jesus, God-made-man, to save humans from damnation. Jesus lived a life of perfect obedience, which is beyond the capability of ordinary, fallen humans. He therefore did not deserve death. However, he voluntarily allowed humans to crucify him, thus giving to the Father that which in justice he is not required to give. Jesus as God died on the cross, so that his payment is infinite; but he is also Jesus the man, so that his payment was for all humans who will accept, by faith, that Jesus has paid their debt of honour or satisfied the necessary demand for punishment on their behalf. God has reconciled them to himself. They can be forgiven, accepted as justified, and enter into eternal harmony with God.

The seeds of this theory are present in the New Testament and in early Christian doctrine, but it became the major emphasis in Christian salvation doctrine with Anselm in the eleventh century. From that time on it has remained the dominant theory of salvation, though it was often held in conjunction with other models.

There are two root concepts behind this idea, both of which are required if the theory is to be accepted. One is that there is an inexorable system of justice in the world, a sort of law or a system of obligation. This may be seen in legal terms or in terms of a debt of obedience and honour. Unless this system is maintained, the moral fabric of the universe would collapse. The sinner may be repentant and ready to amend – though it may be doubted whether, given sinful human nature, our penitence and amendment can ever be thorough enough – but nevertheless the sin, or the lack of obedience, must be atoned for. God cannot simply forgive, for that would be at some level to condone evil. Justice must be satisfied. Since humans are unable to make that satisfaction, God must do so himself.

Thus from a christological point of view Jesus must be God, or the infinite satisfaction which infinite sin demands will not have been made. Only one who is divine, perfectly good, perfectly sinless, can make that satisfaction. This may be argued from two points of view. Because humans are sinful and imperfect, they will be unable to live a perfectly obedient life which alone can satisfy justice; only the God-Man can lead that life. Or the argument may be extended still further to clinch the matter. Since sin has already been committed, even a life of perfect obedience cannot meet that debt to justice or honour, since a human is required to live in perfect obedience anyway, so that the perfect life (even if possible, which it is not) would not repay the debt owing from the past, but only meet current obligations. Therefore again only the God-Man (who because he is God owes nothing to himself), by living a life of perfect obedience and accepting a punishment which is not, in justice, due to him, can repay that debt.

The other root concept is that of human solidarity. Negatively, because one person sins we are all held to be guilty. Adam's sin is the sin of all, either because he is literally our forefather, or because the sin of one human means that all humans share in his guilt. Thus we are all condemned to eternal punishment because of the accumulated sins of humanity. Even if we set that belief aside, the theory demands that one person's virtue, one person's payment of the debt of justice, counts for all. Thus it is essential that Jesus be not only truly divine but also truly human. It is humanity's sin for which he atones, humanity's debt to justice that he repays. Therefore he must be human.

This theory clearly requires the essence of the Chalcedonian Definition. Some budding of the idea, not surprisingly, can be found in Athanasius, and even earlier. As Gustav Aulen remarks,

Tertullian provides the building materials, Cyprian begins the construction out of them of a doctrine of the atonement.[70]

The seeds are in the New Testament, and even, especially with regard to the idea of human solidarity, in the Old. In Genesis 18 we read that fifty, forty, even ten righteous men may cause YHWH to suspend the destruction of Sodom. Just as many are punished for the sin of one (Josh. 7.19–26), so a righteous one may bear the iniquity of us all (Isa. 53.5) and bear our sins. Whether Old Testament Jews believed in any way in substitutionary death is dubious though debatable.

> The ideas of transference and substitution are indeed present in the Old Testament, but . . . in connection with rites of purification and expiation they are not as pervasive and fundamental as scholars . . . often imply.[71]

Sam Williams does not think that the suffering servant of Isaiah 53 has to do with expiation, but with the suffering of a righteous man who is vindicated by God.

It is Paul who has the most explicit ideas in the New Testament about the death of Jesus saving us from the wrath. In developing his ideas, Paul may possibly have had in mind IV Maccabees, where the idea is found. Paul (Rom. 5.12–21) is clear that through Adam's sin we are all subject to death (5.17) and condemnation (5.13) – and through Jesus' victory those who are in Christ through baptism are victorious over death, and judged righteous by, reconciled with, God. (Rom. 5.1, 10). God treats the sinner, although still sinful, as if righteous; he imputes righteousness to us by virtue of our being 'in Christ'. It seems certain that Paul taught the idea of human solidarity, even if, as Dodd argues (somewhat improbably in my view), he did not necessarily believe in a historical Adam.[72]

Whether Paul believed in the concept of Jesus' death being a satisfaction for sin is notoriously a matter of debate. It seems to me that Leon Morris[73] is probably correct in saying that this is what Paul meant by *hilasterion* in Romans 3.24, and that those who claim that Paul meant expiation rather than propitiation are arguing on the basis of their own theological preferences.

Whatever Paul meant, the doctrine received its fullest expression with Anselm's *Cur Deus Homo?* in 1098. The first major systematic treatment of the atonement in the church's history,[74] Anselm's views were to remain dominant for the next millennium. Anselm framed them in terms of the feudal society of his day. Society was held together by a hierarchical system of honour. The peasants owed honour, recognition of his status, and obedience to the knight, who in turn protected them from other violent men; the knight to the baron, who gave his umbrella of support to the knights; the baron to the king. To God, who is the supreme King, we owe honour and obedience most of all. If we disobey God we dishonour him, we fail to recognize his necessary pivotal place in the scheme of things. This has consequences for society and the individual. Because humans as a whole fail to honour God, the fabric, the integration of the cosmos is at risk. The individual becomes subject to rejection by God, spiritual and physical death, eternal banishment to hell. Jesus, however, paid on our behalf to God the debt of honour and obedience which we fail to pay, and the consequences are averted.

Over the years, as feudalism gave way, the theory was modified, particularly by Calvin. Calvin in a new age of cities rather than farms and villages, where justice rather than force of arms seemed to provide the glue by which society was kept together, changed the image of honour paid to God to a more legal image of God's justice demanding satisfaction. With this went a consequent narrowing down of Anselm's focus on the life *and* death of Jesus which both honour the Father to a focus, rather, on the death of Jesus alone, as a legal execution. Thus the demand that in order to fulfil the requirements of justice sin must be punished and paid for is met in the execution of Jesus. Jesus was not a sinner. His death in justice could not therefore be required, and his undeserved death on the cross therefore makes satisfaction for our sins. Whether in its Anselmian or Calvinist form, the theory that Jesus vicariously pays the debt of honour or of justice owed to God which makes forgiveness and justification by faith possible is probably still the dominant salvation theory in Christianity and in the preaching of the church (if not the teaching of academic theologians) to this day, at least at a popular level. It is surely still the basis of most evangelical appeal.

Our criticisms of the theory need not detract from its genius in its own time. Despite some mediaeval excursions into angelology, it ties up many of the loose ends from Athanasius and the Chalcedonian Definition; it includes within itself other theories such as the exemplarist. One major merit is that it shifts the focus from the devil's rights to God's rights. If Anselm's theory is accepted, it makes it logically necessary to believe in the two natures of Jesus. The theory has the great merit of taking human feelings of guilt seriously, and is perhaps psychologically satisfying for that reason. It takes the *skandalon* of the cross and tries to show us its logical necessity from a divine perspective. Undoubtedly, too, despite its emphasis on justice, it makes it clear that God's love is ultimately triumphant.

Nevertheless, my earlier reference to Macquarrie[75] reminds us that for many the theory will not do today. It has always had its critics. Anselm himself provides the first, in the words which he places in the mouth of Boso, his partner in the dialogue. Such is Anselm's genius that Boso's questions have a surprisingly modern ring to them. Does the theory not mean that God's justice overshadows God's love?[76] Does the fact that Jesus had to be the sacrificial victim not deprive Jesus of human free will?[77] Why cannot God simply forgive?[78] Why, if he cannot simply forgive, are we enjoined to forgive those who sin against us?[79] Why should the devil be regarded as having rights over humans?[80] Is God just in punishing the innocent in order to forgive the guilty?[81] Does the theory not make God more concerned for his honour than for our salvation?[82]

Abelard was a severe critic of the theory in the twelfth century, as was Socinus in the sixteenth. Nearer to our own time, Hastings Rashdall and Gustav Aulen revived the exemplarist and classic theories respectively, largely because they were unhappy with the vicarious satisfaction theory.

Boso's criticism that in the theory God is more concerned for his own justice than with love for his creatures is not really answered. Although God's love means that he himself provided the satisfaction for the human debt of dishonour, even this is said in the context that God's plan for heavenly order cannot be thwarted. Although for Anselm Jesus' whole life of obedience, culminating in his death, constituted the representative satisfaction of honour to the Father, it is really his death, which could not logically be required of him since he is sinless, which makes up the extra offering to God to repay the debt of lost honour – since Jesus' earthly obedience is God's due anyway. In Calvin this narrowing down of the focus to the death alone was taken still further, and Jesus' human life is of secondary importance.

Many modern writers take offence at the theory because of the injustice of punishing one for the sake of many.

The fundamental defect of Anselm's attempt to reconcile the traditional scheme with ordinary ideas of justice is that no civilized system of law permits the attribution of guilt to all humanity for the sin of one.[83]

Most text books on atonement theories list the problems with the theory: the alleged lack of relationship between God's honour and God's justice; the trinitarian problem of ascribing different moral qualities to the Father and the Son; the somewhat external or 'commercialized' concept of sin; the lack of overt scriptural reference.

Our question is, however, posed from Sipho's point of view. How can the theory help him? I have argued in defence of Anselm that far from emphasizing only the justice of God, he claimed that his theory shows that God in his mercy has provided the way for love to triumph, so that sinners can be forgiven. Once Sipho is old enough to be regarded as responsible for his own actions, it is very likely indeed that he will commit fairly grave 'sins'. However, the extent to which he can be held personally responsible for them is questionable. Overcrowding, misery, poverty, lack of stable family life, make sexual immorality, violence and theft almost inevitable. In what way does Sipho owe a debt of honour to God? How has he offended against God's justice, or earned God's wrath? He is more sinned against than sinner, more to be pitied than blamed. His sins are hardly his fault, but the fault of those who oppress him, and the fault of a system which puts Sipho into a hopeless social environment.

Anselm as Abbot of Bec or Archbishop of Canterbury, Calvin as leader in Geneva, represent the reasonably well-off and reasonably free people of any era who more or less direct their own lives and can therefore more or less be held accountable for them. Such persons can find comfort in the penal theory; aware of their culpable guilt, they need an assurance of forgiveness. The theory does not seem, however, to have the poor and 'unfree' in mind. It is essentially theology for the *bourgeousie*. The theory assumes a corporate human guilt for the sins of humankind; but to what extent do the victims of human greed and lust for power share in that corporate guilt? The penal theory is a concept which offers forgiveness to Sipho's oppressors, but it carries no assurance of God's love for Sipho and those like him.

Its supporters claim that the theory intends to uphold basic justice in the universe; that to forgive sin only, without demanding payment or satisfaction, is to imply that sin is relatively trivial and unimportant. They claim that the charge that the theory drives a wedge between the Father and the Son, making the Father vengeful and the Son loving, is untrue, since both Father and Son will that sin should be thus atoned for. God's love is shown in that he sends his own Son to be the willing victim. But what cannot be escaped from is that the theory has a primarily retributive view of justice, a belief in a world not unlike the Hindu world of *karma*, where an impersonal system of law and obligations takes precedence over everything else, and God himself is as much obliged to keep this law as any of his creatures. In this regard, Anselm did not move on beyond those who believed that, because of this law, sinful human beings belonged by right to the devil. Perhaps for Anselm they did not belong to the devil, but they did belong to destruction and perdition, to which God would be obliged to send them if satisfaction were not made.

Retributive justice is the last thing that Sipho deserves or needs. He lives in a world where retributive justice, an eye for an eye, is the name of the game in township violence and black/white politics. In the black suburbs of the city where he and I live, as I have said, literally hundreds of people, many of them schoolchildren, have been killed in the past year; not by police or army, but in battles between the Inkatha movement and the United Democratic Front.[84]

Sipho's mother Claudia and her children have no preferences either way. Claudia, like many in her position, knows and cares little about politics but wants her children to have an education and to live in peace. This however, is not possible. Their house is situated in a block which is regarded as Inkatha territory. The local school is therefore by association an 'Inkatha' school. Periodically UDF supporters lie in wait for these Inkatha scholars and kill them. Three children at the primary school which Sipho's brothers attend were killed in 1987. Were they to live in a UDF block, there would be no difference. As one group inflicts violence on the other, so the injured group must fight back the next day and kill an equal number of persons. Neither the Inkatha nor the UDF leaders officially sanction these happenings, but they are also unable to stop them. Although UDF–Inkatha clashes are responsible for most of the violence in my town, there are other equally violent clashes elsewhere: *witdoeke* versus Crossroads residents in the Cape, Crossroads versus the squatter community called KTC. Retribution demands an ever-increasing spiral of violence.

Rigid military control prevents blacks from venting their anger on whites or other race groups, which is probably part of the reason why there is so much frustrated inter-black violence. Occasionally, however, there are bomb attacks, sometimes in white shopping areas, presumably as part of an attempt to terrorize whites into power-sharing. Whites, too, then demand retributive vengeance. Every time there is a major bomb explosion in a street or shopping centre, it has become almost predictable that within days there will be an army raid on alleged African National Congress bases in a neighbouring country, presumably in order to show alarmed government supporters that the government has not lost its grip.

Retributive justice rules the day. If retribution must be demanded to preserve the difference between right and wrong, then God help us all. The principle of retributive justice is already very strong in South Africa, with disastrous consequences. If retributive justice is to be maintained as central to the good ordering of society, it is likely to exact a terrible cost, not only as blacks seek vengeance from whites but when rival black groups seek vengeance from one another. It is likely to make a peaceful post-independence society quite impossible.

The substitutionary theory does not, of course, teach that human retribution is called for; clearly it is God alone who is to be both victim and judge. Nevertheless, the principle of retributive justice lies at its very heart. Surely what is needed, if Sipho is ever to find peace and happiness, is a very different concept of justice, a justice which is concerned with reform rather than retribution, a justice which is aware that our behaviour is governed not so much by unalterable embedded natural principles or divine *fiat* which we either obey or disobey, thus deserving reward or punishment, but by social conditioning, parental upbringing, the effects upon us of the behaviour of others. We are not always responsible for our own decisions. We are influenced in our behaviour by many factors beyond our consciousness or control. What is needed is not so much payment for our sins, as new insights into our own behaviour and that of others, help in changing our present behaviour, encouragement to mutually forgive and rebuild.

Jesus in his teaching emphasized that we should forgive, just as God forgives us – until seventy times seven if needs be. He, being reviled, did not revile in return. He abandoned retributive justice on his own behalf. We are back with Boso's question: Why cannot God simply forgive? Jesus' message seems in fact to have been that God does, and that through Jesus' own readiness to forgive his persecutors, a new kind of human relationship is born which has nothing to do with an eye for an eye. Anselm presents us with two alternatives. In the face of sin, God cannot forgive, for to do so is to condone; therefore he must either punish, or demand satisfaction.

Jesus seems to have contradicted the first premise. He forgave, but there is no impression that in doing so he condoned sin, nor that sin was thereby made less sinful. Bernard Shaw once said that forgiveness promotes moral laxity; John Baillie takes issue with this and quotes 'To whom little is given, the same loveth little' in return.[85] To forgive does not necessarily mean to drop one's demand for repentance (we shall return to this below), but where repentance is expressed, reformative justice suggests that the purpose of justice has been met, and forgiveness is possible.

Then, too, since in the substitutionary atonement theory Jesus alone is able to make satisfaction, the human role in our salvation is reduced to an entirely passive one, and the salvation envisaged is exclusively the idea of personal reconciliation with God. There is little room in the theory for human endeavour, or for developing mutually forgiving human relationships, about which Anselm says nothing. God's relationship with humans, demanding that justice and honour be requited before forgiveness can take place, bears no relationship to what we have learned to regard as loving human parent-child or friend-to-friend encounters. There is no model here for Sipho to develop his own human relationships – which are already so sadly deformed. The salvation is entirely heavenly, having nothing to do with the kingdom of God here on earth now. If accepted, the theory encourages Sipho into a personally pious but quiescent, passive religion which has no emphasis on social responsibility.

For all these reasons, the substitutionary atonement theory seems to be of more harm than help to Sipho and to those like him. In a subsequent section I argue that there is even a link to be drawn between this theory and the development of apartheid.

(b)   The idea of victory

Gustav Aulen[86] brought this theory back into prominence, though he quite correctly showed that it had already been the dominant theory in the early church until Anselm, at least in the East. He concedes that in its original form the theory was expressed in ways that would not now be acceptable,[87] but believes that, properly understood, it is the best way forward for a Christian understanding of salvation.

For my own part, I am persuaded that no form of Christian teaching has any future before it except such as can keep steadily in view the reality of evil in the world and go to meet the evil with a battle cry of triumph. Therefore I believe that the classic idea [Aulen terms this theory the 'classic' theory] of the Atonement and of Christianity is coming back.[88]

Macquarrie, while also conceding that the theory as originally expressed needs demythologization,[89] says that it seems 'to offer the most promising statement of the work of Christ.'[90]

The nub of the theory is that Jesus is victor over the enemies that beset us: sin, death and the devil. Again the seeds of the idea are in the New Testament: in the Gospels Jesus is shown as having authority over demons; he has tied up the 'strong man', i.e. Satan (Mark 3.27 and parallels). Paul says that Jesus has broken the tyranny of sin, law, flesh and powers. As in the satisfaction theory, Jesus is seen as in a sense a substitute for us, not, however, as one who pays the penalty on our behalf but as one who achieves a victory on our behalf in the struggle against all that troubles us, limits us, imprisons us.

The concept of divine victory is strongly emphasized in the Old Testament, which says that God intervenes to rescue his people from enemies and oppressors. The experience of deliverance from Egypt led to the expectation that God would deliver his people again, to rescue them not just from external enemies but from their own sinful self-destruction, and to rescue not only the people of Israel but the whole creation: land, animals, plants and people from destruction (e.g. Isa. 65.17–25). God will build a new kingdom on earth. From these expectations comes the expectation in due course of a Messiah who will usher in the kingdom. And this understanding of messiahship underlies some of the New Testament interpretations of Jesus as the Messiah.

There are a number of twists and turns in the way the theory subsequently developed as to over whom or what the victory is achieved. A personal devil features prominently, often conceived of as having rights over humans who, having sinned, now belonged to the devil. The ransom paid by Jesus in his death was thus paid to the devil, to buy humanity back. The devil was deceived and trapped by Jesus who in his humanity appeared to be easy bait for the devil. The devil discovered too late the divinity of Jesus as the hook within the bait. These are presumably the elements that Macquarrie thinks need to be demythologized.

However, not all the early fathers agreed with this version of the theory. For example, Gregory of Nazianzus denies any idea of the devil having rights.[91] The theory can be restated in less mythological form. In essence, it is that Jesus is victor over evil and all the consequences of evil; physical death, but also spiritual death, separation from God, the spoiling of the image of God in humans, the despair and hopelessness of subjugation to the law, to 'powers' that usurp God's authority over humankind, etc. The 'powers' to which Paul refers probably meant spiritual powers, angels or demons, but as Caird argues,[92] this can be extended to human authorities, which is of relevance to South Africa.

Aulen therefore suggests that even the idea of a ransom to the devil, interpreted correctly, has some validity. The demands of the 'powers' for justice, for fair play, in so far as they are just demands, must be met. There is therefore a double aspect to the victory theory. God is both the judge who imposes due penalty for sin, and the redeemer who releases us from that penalty.

> When the suffering which Christ endured is treated as the endurance of the punishment which men deserved, that is another instance of the same double aspect. When Christ suffers the punishment involved in God's judgment on sin, this is the accomplishment of God's own work of redemption whereby the tyrants are overcome and the reconciliation takes place.[93]

Let us concede immediately that the theory appears to avoid the weakness of the substitutionary atonement theory, and yet shares the great merit of that theory, i.e. that evil and sin are to be taken seriously – not, however, because of offence to God's honour but because of the consequences for humans. It still maintains that God will act justly, that justice and mercy are combined in our redemption, and that the demands of justice are met by Jesus' death. However, the idea of punishment, though still present, is not dominant. There is not the same stress on retributive justice. The victory does not only entail meeting the demands of justice, but involves transforming human nature and the human situation. It is far wider in its implications than the substitutionary theory.

It seems to require that Jesus be God as well as man. For who but God could achieve this victory? Who but God could remake humans in his own image? Who but God could restore immortality? Because of its double aspect – God is both judge and redeemer – it is again necessary that Jesus the redeemer be God, or we drive a wedge between judgment and redemption.

Logically we might pose an objection. Since Jesus did live a perfect life (let us grant a reliable reconstruction of the human life of Jesus for the moment), we might argue that this is proof that humans can achieve moral perfection and achieve victory over sin as humans, rather than proof that Jesus, because victorious, was God. But in answer it might be argued that salvation is not only about victory, and that other soteriological demands make a human superhero inadequate.

We might pose other objections. The Jewish expectation of deliverance and the establishment of a kingdom of justice and prosperity for all never materialized. We might claim that the theory is therefore perhaps invalidated. But for Christians the understanding is that the fulfilment of the expectations came with Jesus, who while ushering in the new kingdom also reinterpreted it to mean a kingdom not of this world. Thus the expectations, although changed, are still met, or may be met alone in the *eschaton*, the life to come.

The theory has its strongest appeal to people who are oppressed by forces they cannot control. In a technologically skilled age, humans are more able to achieve mastery over such forces by their own abilities. The theory is therefore not so attractive to a self-confident middle-class Western society. But then we may say that the real forces of destruction in the world are as powerful, even more powerful, than ever before, for we are unable to control human nature. In a post-Nazi, post-Holocaust world, living at present under the threat of nuclear self-annihilation, the need for a divine victor is greater than ever. In any case, many Christians are not self-confident middle-class Westerners but poor and oppressed, for whom the theory is presumably still very attractive.

Let us examine again whether this theory helps Sipho or not. Surely one day Sipho will ask, as many young black people in South Africa are asking, 'If in Jesus' victory the lives of humans, or at least of Christians, are transformed, where is the evidence of that transformation?' It is Christians who oppress Sipho: disobedient Christians, it may be, but Christians who are supposed to have been transformed by the power of Christ, to have been made part of the kingdom of God. We recall again Athanasius' proof that Jesus is saviour – that Christians are braver, more chaste, more faithful to their God, than others[94] – and extend it. If the victory over sin is real, where is the evidence of it for Sipho? Surely Athanasius was right to expect transformation of character in those for whom Jesus had wrought the victory? If it is Christians who oppress Sipho, how can we talk meaningfully of victory for Sipho or for his oppressors?

What does victory over death mean for Sipho? If Sipho dies – as many African children do in early childhood – from malnutrition and the poor hygiene that are inevitable for those living under grinding poverty, unlike Jesus he will not be raised again in three days. Can we honestly say that Jesus has brought salvation to him? He may have the promise of ultimate resurrection, but that will not help his mother. It seems the height of cynicism to say to a community where infant and child deaths still run at 86 deaths for every 1000 births, almost five times greater than comparable white infant mortality,[95] that Jesus has given victory over death. That is not to deny that belief in a resurrection is of comfort to the mourners; but the comfort may be of an opiate kind if it encourages them to accept fatalistically an unacceptably high infant death-rate. Resurrection notwithstanding, child mortality remains a tragic waste of potential.

Possibly the victory theory offers help of another kind to Sipho. It may be interpreted as meaning that Jesus is victor over the evil secular powers of this world. This was not the primary focus of the theory in the Fathers' minds, but as we have noted it may have been present in Paul's thoughts, and is certainly part of Old Testament expectations. It is a theme that emerges quite often in South African black theology.

> It may seem as if the dictators, the powerful and the mighty have full control over this world. Their arrogance seems to have no bounds. But the Church knows . . . Jesus Christ is Lord of history, he is Lord of life, and his truth shall have the final word.[96]

> [Jesus] discloses his will to restore wholeness to the broken and fragmented lives of those who trust in him for liberation. And, as at first, he shall not fail them.[97]

> Real peace and security will come to our land only when apartheid has been dismantled. I have no doubt that this will happen. If God be for us, who can be against us?[98]

> God cares, and God will act decisively to bring justice, peace and reconciliation to our land.[99]

The promise is a powerful one which on the face of it is very relevant to oppressed persons. There are, however, some problems. For one thing, the victory is won by God; more specifically, it is won by Jesus as God on behalf of humans. This is in fact why, in this theory, Jesus must be God, for only God can achieve the victory if we are to avoid auto-soteriology. Does this view not encourage human passivity, leaving everything to God, especially since the stress is that Jesus could only accomplish the victory because he was God? Is this not very similar to what the Pharisees believed: that only God could establish Israel, and that faithful Jews should therefore leave active politics alone and concentrate on their faithful religious observances?

This is not to deny that Jesus was personally victorious over evil. Despite the problems of establishing the historical Jesus, we may surely claim that tradition is very strong about Jesus as an example of one who is victorious over the powers of oppression and hatred, in the sense that he is crucified but not cowed, nor brought down to the level of his persecutors. 'When he was reviled, he did not revile in return' (I Peter 2.23).

Even if there has been an element of hagiography in recording the victory, it seems likely that Jesus espoused these values and taught his followers to do so. Those who perceive in Jesus an example of one who is victorious over the powers of oppression and hatred find strength and inspiration in that example. There is no doubt that Christian belief has been a source of courage and determination for many black South African leaders, from Albert Luthuli to Archbishop Tutu. Those who perceive in the death of Jesus, the anointed servant of God, a reminder that God is on the side of the oppressed, find affirmation for their own inherent worth in that example. But if our emphasis is on Jesus achieving that victory as God, the problem of human passivity remains. If our emphasis changes, to say that Jesus as man achieved this victory as an inspiration for us, then this is no longer the classic victory theory. It is a version of the exemplarist theory, to which we shall return below: that is, by his example, Jesus inspires us to take up the battle and win the victory for ourselves.

The whole concept of God acting in human history is a problematic one anyway, as Maurice Wiles has shown us in his recent Bampton Lectures.[100] Latin American liberation theologians seem to accept this. Committed as many of them are to a Marxian interpretation of history, these theologians still confidently expect ultimate victory; not, however, because of God's direct intervention, but rather through the economically determined processes of history.

> The Messiah under no circumstances deprives people of the creation of their own history and their society . . . [Jesus] does not free us from . . . history and patience.[101]

For Marxists, the nature of the economic/material world is such that it will culminate in victory for the oppressed. For Christian Marxists, presumably, this is how God made the world, so that God is still the author of our victory, although he achieves the victory indirectly, through the economic process. We need to ask how the liberation theologians think that Jesus is involved in this victory, but we shall consider that later.

A serious objection to understanding the victory of Jesus as a victory over secular enemies and oppressors is that this view can easily lead to arrogance and insensitivity towards those who are regarded as the enemy, particularly once the victory has been won. Is this not the kind of thinking that led to the crusades? I will be arguing in a subsequent section[102] that the Afrikaner nation in South Africa was greatly influenced by a form of the victory theory in its attitude towards black people. The theory provides a tempting rationale for Christians to sacralize their struggle against their enemies. One's enemies become God's enemies, and therefore are no longer entitled to consideration of their point of view or indeed to be treated as fellow humans. This enables many Christians in South Africa to avoid any sympathetic consideration of the position of the African National Congress. It also enables Christians on the black side of the struggle to ignore the genuine difficulties of the Afrikaners. 'A regime that has made itself the enemy of the people has thereby also made itself the enemy of God.'[103] There may be situations in which such a judgment would be valid, but the temptation to righteous arrogance is a real one. Belief in the victory theory was certainly one of the factors enabling Afrikanerdom to overcome its problems following the Anglo–Boer War and its aftermath. It may well help black people to achieve their victory now. But it may well turn that victory, as it has turned Afrikaner nationalism, into a triumph not of righteousness but of *self*-righteousness and oppression of other groups.

Perhaps this is not of immediate relevance to Sipho, for whom the revolution has not yet happened. Perhaps it is expecting too much to be concerned about dangers following the revolution. There is another, and even greater, difficulty with the victory theory if we look at it through Sipho's eyes: the revolution has *not* happened. How then can he believe that Jesus is victor in the matters that concern him most? Even if the revolution should eventually succeed, thus vindicating Jesus as victor over the forces of oppression, it will have succeeded far too late. What justification can black theologians have for any confidence that God through Jesus will intervene? If God intervenes in some events, he must surely intervene in all, wherever there is injustice. If he will soon be responsible for throwing off the apartheid regime, why has he stayed his hand for so long? Whole generations of black people have lived and died in unfulfilled misery.

In the South African context, if we are to draw conclusions about God's intentions by looking at history, we shall surely have to say that so far he has been on the side of Afrikaner nationalism, not black nationalism. He has not intervened to save the black oppressed. If he can do so, and does do so at some future date, is it not a scandal for us that he has waited so long?

We may, if we will, say that it is not for us to question God's morality or God's reasons. That is part of another debate, although Stewart Sutherland's remarks quoted earlier come to mind.[104] My point here is not to debate the *Euthyphro* problem, but to show that the victory theory, if interpreted as meaning victory over political oppressors, cannot easily be sustained. No political victory has been given to black South Africans. There can therefore be no basis for confidence that it will be given in the future.

We may, if we will, say that such a victory is part of God's intention but that God will not intervene by forcing human hands. We may see victory as a future hope and not a past achievement. We may say that God desires peace and justice on earth, but awaits our voluntary co-operation, and will do no more than offer guidance which he pleads with us to follow. Whatever the merits of this belief, I cannot see that it is a belief in Jesus' objective victory over the power of evil. It is no longer a *victory* theory.

We may say that the victory has indeed been won, and the power of evil broken, but that the 'mopping up' battles still need to be waged, although the decisive change has already been accomplished (to borrow Cullmann's analogy).[105] This is of little relevance to Sipho, and of even less to those who have gone before him – except that they will be happy in heaven. Perhaps the global victory has been won, but that does not help those suffering in the present moment. It is a point of view which assumes that God views events through the eyes of the 'great ones', of generals and statesmen who are concerned with overall strategies, and not the eyes of the 'little ones' who are hurt in the process. It seems to me to be morally outrageous to say that God in Jesus is victorious over evil, has broken evil's power, but that God will only grant to us the fruits of that victory in the *eschaton*, in the end days, when there is so much suffering now.

The concept of a battle with and a victory over evil is a dramatic and appealing one. It certainly seems to fit the New Testament interpretation of the life, the teaching, the death, the resurrection, of Jesus. My criticisms of some versions of the theory are not meant to deny that Jesus does give hope in a hopeless world. I do not think we have yet been shown by anyone, however, how Jesus' victory is an 'objective' victory over evil for us. It is very clear that many Christians have not been victorious over evil's grasp on them, have not had their lives transformed by the power of God in Jesus, whether we interpret the victory as being over death, over spiritual or moral temptations, or over socio-political considerations.

In his personal victory, Jesus is a model for us and a reason for hope. He shows us that God's grace is available and sufficient to overcome personal temptation towards hatred, revenge, selfishness, and all the rest of that gloomy list. He shows us that a different kind of life is possible. Interpreted in this way, the model has a great deal of relevance to Sipho, and has in fact been of very great power in the lives of Christians through the ages. This interpretation no longer looks to God to intervene directly, except by enabling the individual who seeks God's help to overcome hatred. But it is no longer the classic victory theory. Nor does it appear to require that Jesus be divine. On the contrary, if Jesus is to be a model of hope for humans, his victory needs to be a human victory achieved by (God-enabled) human strength, or it cannot be emulated and therefore is not pertinent. The Jesus who is relevant to the raw facts of Sipho's life is a Jesus who is helped by God in no other way than that in which God will help all who turn to him when faced with life's burden and pain.

(c)   Some South African consequences

It seems to me that versions of the substitutionary atonement approach and of the victory theory have in different but complementary ways helped smooth the way for the establishment of an apartheid regime in South Africa, and I propose to try to illustrate my case.

I am not suggesting that these theories are the cause of apartheid: that would be ridiculous, since racial discrimination has existed and still exists in many places other than South Africa, some of them clearly not influenced by any Christian theology at all. The causes of racial discrimination in the world can be attributed to many things – desire to control the means of production in society, xenophobia, a drive for power – depending on one's sociological preference. I am only suggesting that particular views of the saving work of Jesus have helped towards the development of an apartheid mentality. It is impossible to prove that this is so, and there are no doubt many indications to the contrary, some of which I will mention. I hope that I can show that nevertheless there is some evidence of the truth of my charge.

The European colonists of the Cape in South Africa arrived fairly late in the story of world colonization. When Europeans came to the New World in North and South America, inevitably they came into conflict with the original inhabitants. Sometimes, as in parts of North America, the colonists went to the new land to escape from poverty or religious persecution at home. Sometimes the motive was profit: to extend trade, or to garner natural resources. Both of these motives were present in the establishment of the Cape Colony by the Dutch, and subsequently by the British.

Sometimes the motive for colonization was more overtly religious – to evangelize the 'natives'. The *Cambridge Modern History* suggests that for some – the Portuguese Henry the Navigator, and Christopher Columbus are the people specifically referred to – the desire to colonize was a 'final effort of the crusading spirit',[106] a continuation of the war against the Moors. But Spain and Portugal probably had more genuinely evangelistic motives mixed up with their desire for profit in their conquest of Latin America. Bernal Diaz in his diary of his journey with Cortes says that when offered maidens as a bribe by an aboriginal chief,

> Cortes replied that he wished first to do the will of our Lord God . . . and to perform the task which our Lord and King had set us: which was to make them give up their idols and cease to kill and sacrifice human beings, cease also the other abominations which they practised, and believe as we believed in the one true God.[107]

The evangelistic motive *may* have worked to soften the exploitative element of the profit-making motive. In the well-known debate between the philosopher de Sepulveda and the Bishop of Chiapas, Bartolomeo de las Casas, the latter insisted that the South American Indians were not mere animals, and should be treated fairly since they were human and capable of conversion to Christ.[108]

In South Africa neither the Dutch nor the British came primarily to evangelize, but evangelistic efforts quickly followed the British traders and farmers and possibly achieved some amelioration of the lot of the Khoi and in due course the Africans, though some would dispute that and would allege that by pacifying the converts, missionary endeavour made colonial conquest more easy to manage. For example:

Missionaries can also be seen as the forerunners of British imperialism in Bechuanaland.[109]

The white man's God has been used to tame the black people.[110]

Nevertheless, whether for purposes of colonization or of evangelization (and the latter was rarely the sole motive), Europeans found themselves in contact with the original inhabitants who were not Christian and whom they therefore regarded as being inferior to themselves. The distinction was one of religion rather than race. Since the original inhabitants were not Christian, that was reason enough to annex their land.[111] In the Christian church alone lay salvation. Those outside the church, those who had not accepted Jesus as saviour, were still under the course of original sin. Their culture could be of no value, their civilization of no account, in God's eyes. That did not mean that the colonists were always contemptuous of the native civilization. The *conquistadores* seem at times to have greatly admired some of the civilizations they encountered – although that attitude was the exception rather than the rule. But in God's eyes such civilizations had no saving value. Christian colonists and their Christian empires must therefore obviously be required by God to take over the land and its administration, convert the inhabitants, and add the colony to the jewels in the crown of the Spanish, Portuguese, or later the Victorian British Empire, ordained by God to establish his kingdom over all the earth.

It is obviously not logically necessary to interpret the Christian gospel in this way, nor have all Christian missionaries thought along these lines. But is it not clear that the Christian gospel, and more particularly the Christian theory of substitutionary atonement by which alone we are justified in God's eyes, can very easily be interpreted thus? All humans have sinned: all fall under God's wrath. The works, the culture, the civilization of fallen human beings, however meritorious by human standards, have no merit in God's eyes. Only in Christ is the curse removed, only by justification in Christ are we acceptable. Therefore only Christian rulers, and Christian civilization, are of any value – or so we might logically argue.

Thus in the early days of the settlement in South Africa, the Dutch authorities seemed to have no racial prejudice. The distinctions drawn were not between white and black, but between Christian and non-Christian, between free and slave (since political resisters to Dutch rules in Indonesia were sent as slaves to the

Cape). Converted and baptized Khoi, and those amongst the imported slaves who embraced Christianity, were granted more or less equal rights in the community with born Christians. Once baptized, a person who was not European was accepted as a member of the Christian community. There was no barrier on marriage with other races, nor were baptized mixed-race children excluded from society. Or at least this was the theory:[112] Giliomee points out that mixed-race children were only accepted as Christian and equal if their parents were legitimately married, which was often not the case.[113]

However, even if in those early years discrimination was on grounds of religion and not of race, the principle of discrimination was well entrenched, and rationalized on the basis of soteriological theory. A fellow-Christian should not be enslaved, but no such restriction was placed on enslaving Moslem Indonesians. Here surely is evidence of the implication of an exclusive substitutionary soteriology. Only Christians have appropriated the benefits of the death of Christ. Only Christians are therefore justified and worthy of mercy in God's eyes. Other humans, being still under the curse laid on Adam, have no claim on human rights.

Neither the Dutch East India Company nor their officials in the early years of the Cape were interested in serious colonization of the interior. Their interest lay in the East Indies, and Cape Town was merely a fuelling station on the route. Therefore they were not in serious competition with the original inhabitants. Once the decision was made to colonize the interior, however, the picture changed. The San, the Khoi, the amaXhosa, were in competition with the white farmers who wished to appropriate their land. At this point, perhaps, religious exclusivism slipped into racial exclusivism, while the justification remained the same.

> Some would maintain that the belief of the Christian church in a privileged and unique truth in its care . . . fosters exclusiveness, prejudice, and in certain instances, racism.[114]

Very quickly we find the colonists attributing to the black people all the negative values which we previously noted being attached to non-Christians. The basis is now race as well as religion. The fact that by virtue of superior arms the colonists usually won the battle was taken as a confirmatory sign.

> The settlers prospered, the indigenous people and imported slaves suffered. The Christian faith seemed to provide the rationale necessary to justify the situation.[115]

Most of the colonists probably held these attitudes: not only those of Dutch/French descent (later to become the Afrikaners) but also the British who took over the Cape at the start of the nineteenth century. They were all Christians, and most tended to interpret Christian exclusivism in this way. But for the early Afrikaners there was the additional factor that they were all Calvinists. Not only, following Calvin, did Afrikaans Calvinists believe the penal substitutionary theory, as also did the British settlers though perhaps less strongly. They also followed the Synod of Dort. They believed that God predestines some humans to salvation in Christ and some to heathenism, not on the basis of merit but by divine arbitrary decree.

The Dutch Reformed Churches in South Africa still tend strongly to follow that approach. R. Buis sums up what he regards as standard Dutch Reformed Church teaching as follows.

All Adam's descendants having fallen to sin by the sin of their first parents have the mercy and justice of God revealed to them. God is merciful and just because he saves from total destruction all those whom out of goodness and mercy and in accordance with his plan he has chosen . . . God is just in leaving others in the sin and ruin in which they have involved themselves.[116]

Again it is possible that many British colonists believed something of this too. In the words of a verse usually omitted in modern hymnals from Mrs Alexander's hymn *All Things Bright and Beautiful*:

> The rich man in his castle,
> The poor man at his gate;
> God made them high and lowly,
> And order'd their estate.[117]

However, this belief was less formal and explicit amongst nineteenth-century English Christians than in the Dutch Reformed Church, and in any case it is the descendants of the latter who now call the shots in South Africa and whose opinions therefore affect us all.

Thus not only were black people not Christian and therefore not entitled to equality with Christians, but God had eternally preordained it so. To grant to blacks an economic and legal equality would be to go against the plain will of God – or so it could be easily argued.

The natural role of the non-Christian . . . was to labour for the European, to be at the beck and call of any Christian who required his services.[118]

By virtue of his religion, he justified his right to dominate the heathen by whom he was surrounded . . . The idea that Christian and non-Christian were in any sense equal before the law . . . was entirely foreign to frontier mentality.[119]

To present the other side of the picture, there is evidence to contradict MacCrone's somewhat generalized claim, and it is likely that these religious views provided a rationale rather than a cause for such beliefs.

The missionaries at the Eastern Cape frontier and in Natal, motivated by their gospel, were strong defenders of the rights of the Khoi, slaves and Africans to education, freedom to work where they pleased, and equality before the law. However, missionaries took a paternalistic approach to their flock, and could act brutally if their authority was questioned. Robert Moffat, father-in-law of David Livingstone, believed that his newly converted congregation was threatened by what he regarded as a lawless and work-shy group of Mantatees nearby. Together with Melville, another missionary, he met with local Griqua chiefs, armed them, and set them to attack the Mantatees. Between two and three hundred Mantatees were slaughtered at the battle of Dithokong. Moffat used another Griqua to round up the surviving women and children, on the grounds that he was protecting them from their savage foes (and presumably to protect the missionaries from the questions of the London Missionary Society), and sent them into slavery in the Cape, retaining one boy for service in his own household.[120] One can only explain this extraordinary story on the assumption that for Moffat, non-Christian Mantatees were expendable.

It is also true that in its earliest days the Dutch Reformed Church itself insisted that within the church no distinctions should be made on the grounds of race. After a dispute in Somerset West about the acceptance of a mixed-race baptized person at the Lord's Supper, the Cape Town presbytery and a subsequent synod in 1829 advised that the church should make no such distinctions. But as frontier pressures grew, the church by 1857 would change its mind and agree that the 'weakness of some' meant that separate church institutions and buildings for different races might be allowed. In due course, social and religious segregation would become official Dutch Reformed policy and not just a dispensation for the weak.

We were first with a policy of separate development which began in the 1850s when separate church structures were provided for each separate racial group.[121]

It would be true to say . . . that the NGK [Dutch Reformed Church],[122] through its theological interpretation, provided the Afrikaner government and parties with the Christian justification for policies and actions that they needed, and thus in a sense the NGK prepared the way for party and for government, which later evolved an apartheid policy called separate development.[123]

Perhaps the closest indication that MacCrone is not being unfair in his remarks about the link between religious exclusivism in colonial attitudes are the words of Anna Steenkamp, the niece of the *Voortrekker* Piet Retief. By the early nineteenth century the British colonial administration was insisting on the emancipation of slaves and on somewhat better conditions for the Khoi and African labourers on the Eastern frontier. Anna Steenkamp complains, as did a number of farmers, that they were not paid out as much compensation for freed slaves as they had been led to expect, and that the British army was slow to help recover stolen cattle from marauding tribesmen. Many 'Dutch' farmers chose to leave British rule and embark on the 'Great Trek' northwards, away from meddling missionaries and colonial officials.

Yet is is not the freedom [of slaves and Khoi] that drove us to such lengths, as their being placed on an equal footing with Christians, contrary to the laws of God and the natural distinction of race and religion, so that it was unbearable for any decent Christian to bow beneath such a yoke: wherefore we withdrew in order to preserve our doctrines in purity.[124]

Of course none of this is what Calvin taught. Calvin did not have to confront the issue of racial discrimination. He did believe that only those who are justified by faith in Christ can be saved; and it seems clear to me from the *Institutes* that he also believed that God predetermined who would turn to faith in Christ so that not even their faith could be seen as merit. But the identity of those predetermined for salvation was firmly seen by Calvin as a mystery which only God knows, and he certainly did not believe that God preordained some to earthly privilege.

The fruits of election are in no respect visible in any outward advantage or prosperity enjoyed in this life, where impiety prospers and the pious are forced to bear a cross. The blessing of the elect lies rather in their assurance of God's sufficiency and unfailing protection amid their afflictions, and in the happy anticipation of the life to come. [125]

Nevertheless, despite Calvin's qualifier, I suggest that it is clear that belief in the penal theory and in predestination were factors which enabled the *Voortrekkers* and their political descendants to justify racial distinction and discrimination, and have thus been of great harm to Sipho.

The Voortrekkers believed not only the substitutionary atonement theory but also in their own version of the victory theory, a bizarre version which is still embedded in South African white consciousness. Piet Retief, Anna Steenkamp's uncle, in due course came to the territory of the Zulus. He tried to persuade the Zulu king to give his group of Trekkers the right to settle and farm. The King, Dingane, was not unnaturally suspicious of what the presence of a large body of armed men would do to his kingdom. Pretending to welcome them, he had Retief and his companions seized and killed. He then sent out his warriors to find the rest of Retief's party. The warriors surprised the unsuspecting camp and killed the great majority of them at the place now called Weenen ('weeping'). Other Trekker leaders, enraged by the massacre, gathered a larger party together and set out for Dingane's territory. The Trekkers and the Zulu regiments met on the banks of a river in Northern Natal. The Trekker leaders prayed for victory, and promised that if God gave them victory they would erect a church in his honour and each year on the day of the battle would remember and thank him.

Although much fewer in number, they did, of course, have guns. So many Zulus were killed that the river ran red, and was named 'Blood River'. The Trekker prayers were answered. The battle was won; the church was built and still stands in the city where I live; and each year on 16 December, the Day of the Covenant (the use of the Old Testament phrase is significant), all of Afrikaans South Africa observes a holy day of sabbath. God acted, it seems, to save his people.

Indeed, of course, if God is Lord of history in South Africa we would have to say that God has made the Afrikaner mighty. He has put down not only the British imperialists but also the black people from their seat, and has exalted the Afrikaner nation. This is exactly what many Afrikaans Christians have believed.

The Trekkers went on to found new republics. The two largest became the Transvaal and the Orange Free State. They saw themselves, like the Israelites in Canaan, as destined by God to overcome the heathen and to rule over them. God had chosen them, and God would give them victory. Despite the somewhat contradictory fact that they were also called to evangelize these same heathen, a task for which ordinary citizens sometimes had little sympathy –

> We will have no servants who go to Church on Sundays dressed as ladies and gentlemen, to hear sermons on their being just as good as we . . . [126]

– somehow whiteness continued to be associated with being Christian, black with being pagan. The republics were to lose the battle against incorporation into the British Empire, but in 1948 their story reached its promised end. The Afrikaner Nationalist Party came into power, and eventually became a republic once more. The scene was set for the reassertion of Trekker values, and for an ever increasing rigid apartheid or separation between the races, and Dr Malan, the first Prime Minister of the new Nationalist dispensation, could say:

> The difference in colour is merely the physical manifestation of the contrast between two ways of life, between barbarism and civilization, between heathenism and Christianity. [127]

Even educated, converted, baptized black people are not 'civilized', and are somehow still 'heathens'. The doctrine of a distinction between saved and unsaved, elect and non-elect, begins as a religious distinction, and is pressed into service to justify a racial distinction in a situation of economic competition for land, until eventually a God-ordained racial distinction becomes primary even when religious distinctions cease to apply.

There is another way in which the substitutionary theory has affected South African attitudes. It is associated, at least in its Calvinist form, with the idea of human depravity. Unsaved human beings cannot be trusted to live together in peace: their depraved instincts will make that impossible.

What is not generally understood outside South Africa is that the modern defence of apartheid form is no longer that of Verwoerdian racial superiority, though that may still lie unacknowledged in the background, but the belief that persons of different cultures cannot live together in peace without wishing to dominate and destroy one another. Thus it is held that for the protection not only of Afrikaner but also of black society, race groups must be kept apart in separate but theoretically equal blocs. The Dutch Reformed Church has often accepted this as a regrettable but realistic political solution to what must otherwise, in their view of human nature, be a scene of perpetual conflict. They do not any longer claim that the Bible teaches racial separation, but that in view of the weakness of fallen human nature the Bible permits it.[128]

Now of course we can find logical fallacies in the argument. The solution is not economically viable. Black blocs are not given equal access to finance. If the solution is inevitable it should also mean that Jews must be kept apart from Christians, Hindus from Moslems, those of Portuguese culture from those of English: each should have its own separate state or 'bantustan'. That, however, is not my point. My point is that the theory is justified by direct reference to a particular Christian interpretation of fallen human nature. The doctrine of total depravity provides a neat justification for apartheid.

Before Dr Malan came into power, the Afrikaner nation went through many difficulties. Having overcome the threat of the surrounding African kingdoms, once gold had been discovered in the Transvaal it also faced the acquisitiveness of the British Empire, and was defeated in the Anglo–Boer War. The story of that war is long and complicated, but the memory of farms being burned and women and children being herded into the world's first concentration camps, where many died of sickness, is still vivid in Afrikaner folk memory. A relatively magnanimous peace still left them impoverished, and in the subsequent union of Trekker republics with the British colonies of Natal and the Cape, they were very much the junior partners in the increasingly industrialized and urbanized Union of South Africa. The depression of the 1930s saw many Afrikaans families reduced to beggary. But they never lost their belief in their destiny and in the promise to them of victory.

The roots of apartheid in South Africa go in many directions, of which the Calvinist penal theory is but one. J. Kinghorn, while agreeing that the idea of a spiritual separation between Christian and heathen is part of the background for Dutch Reformed identification with apartheid, points to a number of these other factors: the socio-economic problems of the Afrikaner poor, the influence of the Romantic movement and the influence of Nazi race theories.[129]

To these we might add the insensitivity of Lord Milner and his Anglicization policy following the Anglo–Boer War. But in all these troubles, Calvinist theology helped provide an answer. Kinghorn reminds us[130] that the Dutch Reformed Churches in South Africa are not just Calvinist, but have been strongly influenced by the reinterpretation of Calvinism by Abraham Kuyper.

Kuyper would not have supported race discrimination.

> . . . we cannot recognize any distinctions among men, save such as imposed by God himself, in that he gave one authority over the other or enriched one with more talents than the other, in order that the man with more talents should serve the man with less.[131]

But Kuyper, reflecting Netherlands nationalism after long periods of belonging to other empires, also believed that God ordained nations as part of his creation.[132] For Kuyper, Jesus is Lord of all life, political and spiritual. While state and church institutions are to be kept separate, the pietist separation of religion from worldly and political affairs was rejected. Church and Volk, ecclesiastical and political community, are both of them created by God, chosen by God, for victory over the forces of humanistic, ungodly liberalism.

The Kuyperian version of the victory theory had a profound influence on the development of Afrikaner nationalism. The Afrikaner nation came to believe in itself as God's chosen, a nation to whom not only spiritual but political victory was guaranteed. This faith enabled them to bond tightly together to throw off British colonial oppression, and to throw off the internationalism of Jan Christiaan Smuts, whom Malan replaced when he came to power. It provided a most powerful antidote to the demoralized state of the Afrikaans community in the first half of the twentieth century. It enabled Afrikaners to interpret their history as one of God-given victory over the black heathen nations, and to have hope for the future as one of God-given victory over the financial and political hegemony of the British Empire, over English and Western influence in Afrikaner affairs, and over the influence of post-Enlightenment, secular, godless and immoral Western society. To this day it enables Afrikanerdom largely to disregard world criticism of South Africa and the imposition of sanctions as being inspired by godless liberalism and Communism. For God, they believe, will still not desert them. To quote Dr Malan again:

The history of the Afrikaner reveals a will and a determination which makes one feel that Afrikanerdom is not the work of man, but the creation of God.[133]

There is no doubt that the belief was of major assistance in rebuilding the Afrikaans community. But it also exacts a price. Having achieved its own victory, Afrikaner Christianity has found it hard to accept that other people may be enabled by God to achieve victory over it. The Israelites under Joshua, certain that God would aid them in their battle to secure a foothold in the Promised Land, showed scant appreciation of the fact that, once they had gained the upper hand, the Amorites, Canaanites, Perizzites, Hivites, etc., became the oppressed. The successors to the Voortrekkers showed a similarly scant appreciation of the oppressed status of black South Africans, though the parallel is today frequently pointed out to them.

In this way, the victory theory has in fact been a factor which has militated against the recognition of black rights. It has provided, as did the substitutionary satisfaction theory, a way of theological and moral justification for apartheid doctrines, even though the actual causes for these doctrines lie in socio-economic factors.

At present the Afrikaner Nationalist government is slowly moving towards some sort of recognition of the need to accommodate black aspirations and some sort of reform, though still with little clarity of vision or intention. They are opposed by conservative Afrikaners. Just as Dr Malan, himself a dominee (minister) of the Dutch Reformed Church, broke the power of Smuts, it is possible that the power of the Nationalists could be broken by another dominee, Dr A. P. Treurnicht, leader of the Conservative Party. He continues in Kuyperian fashion.

Your own particular character is therefore your 'law of life', and obedience to it is justice. . . . we say that autogenous development is the best exercise of justice. Justice is plurality.[134]

Plurality means apartheid. Apartheid means white power. God still protects his people and leads them to victory!

Of course we may say that this development of soteriological theory is a false one; that neither the substitutionary nor the victory theory need lead us to such conclusions; that it is a skewed outgrowth from Christianity, from Calvinism, from Kuyper. Thus we may claim that apartheid is a heresy. But it has found justification from attitudes generated by these theories. In view of the very great harm that apartheid does to Sipho and his people, Christians need to be very sure that they need these theories which have proved so easy to use or misuse in this way. The theories carry much potential danger. They have been of no help to Sipho.

(d)   The idea of example

Hastings Rashdall, like Aulen, was dissatisfied with the substitutionary theory of the atonement, and brought back to our notice the exemplarist theory. He acknowledges that the strength of the substitutionary theory is that it provides a connection between the death of Jesus and our salvation, thus providing a demonstration of God's love; but in its interpretation of that connection the substitutionary theory drives a wedge between the persons of the Trinity, between the juridical function of the Father and the redemptive function of the Son.[135] It was not taught, Rashdall claims, by the early Fathers, nor by the New Testament with the exception of Paul.

In Rashdall's view, the simplest explanation of the connection between the death of Jesus and our salvation is that in his death Jesus shows the love of God for us. That example of love cannot fail to excite our own response of penitence, conversion and commitment to God in return. While Abelard gives the definitive expression of this exemplarist view, it goes back, Rashdall claims, to the early Fathers, especially Origen, and is supported by modern theologians (modern for Rashdall: he mentions Coleridge, Schleiermacher, Ritschl, Colenso and Westcott).

The view is summed up in the well known words of Peter Lombard.

> So great a pledge having been given us, we are both moved and kindled to love God who did such great things for us, and by this we are justified, that is, being loosed from our sins we are made just. The death of Christ therefore justifies us, inasmuch as through it charity is stirred up in our hearts.[136]

The obvious question, if one rejects the substitutionary view, is how the death of Jesus proves God's love. Rashdall quotes James Denney, who objects that if someone jumps in the water simply to show his love for me, that is hardly a demonstration of love unless his suicide helps me.[137] If Jesus' death is a sacrifice offered to the Father to atone for my sins, then it is a demonstration of love; but if one rejects that interpretation, how can I say that Jesus died *for me*? How does his death help me? To this objection, Rashdall offers a natural historical interpretation. Jesus did not commit suicide. He did not submit to death as a ritual sacrifice. He was killed by others because he preached an unwelcome message of justice, truth and love to the bitter end.[138] His love is demonstrated in his willingness to live and teach a message of justification and truth, even though it was clear to him that the likely end of such a course would be to be killed. This is what he did for us.

In the face of this love, our hearts are moved to penitence. In gratitude, we amend our ways and are thus loosed from our sins. Our justification lies not in the debt for sin being paid on our behalf to satisfy the Father's wrath, but in the actual change and amendment in our lives.

Following our principle of economy,[139] the simplest explanation, provided it fits the facts adequately, is the best explanation. Does Rashdall's explanation fit the facts? Certainly it seems to fit well with the synoptic Gospels' account of Jesus' progression to the cross. It fits well with the change which Jesus or the synoptic evangelists wrought in the interpretation of the Messiah, modifying triumphal messianism and apocalyptic expectations of a Son of Man with the addition of Suffering Servant imagery.

Major objections have been raised to the exemplarist theory. Is it possible, even if we amend our lives, for God simply to forgive the past without 'satisfaction', without the demands of justice having been met? Does this not imply that sin is condoned? Can humans respond to God? Is not the theory hopelessly over-optimistic about human capabilities? Is it possible for sinful humans to amend? Will the amendment not still fall far short of the perfection which alone will satisfy God's just demands and purposes? And how does Jesus' death, in Rashdall's view, demonstrate *God's* love? Is it not only the love of the human Jesus which is demonstrated?

Proponents of the substitutionary theory will obviously not agree that God can simply forgive. On their view, the principles of justice, to be maintained, require satisfaction. Simply to forgive is to condone and thus to countenance sin. However, the belief that simple forgiveness without satisfaction means that sin is condoned has never been obvious to anyone except Christians. Jews and Moslems have no problem in believing that God can simply forgive, without this in the least weakening their belief in a God of justice. In human terms, forgiving need not imply condoning. Provided that the sinner is repentant and intends amendment, God's justice is surely not weakened by accepting the penitent back into a relationship. There is no suggestion in the parable of the prodigal son that a punishment of the prodigal (or of someone else in his place) is called for, and the reluctant elder brother is rebuked for his reluctance to welcome the repentant prodigal back to the family fold. I have dealt with the dangers of insisting upon retributive justice above.[140]

As to how the love of Jesus demonstrates the love of God to us, Rashdall is quite clear. Rashdall is an orthodox Chalcedonian. For Rashdall, Jesus is God; his actions are God's actions. He concedes that the love and the death of even a purely human Jesus would be salvific, because all love is contagious and inspires imitation.[141] He concedes that in all humanity there is some revelation of God, to differing degrees, since we are all made in the image of God. But Jesus is not just a martyr. He is 'so much more than martyrs because his life was more than other lives'.[142] Because Jesus is God, the love that he shows us is more than human love. It is God's love, making it all the more irresistible and evoking all the stronger a response. Quick's criticism that

> the love of a living and redeeming God can only be fully revealed and displayed in a divine act. If all we can say of Christ's human life and death is that they *symbolize* God's constant love, and are *not* God's own act, then the love which they symbolize is after all something different from what the highest Christian faith has held God's love to be,[143]

is not applicable to Rashdall. For Rashdall, Jesus *is* God, acting out of love.

Immediately, though, Rashdall faces the problem that Jesus' death cannot be God's death. He acknowledges that the suffering and death of Jesus are human suffering, attributable to God only through the *communicatio idiomatum*, the attributing of human actions or experiences to the divine nature and *vice versa* because of the unity of the two natures in Christ, but really only as a manner of speech and not as a real synthesis. While this may be orthodox Chalcedonianism, it raises logical problems. If it is in his human nature that Jesus suffers and dies, how is this human action a demonstration of the divine love? Perhaps this is a quibble. But without a substitutionary or victory interpretation of the atonement (where only God can meet the demands of justice or accomplish victory over the power of evil), why does Rashdall need to emphasize the divinity of Jesus at all? Surely it is not only God who can love?

He needs to emphasize it because throughout, in his interpretation, Rashdall is still thinking more about atonement than about the wider concept of salvation from all of this world's ills. Like Abelard, he is still thinking in mediaeval terms of evil as meaning primarily the breach of the relationship between the individual and God. Where Anselm sought to heal that breach through substitutionary payment, Rashdall seeks to heal it through a restoration of a loving response to God. God must initiate the restoration. Since it is Jesus who demonstrates the love and thus evokes our gratitude and response, healing the breach between God and ourselves, Jesus must be God. Rashdall's concept of salvation is thus limited, as inevitably was Abelard's. He does not seem to be aware of the potential for a wider development of his theory, in a way which does not require Jesus to be divine. We shall return to this point later.

It is the charge of over-optimism about the possibility of human response which seems to carry most weight amongst Abelard's and Rashdall's critics. Thus O. C. Quick says:

> To one who understands the power of sin as St Paul understood it, that theory can never express the reality of God's saving act in Jesus Christ.[144]

The theory, according to Macquarrie,

> . . . Takes no account of what we know as the impotence of the human will, nor does it sufficiently recognize the 'escalation' of sin in human society and the problem of trying to reverse the prevailing trends.[145]

These critics are not denying the truth of the exemplarist theory, but say that it needs to be complemented with the belief that in Jesus, God has somehow intervened to save the situation, not only by providing encouragement and example but by healing our guilt and breaking evil's power. In fact, far from rejecting the exemplarist theory, they point out that it is in itself a necessary complement to the so-called 'objective' theories in that it emphasizes the need for a 'subjective' response on the part of the saved believer.

However, on its own, say the critics, it is inadequate because it underestimates the power of sin, and overestimates human ability to respond. On the face of it, this seems to be a logical criticism. Human beings are weak, and the 'escalation' of sin in human society to which Macquarrie refers is possibly true – I am not sure how one measures it, or judges that Hitler's Holocaust or South African apartheid are more sinful than Genghis Khan. The difficulty with Macquarrie's objection is that it applies just as much to all the 'objective' theories, including his own preferred victory theory. *Christian* human beings are also weak. Many Christians (however false to their faith) participated in the Holocaust, or at least did nothing to stand against it. Christians have devised apartheid. There are, of course, shining Christian exceptions. But there are shining non-Christian exceptions, too. The truth of the matter seems to be that some few humans, Christian and non-Christian, are able heroically to make a stand for goodness; some few humans, Christian and non-Christian, seem to be unmitigatedly wicked; and most humans are a mixture. Believing the Christian faith seems to be no guarantee of behavioural change, whichever theory we choose to adopt.

This is a problem for the credibility of so-called 'objective' atonement theories. 'Objective' theories suggesting that God has accomplished our salvation irrespective of our own feelings on the matter, that salvation is a matter of fact not subjective experience, do not fit the fact that Christian lives are of no better quality, as far as we can judge, than lives of non-Christians. Macquarrie's 'escalation of sin' is as true of Christian society as non-Christian society. There is no evidence, as according to the 'objective' victory theory there should be, of any objective change for the better in Christian society. In the substitutionary satisfaction theory there is not even any expectation that there should be, and this is its weakness.

The great merit of the exemplarist theory as an explanatory theory is that this lack of change does not count against it. In the objective theories it is God who is understood to perform the transformation, who changes the situation. Since God by definition must be reliable, able and consistent, a failure to effect the change rules the theory out. In the exemplarist theory, while God calls for a change in the human situation, God's action is restricted to providing a call, an example, an assurance of his love to encourage us. It is humans who must respond to that initative and make the changes. Since human beings are not understood to be always reliable, able or consistent, any failure on their part to do so does not invalidate the theory. As long as some humans, sometimes, respond, then the theory is still valid.

This is not necessarily to say, however, that the theory is useful. To revert to Sipho as our touchstone: an assurance that God's love for him is demonstrated in the lengths to which the God-Man was prepared to go for him is in some ways very affirmative. Reared as he has been in a society which implies that blacks are worth less than whites, and in an environment where an unstable family life gives little opportunity for the development of a positive self-concept, the knowledge that the Son of God loved Sipho enough to die for him has a very great potential for him. He can begin to believe in his personal worth and to believe that he is lovable. But he will surely begin to ask himself why, if God loved him enough for Jesus to die for him, God does not show his love for him now in a more practical way.

Rashdall's account of the exemplarist theory suggests that we are drawn to respond to God because of the love God shows to us in Jesus' death on the cross. The real problems with this version are:

1. that Rashdall needs to explain how *God's* love is shown through Jesus' human death;

2. that Sipho, and others like him, may ask why God's love stopped at that point, and how Jesus' death helps Sipho now;

3. that Rashdall's concept of salvation is too narrow, dealing only with the restoration of Sipho's one-to-one relationship with God.

We have seen that for Rashdall, Jesus is God, so that the love of Jesus is the love of God. But if that love is shown primarily through Jesus' death, then we must ask: Can God die? Can God even suffer? If not, how does Jesus' death on the cross show us God's love? How is his death a divine act, a divine demonstration of love? This point is not developed by Rashdall.

The sufferings and death of Jesus do provide a link for Sipho with his own sufferings. However, this point is not developed either. Although Rashdall agrees in theory with the notion that 'Christ's whole life was a sacrifice',[146] and insists that we regard the whole life of Jesus as an example of God's love, what he appears to mean by that is that we should not forget that the *teaching* of Jesus was also a gift of great value and that his teaching also touches human hearts. Rashdall makes no mention of the poverty and oppression which Jesus, like Sipho, endured – perhaps not a surprising omission in Rashdall's time and social class.

We may, however, extend the argument and agree that it is the Incarnation even more than the death which is a demonstration of God's love for and solidarity with Sipho. God became human, and as a human being suffered persecution, dispossession, torture, bullying from the Roman imperial power, and maltreatment from members of his own race, just as Sipho does. This may well be a theme which offers great comfort to Sipho.

Sipho will, however, surely have a right to ask, 'So what?' The fact that in Jesus God shared our plight, understands our problems from within, that he is therefore very sympathetic towards Sipho, is in fact still deeply suffering because Sipho suffers – how does that help Sipho? This is the problem with the exemplarist theory if it is too narrowly presented. It does not concern itself with a sufficiently wide concept of salvation. It is concerned only with restoring a loving, worshipping relationship between Sipho and God. Sipho needs more than an assurance of God's love and a restoration to that loving relationship, important though that might be. He needs a way out of his poverty and persecution. He needs practical help with practical problems, or else the love of God for him is merely a sentimental opiate. He needs to see something more in his life of suffering than merely an opportunity for God to show him an empathetic love.

This is why, of course, people have wanted to bring in the victory theory; but we have seen the problem of credibility with that theory. We should therefore look in some detail at Jürgen Moltmann's suggestions in *The Crucified God*. Here Moltmann does extend the concept of salvation, and argues that Jesus' identification with the lost, the socially unacceptable, the poor, the hopeless, is the key to a correct theological understanding of Jesus, of God, and of human nature. Moltmann takes into account, as Rashdall appears not to do, the poverty and political oppression which Jesus endured, as a way of showing God's concern with those who at present are oppressed and rejected. His concept of salvation is one of deliverance from these evils, and is not restricted to the concept of being reconciled to a God with whom we have lost contact because of our guilty feelings.

> By his suffering and death, Jesus identified himself with those who were enslaved and took their pain upon himself. And if he was not alone in his suffering, nor were they abandoned in the pains of slavery. Jesus was with them.[147]

In fact Moltmann's theory is far stronger than that. It is not only that Jesus was 'with them'. Moltmann's christology involves a very orthodox view of Jesus as both human and divine, and includes a strong trinitarianism. If Jesus took the pain of the outcasts on himself, God too took the pain on himself. God is a 'crucified God'. God is 'with them'.

Moltmann believes that we cannot look at the cosmic Christ, of universal significance, without rooting that belief in the historical sufferings of Jesus. We must hold in tension our theological beliefs about Christ and the earthly particularity of Jesus. The cross and the resurrection of Jesus mutually interpret each other. A soteriology or christology which does not take seriously, the historical reality of both, but especially the cross, is missing the point.[148]

To explain this, Moltmann looks at why Jesus died. It was not an accident, nor the result of sickness. Nor did he choose to die, as an expiation of the world's sin or for theological reasons of that kind. Although Moltmann acknowledges elements of truth in the penal atonement theory – that we cannot achieve righteousness for ourselves, that Jesus' death on the cross was 'for us'[149] – he thinks that theories of this kind reduce the horror of the cross. We need to 'abandon traditional theories of salvation which have made the way the cross is spoken of in Christianity a mere habit'.[150] He is just as wary of attempts to bypass the historicity of Jesus' suffering through Bultmannian existentialist interpretations of the death and resurrection of Jesus, which reduce the cross to a speech-event. It is the historical person, not the idea, of Jesus which saves us.

> It is he, the crucified Jesus himself, who is the driving force, the joy, and the suffering of all theology . . . which is Christian.[151]

Jesus died because his teaching and his alignment with the outcasts and powerless stirred up opposition from both Jews and Romans. To the Pharisees and orthodox Jews, Jesus was a blasphemer, because in the face of the Torah and the Mosaic restrictions, he demonstrated God's 'eschatological law of grace'[152] towards those outside the law or who had transgressed the law. Where the Jews and even John the Baptist expected the Messiah to come as judge, Jesus came not as a judge of sinners but as a friend, as a bearer of unconditional forgiveness and grace. And he claimed authority to do this not from religious tradition but from his own direct relationship to Abba, the Father. So the orthodox condemned him for being false to the tradition, a blasphemer.

To the Romans, on the other hand, Jesus was a political agitator. Moltmann does not agree that he was misjudged by the Romans in this. Because Jesus sided with the poor, and because he numbered Zealots amongst his followers, and in Moltmann's eyes took a line very similar to the Zealots, this created the real possibility of a revolt by the poor.[153] Jesus stood as one who opposed what the

Roman empire was doing to the dispossessed. So Pilate needed to kill him to preserve peace and quiet.

Thus Jesus took a radically new and different stance from traditional Judaism, in the belief that this was his message from God. For this he faced death. For this, too, he lost the support of people who might have sided with him in a less radical and novel stance. However, although Jesus was sympathetic in some ways to the Zealots, he did not share their Jewish legalism, or their belief that God would punish the faithless Jews and enemies of Judah.[154] Jesus was equally sympathetic to the collaborating tax collectors. So for the Zealots, Jesus was a traitor.

Thus far Moltmann has followed Rashdall, though stating his case with more force and detail. In Moltmann's account, Jesus' death was no accident, no suicide, but the result of his decision to preach the gospel of God's kingdom, a decision which he made knowing the likely cost. But Moltmann develops the idea still further. Deserted by those who but for his radicalness might otherwise have supported him, Jesus was deserted by God too. The Father did not rescue or defend him. Therefore it seemed to the disciples that Jesus had been wrong, and they too left. In human terms, Jesus' mission had been a failure. Even the Father abandoned him to his fate as a sinner against the law and a disturber of the peace.[155] At his death, Jesus himself felt that the Father had abandoned him. Moltmann places a very strong interpretation on the cry from the cross, 'My God, my God, why hast thou forsaken me?' (Mark 15.34).[156] Because what he preached was so bound up with who he was, or with the person that he was, Jesus felt that because his person was now being killed, all that he had preached was being denied also.[157] This is, for Moltmann, what makes Jesus' death different from all the other heroes who have suffered in the world. It goes beyond their suffering, because Jesus felt that God, Abba, with whom he had been in perfect relationship, had denied him and all that he stood for.

It may be that in some of these observations Moltmann has gone beyond, or been very selective in his use of, New Testament evidence. By no means all New Testament scholars would agree, for instance, that Jesus was sympathetic to the Zealots' cause, even though Moltmann has moderated very much the ideas of Brandon in this regard,[158] nor that Jesus' use of Psalm 22 should be interpreted in this way. However, even if, as I think, Moltmann may have stated his case too strongly, in general his picture of the historical causes for Jesus' death is surely valid, as is his belief that this makes Jesus the partner or fellow-sufferer with those whose cause he adopted: the powerless, the poor, the homeless and despairing. It brings Jesus very close to Sipho, which Rashdall's much weaker version of the theory failed to do.

However, this is only the start of Moltmann's theory. We must also proclaim, says Moltmann, that Jesus rose from the dead. Jesus' life, his person and his teaching were vindicated. Moltmann insists that we interpret the resurrection in terms of the crucifixion of Jesus so that our theology is not a theology of glory, victory and triumph only, but a theology which recognizes that the resurrection is accomplished through defeat, death and disgrace.[159] The resurrection is the beginning of eschatological change in the world. God's intention is to bring the whole world into his new kingdom. The risen Jesus is the first fruits of that kingdom, a proclamation of a proleptic hope.[160] The resurrection is not just the rising to life again of a dead person, but a new creation, a new start of the coming and future kingdom of God. In this way it is a proclamation of hope to all the hopeless. Yet although this has parallels with the victory theory, the emphasis on looking back to the cross as well as forward to the new kingdom is an important modification.

The looking back is important, not just in order to realize what all this had cost Jesus (which would be the old exemplarist theory again), but because the crucifixion also proclaims to us the nature of God. Moltmann suggests that the early church, because of its adaptation of a Platonic conception of God who is beyond change, suffering or feeling, had great problems in giving full emphasis to the sufferings of the God/Man, and had to fall back on a two-nature theory, to say that Jesus suffered and died in his human nature but not in his divine nature. The closest they could come to conceding a divine suffering in Jesus was by association of the divine with the human, the *communicatio idiomatum*. Inevitably the sufferings of Jesus were often minimized in a docetic way.[161]

However, the Old Testament prophets had stressed a somewhat different conception of a God who did feel, and because he was concerned for his people, suffered with them in their adversity. He was thus independent and yet dependent in a dipolar way. Moltmann chooses not to follow up this thought in a process theology way, but instead to stress the Trinity. A suffering God is a mystery; but we can make sense of how God can suffer in Jesus if we remember that the suffering is voluntarily accepted, and if we allow a distinction between the Father and the Son. Instead of a dipolar God, Moltmann uses the concept of the persons of the Trinity,[162] stressing the distinction and otherness of the persons. Jesus, he says, is not 'God' in the generic use of the title, but 'God the Son'. It is 'God the Son' who suffers and dies and is abandoned by the Father. Thus he avoids patripassianism, the old heresy which taught that the Father suffered. The Father does indeed suffer, but in a different way,[163] one having nothing to do with physical pain. He suffers by abandoning his beloved Son, which he does 'for us'. In this way God himself enters into our suffering, although in different ways for Father and Son. Suffering is made part of the nature of God. God sends his Son for us, abandons him on the cross for us, and feels the pain of that abandonment and crucifixion.

For Moltmann this has profound consequences for our perspective on suffering. Not only can Sipho know that God identifies with his suffering, but Sipho's suffering means that Sipho participates in God's very nature. God not only sent his Son to live as human and suffer as human so as to remake the broken world, but in that sending there is an element of denying himself, working against himself, crucifying himself.

> Creation, new creation and resurrection are *external* works of God against chaos, nothingness and death. The suffering and dying of Jesus, understood as the suffering and dying of the Son of God, on the other hand, are works of God *towards himself*.[164]

Just as sacraments can be interpreted as meaning that the Christian, through participation in baptism or the eucharist, becomes part of the trinitarian relationship between Father, Son and Spirit, so through suffering the poor and oppressed are part of that trinitarian relationship. The sufferer is

taken up into the inner life of God.[165]

Left at this, the danger of such an approach is that it so dignifies suffering that suffering loses its horror, and becomes almost desirable and acceptable, becoming the high road to divinization. This is where the dialectic tension between crucifixion and resurrection, looking back and looking forwards, is important. Moltmann, echoing his earlier book, *Theology of Hope*,[166] emphasizes that the resurrection is a sign to us of the future which is breaking into the present. Jesus does not come to preach suffering. He comes to preach God's kingdom, and the resurrection is the coming to fruition of God's kingdom of righteousness and peace, where oppression and poverty have no place. God identifies with us deeply in our suffering, but promises us a kingdom where suffering shall have been overcome. Thus the poor are delivered from fatalism and apathy in the face of their suffering.[167]

This emphasis on suffering and resurrection has implications not only for the individual but for the church, which should never identify with the governing authorities in a Constantinian way. God's identification with suffering means that the church must identify with those who are alienated from society. God's seal of resurrection means that the church must always point critically beyond the *status quo* to the as yet unrealized future.

Moltmann's approach is a very bold one. Where some liberal theologians have felt that the arguments about the divinity of Jesus, let alone the logic of a Trinity, are out of place and without useful value in our modern world, Moltmann sets out to show that belief in the nature of Jesus as Son of God, and in the Trinity, provides a way of seeing modern socio-political issues in a new light and provides precisely the model of salvation that we need. He believes that his way of interpreting God in the light of the cross and resurrection of Jesus provides a way forward in the face of suffering that is provided neither by the traditional concept of God in classic theism – immutable, invulnerable in his aseity – nor the protest atheism of Feuerbach and his like. Classic theism takes all power from humans and gives it to God.[168] God alone is in control; God is utterly strong and self-dependent. Because God is other and transcendent, human nature is of little account. In Moltmann's view, classic theism also reduces much of God's nobility. The truly noble human being is not removed from suffering, but grasps suffering and finds purpose and meaning in his life in so doing. A God who cannot suffer cannot show this nobility. Process theologians have made much the same point. Such a God is too far removed from Sipho's world to be of relevance to him, and provides no model of bravery and self-sacrifice with which to inspire suffering humanity. Such a God-concept makes the suffering of Jesus refer only to his human nature with all the consequent difficulties we have discussed.

Feuerbach argued correctly that this kind of God took all the power from humanity and placed it into the sphere of God, leaving humans weak and dependent. But the protest atheism which rebels against this kind of God also provides no hope for the sufferers in the world. It would not be expected that Moltmann with his concern for the underdog would have much sympathy for Feuerbach. Protest atheism, says Moltmann, puts all the power in human hands, but twentieth-century experience shows us that human power can be used against humans.[169] Protest atheism provides no grounds for hope for the oppressed. Only a faith in God as the crucified God, the God who is revealed to us in the historical sufferings of Jesus and in his resurrection, a God who must be understood as Trinity and as incarnate in the life and suffering and death of Jesus, can provide us with an understanding of the hope that is there for us.

If Moltmann is right, this is of the greatest importance for the concerns of this book. He seems to speak directly to Sipho's situation. Moltmann certainly believes that this kind of Christian faith brings liberation from political impotence, from fatalism, from a feeling of inferiority in the face of this world's governing powers, from low self-esteem, from hopelessness about being able to effect change, and from death itself with its associated fear of transitoriness,

> [The cross] is set up in the cosmos to give future to that which is passing away, firmness to that which is unsteady, openness to that which is fixed, hope to the hopeless, and in this way to gather all that is and all that is no more, into the new creation.[170]

Once we understand God as the crucified God, there can no longer be any question of divinizing human authorities by investing them with God's power. The 'gods' of wordly power, of class and caste and race, are shown up as false gods. The crucified God is not only on the side of, but in an important way shares the nature of, the poor, the oppressed and the alienated. The ideals for which we strive will not be those of stoic apathy in the face of suffering, nor gnostic release from suffering, but victory over suffering through participation in suffering. Moltmann traces some of the anthropological, political and psychological implications at the end of the book.

Salvation then includes the idea that those who are oppressed are given a new vision of their own dignity and godlikeness in their suffering; they know the presence with them in their sufferings of a God who understands and shares, thus ending their alienation. They are also given an assurance that their oppression, weakness and powerlessness will be overcome in the *eschaton*. This is rich theology indeed.

There are some problems. It is not clear why the Father is said to 'abandon' Jesus on the cross. We understand what Moltmann means when he says that Jesus was sent to preach the gospel of the kingdom; we understand that the message was unpopular, that Jesus was therefore crucified, and in this way suffered for us and

shared our world of suffering. We understand, too, although less
clearly because of problems with patripassianism, that because the
Father loves the Son, the pain of the Son causes pain to the Father,
even if we are not sure what 'pain' means when applied to God. But
what does Moltmann mean when he says that the Father, albeit
temporarily, abandons Jesus to endure the penalty of the lawbreak-
er? Is it only that Jesus *thinks* the Father has abandoned him? In
that case he is not really abandoned. But Moltmann says more than
that Jesus only thinks he is abandoned. The death of Jesus on the
cross is, in some sense, God's action.

> He died not only because of the understanding of the law by his
> contemporaries or because of Roman power politics, but ultim-
> ately because of his God and Father.[171]

> The Father himself, going against his own divine nature of love
> and power, rejects Jesus.

> Finally and most profoundly, he died as one rejected by his God
> and Father . . . the cross of Christ divides God from God to the
> utmost degree of enmity and distinction.[172]

Is there still some echo of the substitutionary theory here, that Jesus
had to endure the penalty for sin according to the strict interpretation of the law?

We still have to ask: does the incarnation as understood in
Moltmann's terms help Sipho? Sipho is given assurance that God
shares his pain, and also that in the end his oppression and misery
will come to an end. But in fact Sipho's oppression may very well
not end. The apartheid regime will not easily crumble. When it
does, the identity of Sipho's oppressors may change, but being
poor, ill-educated, the victim of his upbringing, Sipho will still be
likely to be at the bottom of the pile, whoever is king of the castle.
Oppression, poverty, impotence to control their own destiny, have
continued to be the lot of most humans since Jesus. In what way,
then, is Jesus really the first fruits of the breaking into human
history of God's eschatological purposes? I do not doubt that
Moltmann enables Christians to have a different perspective on
suffering. His theology could have a particularly valuable and
salutary effect on those of us who are middle-class and whose
Christianity provides a comfortable confirmation of the *status quo*
tinged with a suitable paternalistic sympathy for the poor. Moltmann effectively blocks that kind of rationalization.

I suspect, though, that for the Siphos of this world, whose penultimate[173] needs are still unmet, Moltmann's approach does not offer as much as it seemed to at first sight. The hope which the cross and resurrection offer are still no more than pious faith, only to be actualized in the far-off last days. When the *eschaton* remains unrealized for so long, can it still offer us real hope?

What is of help in Moltmann's theory is that Sipho may be encouraged, in the face of Jesus' example, to see that every person has the potential to engage with the forces that oppress him or her, and to overcome those forces. If Moltmann's theory ultimately boils down to this, however, there are less complicated ways of reaching the same conclusion.

I have included Moltmann's approach in the discussion of the exemplarist theory. Whether it belongs under that heading depends on the significance we place on the example of Jesus. I think it does belong here, provided we are clear that Moltmann does not mean that Jesus stands before us merely as a human and moral example which we should imitate.

In fact this latter interpretation is not Rashdall's nor Abelard's either. This is not always clearly understood. For these two classic 'exemplarists', the example of Jesus' suffering is not a moral model to be followed, but an exemplification of God's love, which will melt our stubborn hearts and thus achieve a reconciliation.

For Moltmann, the 'example' of Jesus' suffering is also an exemplification of God's love, which will change our whole perspective and understanding of suffering, helplessness, alienation and abandonment, investing our weakness with dignity and meaning, and also challenging our weakness with hope. In this way Moltmann is making the same use of the 'example' of Jesus as Rashdall, but offers a much more sophisticated interpretation, more sensitive to a twentieth-century awareness of Third World and working-class needs, than that of Rashdall.

Since the Enlightenment, there have always been those who have been exemplarist in a quite different way; those who have stressed the power of human beings to make decisions about their own moral acts, and the need for these decisions to be informed by reason and by teaching. Jesus is understood to be human and not mysteriously divine. The significance of Jesus for this approach is that he provides for us an example of goodness. As a result of Jesus' example, we are wiser about the nature of 'the good', and more optimistic about our capabilities for attaining the good. It would be proper to call this approach a 'moral influence' theory, a description which I do not think is accurate for Rashdall. To some extent the ideas come from Kant and his insistence on autonomous individual ethics as basic not only to human life but to human knowledge of God. Knowledge of God is primarily a matter of knowledge of what is good and bad. A moral influence theory of this kind is out of favour amongst theologians, but is probably quite widespread in popular Western, particularly English and American, Christianity as an inheritance from Deism.

As Alister McGrath points out, what Jesus is demonstrating in this view is not the love of God but 'the full extent of the love of one human being for another' which 'encourages and empowers us all to do exactly the same thing'.[174] McGrath, of course, thinks this is inadequate, because it would appear that 'God can be left out of the picture with the greatest of ease, and apparently without making much significant difference to the situation'.[175]

In essence the idea is that Jesus lived a morally blameless and perfect life; that if everybody lived like that all the world's troubles would disappear; and that if we imitate him we shall therefore all be saved. Stated like this, the theory is inadequate, although not for the reason which McGrath gives. The theory does not necessarily leave God out of the picture, for God is the source of the moral imperative. God is the one who 'encourages and emowers us' through the example of Jesus to live out in our lives the quality of Jesus' love. We have in any case seen that the more 'objective' theories which McGrath prefers have their own difficulties.

But the problem with the kind of exemplarist theory which sees Jesus as an example to copy is that we know very little about Jesus' life, having only three years of it presented to us by the evangelists, and that in a very selective and stylized way, so that we do not get enough information for a detailed moral example for imitation. Jesus sometimes behaved in what is, at least on the surface, a rather immoral manner – his curtness with his mother, his harshness with the Pharisees[176] – thus making direct imitation problematic. There are many other examples of people about whom we have much more detailed information living good, godly lives which seem to equal Jesus' goodness. In addition, a purely individualistic understanding of ethics is no longer generally acceptable. The difficulties in our society are not only the result of individual failings, but are also caused by impersonal, or at least non-individual, factors such as economic, political or sociological systems. That is not to say, of course, that the example of Jesus has no saving relevance. We shall return to that later. But the example of one who lived in a very different social context can no longer be taken as wholly applicable.

(e)   The idea of sacrifice

Vincent Taylor,[177] after a careful analysis of the New Testament, concludes that while the authors have different ideas about atonement, the idea that best unifies the various strands of New Testament teaching is that of sacrifice. The idea is found particularly strongly in Paul, least strongly in the Johannine literature, but runs through the New Testament as a common thread. Taylor believes this is not surprising, given the influence upon the first Christians and upon Jesus himself of the Jewish cultic sacrifices and idea of the Suffering Servant from Deutero-Isaiah. However, the New Testament shows little interest, outside the Epistle to the Hebrews, in the details of temple worship. It is the sacrificial principle, rather than the external sacrificial cult, which influences them.

By a sacrificial idea, Taylor does not mean the substitutionary satisfaction theory. He is at pains to say that the whole trouble with a penal type of theory is that it *is* substitutionary, that is, that it carries the notion that atonement is God's work alone with no place in it for human response. The implications of Jesus' death, he says, are not 'legal' but 'ethical and religious'. Jesus' death is certainly representative. He does die 'for us', representing us before the Father, but not so as to exclude the necessity for us also to offer our own penitence and obedience (the ethical) and love (the religious) to God. The best way of categorizing or interpreting the representative offering made by Jesus in his life and death is the sacrificial category.[178]

Taylor is another who rejects the exemplarist theory as being inadequate on its own, although he suggests that an atonement theory based on John alone might take that line. The exemplarist theory is not enough, partly because in Taylor's view it leaves out much of the New Testament witness, but also because it takes insufficient account of the seriousness of sin. Sin takes away our capacity to respond to God's love. Sin makes it impossible for the sinner's heart to be touched.

> It is sin that stands in the way of blessedness, not only making fellowship with God impossible, but also darkening his very awareness of God and thwarting the spiritual possibilities of his being.[179]

Of course it is even more true that sin makes it impossible for the
bruised and hardened heart of one who is sinned against to be
touched, but Taylor does not make that point.

Sinful humans are not able to respond. While one might think
that Taylor would therefore choose a version of the victory theory
as a better model, he opts instead for a model which still emphasizes
forgiveness and reconciliation with God as the main issue of
salvation. The point of atonement is no longer that an angry God
must be appeased. Taylor caricaturizes the penal theory in this
respect: even Calvin did not say that God needed to be appeased,
but that the demands of justice needed to be met. So, too, Paul talks
about the wrath of God, but in a rather impersonal sense: it might
be argued that Paul understands Jesus to be saving us from the
wrath of God rather than from a wrathful God. For Taylor, anyway,
God is not angry but ready to forgive. The point of atonement is to
establish a new covenant between God and humans. We need to be
brought into a relationship of penitence and amendment on the part
of humans, forgiveness and the giving of grace on the part of
God.[180]

Reconciliation, in Taylor's conception, thus has a divine and a
human side to it. In Jesus, God shares our sufferings. Unlike
Moltmann, Taylor does not present the death of Jesus as being the
inevitable historical consequence of preaching a politically and
religiously critical gospel, where Jesus shares the alienation and
lostness of the poor and oppressed. He has quite a different
perspective. He suggests that Jesus himself saw his coming suffering
as being within the providence of God, and as being an offering
which Jesus makes to God, by God's will.

> His passion was not only something to be endured; it was an
> achievement to which his life was dedicated, closely connected
> with the Kingdom or Rule of God.[181]

Jesus' death as a human is seen by Taylor to be an identification not
so much with the consequences of oppression, as in Moltmann's
approach, as with the consequences of one's own sin.

> The witness of the New Testament is that in perfect obedience to
> the Father's will he bore upon his heart the burden of human
> sin.[182]

Jesus accepts death for himself as the consequence of human sin,
not just as a human but as the Son of Man, the mediator of the new
covenant, the Messiah. This makes his offering uniquely significant.

Although Taylor concedes that it goes beyond the words of the New Testament, he supports the idea borrowed from McLeod Campbell and Moberly, that in his passion Jesus made a representative offering of confession and penitence to the Father. This is not a substitute for our penitence, but makes it possible for us to make our own offering of penitence in participation with him.

Taylor comes quite close to Anselm at this point. There is more than a hint that the cross is still something that ought to happen to sinners; that on the cross Jesus endured that which is the just consequence of sin, though he himself was sinless. It is a pity that Taylor did not expand in more detail what he means; it seems that he means that humans in penitence need to show some sign, make some offering of sacrifice and amendment, and that in this way Jesus on the cross made a penitential offering not on his own account but on our behalf. I suspect that an element from the penal theory still persists here. It is not clear why Jesus must die as a sign of penitence, unless death is the due penalty for sin – in which case we are back with the concept of retributive justice.

The dividing line between this concept and the substitutionary penal concept is thus somewhat narrow. The important difference is that in this understanding atonement is not purely a question of satisfying God's justice, but of restoring the relationship with God which sin has broken. That relationship is restored from a human side by penitence and amendment. In his death on the cross Jesus as a human makes an offering of penitence and of ultimate obedience; and the offering is not made in our stead, but as a first-fruits, so that by our participation in his life we can receive grace to be penitent and obedient ourselves. God's attitude throughout is not one of judging love, but of welcoming love.[183] The relationship is restored from God's side by a revelation of that forgiving love, and by God's call to us to respond to that love. Jesus, of course, as God and man, restores the relationship from both God's side and the side of humans. He shows us God's love; but as well as exemplifying God's love, he makes a human offering of penitent obedience to God which enables us to respond with him in penitence and love as well.

Taylor envisages three ways in which we may participate in the sacrificial offering of Jesus and receive its benefits and blessings. We are one with him in faith, that is, in our own prayerful commitment to him. We are one with him in the eucharist, where we recall and participate in his offering and make our own 'sacrifice of praise and thanksgiving' with him. We are one with him in service, as we feed the hungry, clothe the naked, tend the lost, and in so doing minister

to Jesus himself. Taylor is quite clear that although the response to
Jesus is an individual one, the commitment of obedience holds
communal and social obligations.[184]

So far as the divinity of Christ is concerned, it would seem
necessary for Jesus' sacrificial self-offering to be of universal
significance and universally representative, for him to be at least
more than merely human. Taylor would not be happy with even an
adoptionist, or as he calls it, an immanental christology, in which
Jesus is human, but so obedient a human being that God acts in him
to a much greater degree than in any other human being. In Taylor's
view, a reduced christology of this kind would not only be untrue to
the faith of the New Testament writers and that of the creeds and
subsequent centuries of Christian experience, but it would make the
work of atonement a purely human work, since the offerer of the
sacrifice would be purely human; and this would be unfitting.

> Immunity from philosophical problems on the basis of such a
> theology is too dearly purchased . . . It is far better to adopt a
> theology which leaves us puzzled than to buy a clarity at the cost
> of inadequacy.[185]

Thus again an inadequate redeemer means an inadequate redemption. Further, the offering which Jesus makes to the Father is an
offering not only of human obedience but of the divine eternal
obedience of the Son to the Father in the unity of the Spirit. Thus
sacrifice (meaning self-offering) is part of the nature of the
Godhead, as well as a necessary human activity.[186]

However, we may question whether an orthodox christology and
doctrine of the Trinity are quite as central to Taylor's sacrificial idea
as they are to Moltmann's model, or for that matter to Anselm's. A
strong doctrine of corporate personality, so that we can see
ourselves as being one with Jesus, would surely mean that a
degree-christology would work as well. Thus Jesus could be seen as
human, not divine; as being uniquely good and obedient and yet
ready to offer himself to share the consequences of sin with other
humans. These lesser humans could still see themselves as participat-
ing in the offering of Jesus and being strengthened by it. I do not
think Taylor's approach would be weakened if it were modified in
this adoptionist fashion.

One might wish that Taylor had said rather more about how our
own sinful nature is transformed and healed, if it is not by the
example given us in Jesus, and that he had developed more fully the
idea of participation in the offering of Jesus. The model seems to

require filling out in this way. Taylor, however, did not offer it as an exclusive concept, and other models might prove complementary.

It is not my intention to offer a detailed evaluation of Taylor's important work on atonement theology in his trilogy.[187] In many ways his review of the scriptural material offers new and convincing insights, while I am not sure that Taylor's notion of representative sacrifice is as far distant from Anselm as he himself believes.

My main concern, however, is that from Sipho's point of view the approach again has very little to offer. As with other approaches we have examined, the emphasis is on restoring a relationship with God which has been broken by our sin. Again I make the point that though Sipho and his family are not without sin, so that the model is not totally inapplicable to them, they are far more sinned against than sinners. It is not Sipho who needs to be penitent before God, or Sipho who needs a 'representative penitent' before God, so much as those who have made his life so mean and twisted. Sipho's circumstances imprison him more than his own sin. Taylor provides a soteriology for Sipho's oppressors, not for him. The emphasis throughout Taylor's thought is on God's love for the sinner. Where, for Sipho, is the evidence of God's love for those who are sinned against? And where is the evidence that the Christian persecutors of Sipho have, by participation in the faith-union with Jesus or in the sacrament of communion, come to be penitent themselves and intending of amendment?

This last criticism may seem unfair, since no model of atonement suggests that Christians are transformed willy-nilly, without freedom to refuse to change. But again I must say that sincere Afrikaner Christians did not intend to disobey God in the creation of an apartheid society. They intended to obey God, and sought in all seriousness to participate in faith, in word, and in sacraments. They were sincerely penitent for such personal sins as they were aware of, and intended amendment; but this did not change their social attitudes. There are many reasons for this; my point is only that we have still not come across a way of understanding salvation which really meets the situation of Sipho, whom I am using as an individuation of all those who are black, poor and oppressed in South Africa. It still seems to be a theory best suited for those who have more power to direct their own lives.

Nevertheless, as Frances Young has pointed out,[188] there is a good deal of power in the idea of a person dying for others, in the notion of sacrifice as a principle of self-giving for the sake of the other. This is a rather difficult slant to the idea of sacrifice, and one to which I shall return later.

(f) Where have we got to?

We have looked at a number of the more traditional ways of understanding salvation, and found that they do not seem to meet Sipho's situation. It is not that they are totally irrelevant. In most cases we have seen that there are elements in them which appear to apply, but they do not seem to get to the heart of his problems. They deal with what are, for Sipho, side-effects and symptoms of his situation and not the root causes. In some cases they seem even to have contributed to the formation of attitudes amongst black people, or amongst their oppressors, which are actually harmful.

There are, of course, great numbers of black people in South Africa who are quite orthodox Christians and who do find help and power in one or other of these ways of looking at salvation. It would be impudent for me to say that this is all illusory, or over-pious escapism, and I do not mean to imply that. The solace and strength that such Christians gain from their faith sustains them under conditions which I have not had to endure personally. Nor, of course, is the situation for all black people in South Africa as bad as that of Sipho, and I have perhaps chosen to focus on a particularly difficult case study; however, it is one which is perfectly factual and not at all untypical.

Nor would I wish to deny the enormous sociological importance of the Christian churches in South Africa, nor the potential which they have as the only surviving multi-racial organizations to influence the situation for good. They have considerable assets of finance and property to be placed at the disposal of the struggle, and have strong international links to provide both money and muscle. They provide places for black people to meet each other, and are important points of focus in the community. They have provided opportunities for black people to exercise control over their own affairs, and to meet in synods and the like with white Christians on more or less equal terms. Potentially they provide links whereby black and white Christians can meet to learn something of each other's circumstances, hopes and fears – links which exist almost nowhere else in apartheid South Africa. They have until fairly recently provided the only education and health facilities for black people. Most of the older black leadership owes its education and its training in democratic government to the churches. All of this can be said to have resulted from the teaching of

Jesus about love and social responsibility, and I shall return to this theme later.

Nevertheless, any other institution, provided it was committed to ordinary humanitarian values and had wide support in the community – the Scouting movement, Rotary International, etc. – could perform the same functions. These are not specifically Christian or theological functions. For Christian faith to continue to have saving power in South Africa, an attempt needs to be made to give a reasoned account, on the basis of logic and experience, of what salvation in Jesus means and how it is found for people in Sipho's situation. Those who maintain traditional accounts of salvation need to try to provide this. Is there evidence that strength in Christ, strength in Christian sacrament, strength in hearing the Word, is greater than and more effective than strength from other religions and religious figures, or other ideologies for that matter? Is there not in fact some counter-evidence? Judaism, Hinduism and Islam seem to have produced as many courageous resisters to apartheid as Christians. And we have the nagging worry that sincere and regular participation in word and sacrament has not prevented other devout Christians from imposing the apartheid regime. Is there any special, distinctive, Christian help available to Sipho? We do need answers to these questions, for fear that the saving faith that we offer is in fact a false saviour.

Perhaps we could categorize Sipho's problems under the Marxian term alienation. F. W. Dillistone[189] reminds us that Marx is not alone in using this concept to describe the human situation, but that the idea is found, for example, in Hegel and Freud, too. Sipho is alienated from his own society which is so divided, from his own culture which has been destroyed, and from the alternative middle-class Western society from which he is excluded. He has virtually no control over his choice of work, his place of residence, or his level of schooling, so that he is alienated from his own talents and potentiality. In Marxist terms he has no control over the fruits of his labour. His family life is very precarious. He is without the security of a mother (since she is at work most of his waking hours) or father (who is usually absent). He has thus little family support. He has no likelihood of achieving self-esteem; he is alienated from himself. And, of course, he is alienated from God. This is the main point for Taylor; it is the main point for Dillistone, too. And perhaps we could say that if the alienation from God is healed, the other alienations will be put right, since they all stem from a world which because of disobedience to God has lost its balance. In reality, however, it probably works the other way. Sipho is alienated from God because of the other alienations. He is alienated from God because of the situation in which God allows him to live. Of course with a proper theodicy we may explain how it is that God allows this situation, or why God cannot prevent it. As far as Sipho is concerned, however, with so little going for him, his relationship with God is the least of his conscious priorities. If he does have recourse to God, it will be in an appeal for God's intervention to overcome his problems; but God has not intervened, and therefore is not going to intervene in the future, for all the reasons we have explained to ourselves in our theodicy. Or Sipho may have recourse to God, like his mother, in an escapist pietism which allows him, for a while, to forget his problems – but weakens his ability to do anything about them. Until the ordinary everyday alienations are put right, he cannot be reconciled with God, because God's 'failure' to deal with these problems will mean a constant re-alienation.

It is true in the large sense that Sipho's ordinary alienation is the consequence of human alienation from God and not the cause, in the sense that humans create an alienating environment for themselves as a result of their alienation from God. But that is only true of humanity as a whole, not of particular individuals. Sipho has not disobeyed or sinned against God and thus created a lonely world for himself. He already lives in a lonely world and therefore cannot really know what obedience to God means.

A way of salvation that is true salvation for Sipho must begin with helping him to cope with and overcome his everyday environment. Then, when he is more the master of his own destiny, he can be held more responsible for sin and be brought to penitence and renewal before God.

Perhaps, though, Sipho's sufferings will turn his eyes towards God and his Kingdom?

It is through the *sufferings* of this present age that man's affections have been set upon the glories of the Kingdom of God and in this very redirection of his desires there has come to pass what can rightly be called a transfiguration.[190]

To express this in the language of our category of alienation, perhaps his experience of worldly alienation will cause Sipho to long for reconciliation with God, to put his treasures in heaven where moth and rust do not corrupt (Matt. 16.19–21).

However, where the sufferings of this present age mean the sort of conditions for Sipho that I have described, we may question whether he *should* redirect his desires. These conditions deny his potential and that of all his community. They must therefore be contrary to the will of any loving God. The Matthaean exhortation to put our treasures in heaven presumably means not looking to worldly riches or status, or to human approval, for ultimate fulfilment in life; it is a warning against middle-class complacency. It does not mean accepting degradation fatalistically in the hope of better luck in the world to come.

III

Salvation as Liberation

1

Latin American Liberation Theology

We have looked at a number of ways of understanding what we mean by saying that Jesus saves us. None of them seem to bear the weight of relevance to Sipho's situation which we should wish a really usable christology to bear. We should take serious account, then, of a theological approach which sets out to be directly relevant to people in a very similar situation to Sipho. Liberation theology, the theology of many Latin American Christians since the Medellín conference of 1968, takes a situation of alienation and oppression as its starting point. Instead of doing what I have done, starting with certain biblical or traditional pre-conceptions and applying them, however critically, to the experience of our own times, liberation theology starts with the situation of the poor, oppressed and marginalized. It assumes a pre-commitment not to any theological or ontological models (that is, not to right belief or orthodoxy), but to the struggle to liberate the oppressed, that is, of right practice or orthopraxy. Indeed, it assumes that the theologian is himself or herself one of the oppressed. Liberation theologians often claim to have no precommitment to theological models. I shall refer to criticisms later that in fact liberation theology does tacitly assume a great deal of Christian dogma as part of its foundation, as well as assuming the truth of post-Enlightenment humanistic ethics, and of Marxian socio-analysis. Thus liberation theology lays itself open to the sort of attack which Polanyi or McGrath make on liberal theology generally: it does indeed operate with a number of important presuppositions, none of which are adequately examined or defended.

This precommitment to the struggle arises out of what is the factual situation of the Latin American people, who are poor and who are Christian, and who therefore need to see how their given situation correlates with their belief. However, liberation theologians turn the need to escape from poverty in Latin America into a theological 'ought'. Theology 'ought' to start from this situation, because the liberation of the poor is epistemologically central. Theology is essentially about the liberation of the poor. The poor are the people who will most easily understand what the gospel is about. Thus, there is a 'preferential option' for the poor. The concept of the preferential option for the poor does not mean that God loves the poor exclusively, or that every poor person is always right and virtuous, or that the rich cannot be saved or be Christian. All that it means is that it is God's intention to liberate the poor; that is what the gospel is essentially about and therefore the poor have a kind of interpretational advantage or privilege.[1]

This does not mean that in the eyes of liberation theology liberation is only a matter of social change. Gutierrez, for example, says that there are three levels to liberation. First, it is a matter of enabling the poor to see how their situation falls short of God's intentions for human life. Theology must therefore 'conscientize' them, or make them 'critically conscious' to use Freire's phrase.[2] Then, the poor need to be shown that because God is on their side, their situation can be changed, thus giving them hope and determination. But, says Gutierrez, once the poor have regained some human dignity and responsibility for their own lives, liberation or salvation also means to be forgiven and set free from individual sins.[3] The traditional Anselmian concept of salvation is thus not rejected, but put further down in the list of priorities.

There are, of course, a number of different versions of liberation theology, some Catholic, some Protestant, some more radical than others. There is by now a fairly considerable body of writing from the school as a whole, so that in my comments there will inevitably be some overgeneralization. However, what all liberation theology has in common is the belief that in starting from the situation of the poor, we need to analyse the reasons for poverty. The theological enterprise thus starts with social analysis, indeed with Marxian social analysis, since this is held to be the best tool for the job.

This is the issue which liberation theologians believe that Christian theology in Latin America must address. Latin America has long been a Christian continent. Liberation theologians feel that the situation of the poor in their continent gives to Christianity a quite different agenda to that of the North-Western world. Where in the North-West theologians may need to try to convince post-Enlightenment sceptics that religious concepts are still viable, Latin American theologians need to show how Christian faith can alleviate the plight of the poor: not for the sake of religion or keeping up church numbers, but for the sake of the poor.

All of these assumptions may be questioned. If we are to take orthopraxis rather than orthodoxy as our interpretative norm – a concept I shall describe more fully in due course – then we may well ask why an option for the poor is to be chosen. If we start with a particular moral attitude and then interpret the Bible, Christian tradition, and our own experience in the light of that attitude, is the way not equally open for a neo-Hitler to start with a different moral attitude with the same legitimacy? In fact liberation theology, as Bonino for example concedes, does not start with such an arbitrary moral choice as all that, and its initial concern for the poor and its indignation on behalf of the poor is a product in part of biblical and Christian teaching. But then we may well ask whether liberation theologians are correct in saying that their starting point is orthopraxis rather than orthodoxy. We may also question – as indeed one or two liberation theologians do[4] – whether a class-based Marxian analysis of history is the only, or even the best, tool for social analysis available to us.

Liberation theologians go beyond Medellín, where the Catholic bishops, following the Second Vatican Council, insisted that theories of salvation in Christ had to take into account the situation of the poor. The Medellín emphasis, although providing a necessary reminder, did not represent anything very new in theology. For some time theologians such as Maritain[5] had been pushing the Catholic church in that direction. The encyclicals of Pope John XXIII[6] and the pronouncements from Vatican II[7] made it clear that rich nations have a responsibility, in Christian ethics, towards poorer, less developed ones. Medellín reflected this.

For many in Latin America, however, the policies of develop-ment, of *desarrolismo*, a 'controlled upward spiral promised by advanced industrial capitalism'[8] as envisaged in the Alliance for Progress, an alliance between the United States and Latin Ameri-can countries, were seen not to be working. Development aid from North America, far from helping the poor, seemed to have enslaved the Afro-Americans, the indigenous Indians, the peasants and slum-dwellers into a neo-colonialist situation in which the profits from their labour went away to North America.

Maritain's theology, and the well-meaning concern of theologians like him, was seen to be merely endorsing this exploitation. Liberation theologians believe that an interpretation of the situation of the poor along Marxian lines best explains that situation. The aim of liberation is not to persuade the rich charitably to share some of the wealth and power, or to be kind to the poor, since this would still leave the initiative and the locus of control, however benevolent, in the hands of the rich. Liberation means first of all helping the poor to *understand* why they are poor – that it is not their fault or because of their inadequacies but because the way in which society is structured inevitably means they are at the mercy of the rich. Secondly, liberation means helping the poor to *change* those structures.

There can be no question, then, at this stage of the struggle, of trying to work harmoniously with the rich. Instead of having a vision of society as one, and a reforming aim of uniting society in a more equitable and harmonious way, as Maritain might have argued, liberation theology, following the Marxian interpretation of the economic process as being a conflict between classes, sees society as divided in two: the peasants/workers and the *bourgeoisie*; the poor nations of the Third World and the rich nations of the First. Liberation helps the oppressed to see the 'conflictual aspect of the economic, social and political process which puts them at odds with the wealthy nations and oppressive classes'.[9] The aim of reform is to enable the poor to gain control over their labour and the fruits of their labour. Then, the dialectic having been overcome, the aim of liberation may turn towards harmony and the rebuilding of one society.

Previous politically reformist theology had stressed that individual Christians, especially rich ones, needed to share more willingly. It directed its efforts at changing the attitudes of individuals, especially those individuals at the top of the social hierarchy. Even the Medellín Conference had echoes of this, suggesting a balance between encouraging the poor to believe in their own rights, and approaching 'those persons at a decision making level whose actions affect change in basic structures'.[10] Thus Medellín said:

> The uniqueness of the Christian message does not so much consist in the affirmation of the necessity for structural change, as it does in the insistence on the conversion of man which will bring about this change.[11]

Liberation theology clearly takes a quite different line. The situation of the poor is seen to be the result of particular social structures and the distribution of power. The analysis of the situation of the poor is taken to be a sociological, not a theological, task. Christians do not see the situation of the poor differently from those without Christian faith, nor do they perceive political liberation differently. The distinctively Christian and theological contribution is to make the connection between the sociologically determined analysis of the process of liberation from the historical situation of the poor and the nature of God and of the saving work of Jesus. In so doing, it provides a symbolic, mythological, ideological way of speaking of liberation.[12] There is no Christian third way, no specifically Christian way of doing politics. There is no middle ground between rich and poor which Christians can occupy.

We shall have to ask in due course whether liberation theology is correct or justified in assuming that Marxian social analysis is the only way or even the best way to interpret history. It is certainly true that many, though by no means all, commentators think that it does yield the most convincing interpretation. It is also true that Christianity has been reshaped through the centuries in conformity with the prevailing philosophical views of the time. Early Christianity interpreted itself in neo-Platonic terms, mediaeval Christianity in terms of Aristotle. Marx is closer to Christian thought than either Plato or Aristotle. There can be no *a priori* objection to interpreting Christianity in Marxian terms.

Sobrino, as I have mentioned earlier, sees liberation theology as continuing the process begun by post-Enlightenment Christianity in the West. Where Western theologians are still trying to show how Jesus is saviour to a world post Hume and post Kant, liberation theologians try to show how Jesus is saviour in a world post Marx. In fact, liberation theology may be continuing in the tradition of the Enlightenment more than they themselves realize. Since the Enlightenment in the West there has been a suspicion towards authority figures, towards kings and popes and bishops. Ideas, it is believed, must commend themselves on the grounds of reason, not on the grounds of the authority who gives them to us. For liberation theologians, too, there is a suspicion, not of individuals but of institutions: of a church and a tradition and a government. Ideas, they believe, must commend themselves on the basis of whether or not they work, whether they change the situation of the poor. Marx demanded that philosophy should not just explain things, but change things. Liberation theologians demand the same of theology, and judge the truth of a theological doctrine on the basis of whether or not it does contribute towards change. Liberation theologians declare themselves impatient with Western theological concerns for explaining to a sceptical Western world how Christianity can still be believable, and want to have a theological programme concerned with praxis, not philosophy.

> The question, then, is no longer how we are to speak about God in a world come of age, it is rather how to proclaim him Father in a world that is not human, and what the implications might be of telling non-humans that they are the children of God.[13]

Yet all this is really something like an extension of the Enlightenment.

Indeed, the demand that theology be judged on the grounds of its effectiveness is much the same as the demand of the American pragmatists like William James. The insistence of liberation theologians on evaluating the truth of theology in terms of its results distinguishes this theology from a theology concerned with metaphysical or theoretical truth. It is a theology, they say, of *praxis*. Where earlier Catholic political theologians attempted to prescribe ethics on the basis of doctrine, i.e. to let theology determine political and social behaviour, liberation theology sets out to prescribe doctrine on the basis of whether it fits in with a predetermined moral attitude, to let right behaviour determine theology. Similarly, where earlier Protestant theologians were, in the view of liberation theologians, largely concerned with private and individual ethics, liberation theology is concerned with public, corporate action. Yet Fierro is correct when he makes the point that although liberation theology is concerned with praxis, its own contribution to praxis is a theological, not an ethical, one. The ethics are already determined by the situation and by the prevailing world-view within the revolutionary movement. Liberation theology provides a theology and a biblical exegesis consistent with these ethics. It reconnects a contemporary pragmatic ethic with a universal divinely ordained one.

Although this theology will still seek to explain the nature and work of Jesus, the intention is not explanation for the sake of apologetics, but explanation as a means of making changes in the situation. Its christology will not be an attempt to explain how Jesus can be rationally understood as God and man – liberation theologians take this for granted and do not debate the matter. Their christology is an attempt to show how Jesus changes things, in order that we may work with him.

Because they so often insist that an attitude of commitment to struggle for liberation is the interpretative key for understanding the Bible and traditional theological concepts, including christology, it might seem as if these theologians are saying that christology is just another name for an already chosen line of action, that the name of Jesus is being used simply to legitimize what is already being done. Indeed this criticism is often made, and we shall have to discuss it further below. Liberation theologians would, however, deny that they are merely legitimizing an already chosen attitude or course of action:

> Our purpose is not to elaborate an ideology to justify positions already taken . . . it is to let ourselves be judged by the Word of the Lord.[14]

While it is true that most liberation theologians do not think that there is such a thing as a specifically Christian revolution,[15] they do think that Christianity and the Christian understanding of the work of Jesus has a special and unique contribution to make to the understanding of revolution. For Gutierrez, for example, a liberation theology which is a critical reflection on theology's understanding of itself, is also a critical reflection on biblical grounds about society and about the process of revolution[16] and a means of judging the process.

Segundo in particular has the concept of a hermeneutic circle; that is, poor Christians begin from a feeling of dissatisfaction with the *status quo*, with their experience of poverty and oppression. This creates in them a suspicion about the present. In this state of consciousness they look at the Word of God in the Bible and at received traditional theological concepts to gain some better understanding of their situation and of how to be liberated from it. But looking at the Bible and tradition from this perspective they become dissatisfied with their previous interpretation of these sources, suspicious of the received interpretation of the texts.

> There is no such thing as a Christian theology or a Christian interpretation of the gospel message in the absence of a prior political commitment. Only the latter makes the former possible at all.[17]

This does not mean that in Segundo's view the Bible has no light of its own to shed upon the situation. We look to the Bible for guidance as to how to find liberation from our situation. The Bible will not really enable us to analyse the reasons for our situation or identify the factors which compose it. For that we must use the tools of social analysis. The Bible will create a right attitude towards liberation, towards ourselves and the oppressed people generally. It will give encouragement and the assurance that God intends liberation for his people. It fills its readers with commitment and hope.

We shall see later that Segundo has his own quite sophisticated and complicated concept of how the historical Jesus leads us on towards liberation. He does not naively assume that Jesus was himself a political revolutionary, or even that he was particularly aware of political issues. But Segundo does most definitely believe that Jesus is the source, the special and unique source, of liberating consciousness.

The questions we ask of the Bible and of the received traditional Christian faith are to do not with ontology but with liberation: how can we be saved? In this sense the experience of oppression provides the setting for interpretation and for theology, and a new way of doing theology. It provides the set of questions to be asked.

Liberation theology has maintained that active commitment to liberation comes first, and theology develops from it.[18]

The fact that poverty provides us with 'privileged theological data', that is, provides us with the way to understand God's word, does not sanctify poverty or make it acceptable to liberation theologians. There may be virtue in the old monkish concept of spiritual poverty or non-attachment to material possessions, but that is not the kind of poverty to which this theology refers. Poverty is 'a scandalous condition inimical to human dignity and therefore contrary to the will of God'.[19] We are not talking about self-denial here but about the situation of those to whom society denies the power to earn an adequate living. God is to be understood as one who reveals himself in the process of liberating the poor. In fact, until the poor are liberated from their abjectness, God remains so inconceivable that theology must be silent about him. Under these conditions the Christian message is simply incredible. We need to be silent about God, to immerse ourselves in the praxis of revolution. Authentic theology can only take place in a society where the process of liberation has at least begun. In that process of liberation, Christian faith can then make a unique contribution towards overcoming the alienation and self-hatred of the poor. Christians should therefore work for liberation without at this stage worrying about what will happen to the rest of the traditional corpus of theology.[20]

There is some ambiguity in liberation theology on the point of how liberation is attained, an ambiguity that perhaps reflects a similar ambiguity in Marx's thoughts. For Marx, the socialist revolution and the coming of utopia were on the one hand the inevitable product of the course of history, as capitalism crashes to its inevitable end, wealth accumulating in the hands of fewer and fewer people so that the workers no longer have the income to buy what the wealthy are selling. On the other hand, it is the duty of every worker and conscientized member of the *bourgeousie* to work for the revolution. Thus the revolution is both the inevitable product of history and the product of people who voluntarily make their own history.

For liberation theologians, liberation is both the inevitable product of God's actions or intentions in history and the product of faithful Christian men and women who work for liberation. This liberation happens in history, in the political, historical, social events of human life in this world. While liberation theologians believe in heaven, their eschatological expectations are essentially for this world and not the next. The kingdom of God means the liberation of the poor. This theology strongly rejects any division between salvation history and secular history. It looks back to the Old Testament, where the people of Israel saw God as having created the world, as having given them their tribal identity, as freeing them from slavery in Egypt and establishing them in the Promised Land. Here is no division between sacred and secular. Their history is created by God.

> The Lordship of Yahweh is an efficacious word which becomes history and creates history by convoking and reflecting men and peoples in relation to God's purpose.[21]

For many liberation theologians, God's action in delivering the Israelites from Egypt was paradigmatic. It provides a way of understanding how God frees his people throughout history. Modern prophets still speak on God's behalf, calling or 'convoking' people together, condemning those who, on reflection about God's actions and God's purposes of liberation, are perceived to be leading God's people back to slavery or the loss of freedom.

This talk of God acting in history raises for us all the problems mentioned in an earlier chapter about such a concept, and recalls Maurice Wiles' Bampton lectures on the subject.[22] However, liberation theologians do not appear to mean that God directly intervenes in human history, though there seem to be different views about this. Generally, however, the view would be that God does not make our history for us. Rather, he enables us to make our own history. The Exodus is taken as a paradigm of God's actions in history. The God of the Exodus did not do the job of freeing the Israelites himself. 'God expressed himself through Moses, and Moses had to assume that historical and personal vocation to freedom.'[23]

God's intervention consisted of calling on Moses with a demand for justice. Moses himself had to make the history, as do the people of Israel in their turn, once inspired by Moses. God revealed his love for them; he told them that they deserved better things, that they were entitled to a fairer dispensation than their lives of slavery and drudgery. God gave them a sense of their own dignity and the promise of a new life which they could make for themselves; he thus both stirred up their dissatisfaction and gave them confidence about taking responsibility. But the essence of the covenant relationship which God made with them is that humans have a responsibility for making their own history and achieving their own freedom.[24] Instead of being the 'objects' of history, being acted upon by others, the Israelites became the 'subjects', the makers of history. So in our own time the poor, with their own situation in mind, must reread or reinterpret the biblical message in order to find the inspiration and power to remake their own history. Properly understood, the Bible gives us the message of God's gift to us of hope, a gift that renews our ability to fight for and achieve liberation. 'It is to have trust in a God who summons things that do not exist into existence, and makes the barren fruitful.'[25]

With the coming of Christianity and the conversion of the Gentiles, say liberation theologians, Christians within a few generations were tempted to see their secular history as irrelevant to God's purposes. In the West, theology opted for a kind of dualism which continued to trace God's actions in the spiritual, personal lives of Christians but saw the events of their secular history as being of little interest to God or to theology.[26] But this dualism is contrary to scripture and to our own experience of God working in the history of our own lives. All human history is salvation history, it is the arena of God's liberating action. God has been at work in the history of humankind from the moment of creation onwards, leading his people on to fulfilment. The fruition of his promises will be experienced in this life in what liberation theologians sometimes call Utopia. Utopia is,

a place of encounter between political liberation and the communion of all men with God. This communion implies liberation
from sin, the ultimate root of all injustice, all exploitation, all
dissidence among men.[27]

Utopia, while not identical with the kingdom of God which is a
somewhat wider concept, is nevertheless closely related to it.
Liberation is more than political liberation. The kingdom of God is
more than a better social dispensation, more than Utopia. But
political and social issues are a very important part of what is meant
by liberation and salvation. Salvation is not a matter of numbers, of
how many people have been converted, but is about the value or the
quality of human existence and the intensity of God's presence
among us. Thus, a vision of a political Utopia is part of what is
meant by the quality of human existence. It is the vision of Utopia
that causes us to be restless and dissatisfied with the *status quo*.
Jesus' promises concerning the arrival of God's kingdom are very
much concerned with the arrival of liberation in a practical sense.
'Christ does not spiritualize the eschatological promises; he gives
them meaning and fulfilment today.'[28]

But here is a problem. Since liberation theology holds that God
has been involved in liberating us in history ever since the creation,
through the history of Israel, and through all human history, how
then can there be a place for christology? God was already doing the
work of liberation before Jesus, especially in the Exodus, and is
always liberating oppressed humans in all history. What need is
there then to emphasize the role of Jesus, limited as the human
Jesus is to his own time and place?

There are a number of different ways in which liberation
theologians perceive Jesus, but a general emphasis is that Jesus is
the *objective* expression, the incarnation in human nature, of what
God does in all history and of God's option for the poor. There is
little discussion about whether and how Jesus is both God and
human, or of the relationship between the Son and the Father.
Orthodox beliefs about Jesus and about the Trinity are taken for
granted, and there is little parallel to Moltmann's tying of trinitarian
belief into their expounding of how Jesus saves. There is an
emphasis, rather, on Jesus sharing in our poverty, and speaking to
us from his own life of poverty about God's solidarity with the poor.

[Jesus] encourages us in our struggles, comforting us in our
weakness and nourishing our hope that it is worthwhile to
struggle for the creation of a new heaven and a new earth. The

liberator is the expression of our anxiety, it is the sign of our hope.[29]

In our attempts to interpret Jesus, as with all theological interpretation, we come to the gospel records out of our own experience, and with the hermeneutical questions which arise from that experience. Thus Sobrino says that we cannot begin with traditional christology and then ask, how is this relevant to our situation? This would make our christology 'historically alienating and open to manipulation, completely lacking in human relevance'.[30] We begin with our own situation and then ask in the light of this what the New Testament texts have to say to us about Jesus. However, although we shall have to interpret the New Testament texts, it must be clear that since God saves in ordinary history, we are not free to invent a mythical, non-historical, existentially interpreted Jesus with no historical grounding. It is the Jesus in history who saves. Sobrino is therefore very insistent that what we claim of Jesus should be consistent with the New Testament records. He, and even more Gutierrez, believes that on the basis of the New Testament we can legitimately see Jesus as a prophet denouncing the religious and political *status quo*, a preacher of the kingdom of God, who in all that he did, whether teaching, healing, or whatever, proclaimed that humans were loved by God and were called by God into a new dignity. His ministry was aimed at the poor, the despised and the marginalized, not only among Jews but all people. In this way Jesus is the incarnation of God's love for these people. In his teaching, Jesus stressed that our access to God was not primarily through cultic practices but through service to the poor. Inevitably, much stress is placed on Matthew 25.31–46. Even in his appeals for conversion, therefore, Jesus was really calling for a commitment to social action and to solidarity with the poor.

Liberation theologians see Jesus as having a concern for politics, including the politics of living under Roman dominance. Like Moltmann, they see Jesus as having been sympathetic to the Zealots, although Jesus did not identify with the Zealots' narrow nationalism. Like Moltmann, they see Jesus as being crucified because his concern for the marginalized brought him into conflict both with the Jewish and the Roman leaders. He challenged the legitimacy of both authorities, and thus encouraged revolutionary ideas. His death is interpreted as a political killing. Indeed much of Moltmann's reconstruction of the life of Jesus is identical with that which we find in liberation theology.

However, although liberation theologians believe in the resurrection, they do not appear to make the same use of the idea of
resurrection as Moltmann. Saul Trinidad suggests that a christology
which is relevant to the poor will not make too much of the idea of
Jesus as the risen and glorious king, because this emphasis in the
past in Latin America has led to a christology that glorifies those
who are glorious and powerful, and encourages the poor to glorify
those who lord it over them. A relevant christology will also not
emphasize the 'suffering servant' kind of idea, Jesus as the humble
and obedient sufferer doing the Father's will in accepting his
humiliation in patience and in love for his persecutors – for such a
christology encourages the poor to accept their fate and be
everybody's footstool.[31]

Earlier liberation theology theories can be criticized for ignoring
the results of biblical scholarship. It must be clear that, both in their
use of the Exodus paradigm, and in their reconstruction of the
historical Jesus, some liberation theologians show little awareness
of biblical criticism, and naively accept the Bible stories of Moses
and Jesus as factual history. They also add to what can be said from
a purely historical point of view: the figure of Jesus which is often
painted in liberation theology, seeing him as a political revolutionary or a Zealot sympathizer, goes considerably beyond New
Testament history. I shall give more attention to this below, but
need to remark even at this stage that this is a potential weakness in
the liberation theology argument. We have to ask ourselves
whether this politically liberating Jesus bears very much relationship to what the historical Jesus actually said or did.

Segundo is aware of this naivete, which we find in Sobrino and
Gutierrez particularly. He says of Jesus:

> Jesus himself seems to focus his message on liberation at the level
> of interpersonal relationships, forgetting almost completely, if
> not actually ruling out, liberation *vis-à-vis* political expression.
> The same would seem to apply to Paul.[32]

He agrees that Jesus was probably unaware of 'the pervasive
influence of politics'[33] and was probably not a Zealot sympathizer.

> I personally think that their interpretations [i.e. theologians who
> hold these views] are a bit forced.[34]

As far as the Exodus paradigm is concerned, he says that the
liberation view of the Exodus is an historical reconstruction and was

not the usual understanding of the significance of the Exodus in subsequent Old Testament writings.[35]

I think Segundo is right. This might seem to cut the ground under the feet of liberation theology. However, there are more sophisticated arguments which are offered, both by Segundo and by Assman. First of all, the literal meaning of the text is not what is ultimately important for us. Assman makes use of Paul Ricoeur's ideas on distantiation from the text and on 'surplus of meaning'; a text needs to be interpreted not only in terms of what the author meant, or how the first readers understood it, perhaps not at all in these terms, although this is largely what biblical criticism sets out to discover and tell us. A text needs to be interpreted, largely independent of its original meaning, in terms of what it means now, in our situation, seen through the eyes of our mind-set and our ideology. Although biblical critics may tell us that the author of Exodus, or the evangelists, did not have in mind overtly political interpretations of the events which they describe, that does not mean we should not interpret them in this way, even if this was not their original significance. In fact because ideology is inevitable we shall inevitably interpret them in the light of our ideology, whether we consciously intend to do so or not.

Ricoeur is helpful to liberation theologians, since he takes a middle line between limiting the meaning of a text to what the original authors intended and allowing the text to mean anything we want it to mean. He chooses neither the 'intentional fallacy' which says we are bound by the intention of the author, rather as biblical critics have tended to say, nor the 'fallacy of text as authorless entity' like Derrida.[36] The original event, the writing of the text, does have a real but limited autonomy, but is at a distance from us from which we need to rescue it by appropriating it to our own circumstances. Thus, for Ricoeur, we need a dialectic between distantiation and appropriation.[37]

He does not reject the work of the earlier biblical critics who sought to recover the 'Sitz-im-Leben', the life-situation of the pericope, the various Bible passages, etc. We are not free to interpret the text as we please. Not all interpretations are of equal validity.[38] But the intentions of those original authors are often lost to us, or are irrelevant to our circumstances, or even harmful.[39] The original meaning may therefore not be the meaning we ourselves derive from it.

This is partly because the scriptures use human language, which is couched in symbolic words and metaphors. Metaphors derive their meaning from the context of the listener. Since our circumstances are not the same as those of the original authors, our context is different. This discordance of the context extends the meaning of the metaphor,[40] and tells us something new not only about the meaning of the text but about the meaning of our own circumstances. Thus Ricoeur provides the framework for Segundo's idea of the hermeneutic circle.

The work of biblical criticism, in this view, should be regarded with some suspicion, since it seeks to objectify biblical truth and thus to imprison us in a dead past. This does not mean that Segundo is abandoning the Jesus of history altogether any more than Ricoeur abandoned the original meaning of the text. He suggests that even if biblical criticism does show us that neither Jesus nor Paul was in fact as aware of socio-political issues nor as aligned with radical political attitudes as some theologians have wished to maintain, what we do learn from Jesus is still the key to liberating consciousness. Jesus taught us the concept of what Segundo (following Freire) calls 'deutero-learning',[41] or 'learning to learn'.[42] That is, Jesus said he would go away so that the Holy Spirit could guide us into all truth. Segundo says that on the one hand there is our conception of God passed on to us from scripture and tradition; and on the other hand are all the real-life issues and problems which each generation must face in its own history, and the conception of God which we formulate to cope with these problems. The bridge between these two theses is our 'ideology'. Since our issues and problems change, so too ideologies need to be constantly broken down and modified. In saying that he was going away and sending the Spirit, Jesus was teaching us that his words would have to be recast, reset, in successive changes of circumstances. We would need to learn anew what his word meant in the light of those changes – the deutero-learning process. Thus it may be true that the historical Jesus was not very concerned with politics, but that does not mean that his Word has nothing to do with politics. Jesus taught us, for example, to turn the other cheek when we are struck; in saying this he was abandoning what the Old Testament sometimes taught about slaying one's enemies. Jesus himself was therefore modifying his ideological interpretative key, in the light of his experienced circumstances. It might well be that in changed circumstances again, we in our time would decide to go back to the Old Testament teaching instead.[43]

This view of the matter gives liberation theology greater freedom to move, in principle, through the scriptures and to work with the faith.[44]

It is not, therefore, the content of Jesus' teaching that ultimately matters, although we need to take that, and scriptural teaching in general, into serious account; we need to live in a kind of dialogue between scripture and our circumstances (the hermeneutic circle). But what is of greater importance is the process of the dialogue, the process of renewed interpretation, of deutero-learning.

> The Spirit of Christ, that is, the dynamic, intrinsic result of the revelatory process, ensures a process that will lead to the full and complete truth.[45]

This raises some questions for us about how important the place of Jesus really is in Segundo's soteriology, to which we shall give attention a little later. It does mean that Segundo goes much further than, for example, Sobrino, in reinterpreting the significance for us of the historical Jesus.

It should not be assumed from the above that Segundo, or liberation theology in general, is in favour of violent armed revolution. They certainly envisage a conflict situation in which the poor struggle and fight to gain power over their own lives and the fruits of their labour, but the struggle may well be one of trade-union action, or civil disobedience, or passive resistance. In fact liberation theology on the whole does not discuss the question of justifying armed revolution; possibly since as most are Roman Catholics they assume that the Catholic criteria for a just war can be applied to a just revolution. The contribution that they do make to this issue is to point out that 'violence' is not necessarily limited to guerrillas or to soldiers. Where the poor are forced unjustly to live where they do not wish to live, or are denied access to education which would uplift them, a kind of educational or structuralized violence is being done to them, so that the situation already encompasses violence, and any violent revolution would only be a response to this.[46] The issue is not, however, discussed with the same intensity as in South African black theology.

Perhaps part of the reason why liberation theologians do not discuss the legitimacy of violence is that the answer differs from one set of circumstances to another; it is a kind of local issue for which there are no global directives. In fact, liberation theology can be criticized for its general lack of specific socio-political directives. Its answer would be that it is only at a local level that such specific discussions can be made, and then only by those living in the situation. Liberation theology, then, at least in theory, is essentially done by local Christian people meeting in 'base-community' groups to work out together the meaning of the gospel for them in the light of their situation, and to consider their situation and what action is called for of them in the light of the gospel.

The professional liberation theologians, the authors of the books, see themselves as spokespersons for these groups, and as merely putting into a logical whole the theological initiatives taken by the base communities. That is, at least, the theory. Critics have alleged that most of the authors are themselves the products of European seminaries and universities; that they are not as independent of the sort of theology taught in Europe, especially in Belgium, as they think they are, and that the degree to which they are spokespersons for the indigenous poor is limited. Edward Norman goes even further, and accuses them of importing European post-Enlightenment political theories, transient, arbitrary and merely fashionable, into Latin America and imposing these essentially European views on to a sort of innocent *tabula rasa*, a virgin slate, of Third-World peasantry![47] I think this is overstating the case, though there are elements of truth in this view. Even the much more sympathetic McCann declares that liberation theology has become 'virtually indistinguishable in nature and content from that of some European progressives.'[48]

What is true is that not all Latin American Christians, not even all, or most, poor Christians in Latin America, have actually been caught up into the base communities of espoused liberation theology. Partly this is because the expected liberation did not come quickly, partly because repressive regimes quickly stifled resistance, and partly because of conservative church reactions. McCann points out that this raises the problem of distinguishing between the base communities and the church. Are the base communities the true church, a faithful remnant, or are they an elite within the church, a leaven in the lump? In the former case the difficult implication is that those who are not sufficiently conscientized are dischurched. In the latter case liberation theologians cannot be acting as spokespersons for the church, as Gutierrez claimed, or even the poor in the church, but for an intellectual elite within the church.

Segundo is clear on this point. Whether consciously or not, he follows Marcuse, the Frankfurt school and Che Guevara. Marcuse was somewhat critical and scornful about the world-wide proletariat for having sold out to a capitalist establishment by co-operation with it.[49] The proletariat was, in his eyes, unable to see how capitalism manipulated them. Marcuse was concerned about the workers and Guevara in his turn with the peasantry in a non-industrialized Latin America. Guevara believed that it would take too long to conscientize the peasants. 'It is not necessary to wait until all conditions for making revolution exist'.[50] They both believed, therefore, that an elite group of conscientized people – for Marcuse a group of young middle-class intelligentsia – who understood the situation properly, and could initiate the struggle, would be necessary. This elite group would have to seize power in order to establish a true democracy.[51] In so doing they would, of course, be acting undemocratically, but would open the way to re-educating the masses so that eventually a true democracy could result.

There are echoes of this in Segundo, who sees the base communities' role as being the creation of an elite who will, once conscientized, be able to 'channel the spontaneity of the masses into the struggle for liberation'.[52] Segundo accepts that political conscientization is more difficult than the educational conscientization with which Freire was involved and from whom the vocabulary is borrowed, because the skills involved are more difficult. Therefore, the masses will have to be helped to liberation by an elite which alone possesses these skills. He sees this as consistent with the New Testament ambiguity about the whole world being saved in Jesus and yet only a few being saved.

> On the one hand it [the New Testament church] was proclaiming the unrestricted victory of Christ's grace . . . On the other hand it spoke about the rejection of grace by and the consequent damnation of the vast multitude of those who refused to join the ranks of Christ's disciples.[53]

Segundo is not suggesting that the non-elite poor are excluded from liberation or salvation. In fact, he says, the achievement of liberation demands both the awareness/intelligence of the elite and the sheer weight of numbers of the masses once they have been led into action by the elite. He recognizes that this could mean that the elite itself becomes a new oppressor of the poor, extending its necessary but limited period of power into a permanent dictatorship – which is why the elite, which is made up of precisely those involved in the hermeneutic circle, *needs* the Bible and church tradition as one pole in that dialectic. 'We have reason to believe that we are confronted here with a hermeneutic circle that is rich in promise.'[54]

2

A Critique

I said at the start of this section that since liberation theology arose out of a situation very similar to that of Sipho, it might provide a way of understanding salvation that would fit his circumstances. We need to consider whether it fulfils its promise. A number of criticisms can be made of liberation theology. I have mentioned already that the opening stance of liberation theology, i.e. that it starts from praxis, from a commitment to the liberation of the poor, raises questions as to where the norms for this commitment come from.[55] Karl Barth, although deeply committed to social justice, would have said that our knowledge of this duty to love the weak and oppressed is laid upon us by revelation, in which case scripture, or church teaching, or personal experience of God is the starting point and our praxis the fruits of that prior commitment.

This is not a criticism I would wish to press, since I have already said that a religion which is not concerned with practical issues in the here-and-now is irrelevant to those who are so poor that other issues cannot be considered by them. I also agree that while there is so much poverty and injustice in my own part of the world, South African theology must take the oppressed as the 'interlocutor' of theology. Liberation theologians say that their theology is a wholly new endeavour, since it deals with the questions raised by the poor, not by bourgeois rational critics. But we shall see that one of the problems with liberation theology is that the poor do not necessarily ask the questions liberation theologians think they should. I believe that theology must still answer to rational criticism. Nevertheless, a theology should be evaluated not only on the grounds of reason but from a consideration of the plight of the oppressed.

I assume, then, that this plight is indeed a major criterion by which a christological theology should be judged. This does, however, leave one open to the charge that one is choosing one's basic stance, i.e. commitment to the poor, on the basis of one's own conscience or advantage. Liberation theologians choose to take belief in God's option for the poor as their starting point, either because they are poor or because they are speaking on behalf of the poor. Having chosen this as their hermeneutical basis they then, not surprisingly, find that scripture can be interpreted in such a way as to agree with them. Well-established middle-class Christians have at other times started with an assumption of God's option for the middle class and God's approval of the powers that be, and interpreted scripture, possibly with equal validity, to support their own cause. Can individuals then choose whatever starting point they think is most advantageous to them? Although advocating 'suspicion' about the motives for ideology and theology, liberation theology is not always sufficiently suspicious of its own motives. Edward Norman implies that the enthusiasm for liberation theology in some Catholic and World Council of Churches circles arises not only out of concern for the poor but because the Catholic church in Latin America was losing its power and monopoly, and saw the espousal of revolutionary causes as a way to stay on the winning side.[56] Norman's book was written before Cardinal Ratzinger and Pope John-Paul II had made it clear that the Catholic church is not unanimously enthusiastic about liberation theology, though I suspect that to some small degree Norman is right.

Liberation theologians would justifiably respond, however, that their adoption of the cause of the poor is not an arbitrary stance taken regardless of scriptural norms. The point of the hermeneutic circle is that the opening stance of commitment to the poor is then held up to examination in the light of scripture, and that it turns out to be not only consistent with scripture, but more consistent with scripture than, for example, a stance endorsing a capitalist or developmental *status quo*. It is true that the poor will perceive this more easily than the rich, but that is no different from saying that sinners who know they need forgiveness responded more easily to Jesus' call to repentance than the righteous who were less aware of their frailty. If it could be shown that their interpretation of scripture was throroughly wrong or entirely arbitrary, then the basis of liberation theology would fall away.

However, the issue is not quite as clear cut as liberation theologians sometimes suggest. We find basically three approaches in liberation theology. Very occasionally we find a liberation theologian like Couch saying that Christians should start with the Bible and then turn to the social situation; and that in the Bible we shall find that God urges upon us a preferential option for the poor.[57] Much more commonly, we find theologians like Sobrino or Gutierrez who say that while they start with a commitment to the poor and then turn to the Bible and tradition, they find that the Bible itself confirms the commitment to the poor, for example in the Exodus paradigm or in the life and teaching of Jesus. In either case, provided they are correct in their view of what the Bible teaches, there is not much problem for theology. More recently, however, some liberation theologians like Croatto and Segundo concede that the Exodus and the life of Jesus do not fit quite so neatly into a liberation pattern. Then the problem becomes quite acute.

Gutierrez in particular has been accused, with justification, of distorting the emphasis of scripture, of seeing in the exodus story or in the life of Jesus political meanings that are not there. The exodus is sometimes seen in liberation theology as a direct intervention by God in the history of the people of Israel, carrying the promise of his intervention in the near future for the poor of our own time. This interpretation raises all the problems which we have looked at previously surrounding the concept of God acting in history, and the question of why, if he is going to intervene, he has stayed his hand for so long.[58]

If God intervened actively and directly in the exodus, then why has he not done so again; and since he has not done so again, does that not prove the Jewish point that Jesus is not the Messiah who is to usher in the new age of human history when God will intervene to put things right? In any case the actual promise in the exodus was not that God would intervene to save the poor of the world, or the working classes, but that he would save the people of Israel, in order to create and maintain them as a people apart from others. If we use this text to show that God is on the side of the poor Latin Americans, or poor Africans, etc., that is a reinterpretation of the text. It is turning an historical account into a spiritual account.

In most liberation theologies the Jewish exodus is used as a paradigm of revolution, but contemporary Jews are nowhere to be found in the writings of the theologians. This continues an age-old Christian tradition of seeing the Jewish people as bequeathing the 'Old Testament' and Jesus and then disappearing from history.

Marc Ellis here echoes our question of why, if the exodus is understood as showing that God intervenes to save his people, God does not intervene in present need. He raises the obvious and grave problem which the Holocaust poses for this point of view, and suggests that to interpret the exodus in this way is to legitimize what is basically a demagogic drive for power:

> On the one hand the exodus – God who rescues his people from bondage – is contradicted by the holocaust event: on the other hand, the need for empowerment renders prophetic voices naive and even dangerous.[59]

Sometimes, in my view more helpfully, the exodus is seen to be the result of the action of Moses and the Israelites, acting by the grace of God, but making their own history.[60] This gets us out of the problem of God's direct intervention in history. The difficulty with this view is, however, that it is not what the Old Testament itself teaches, as Fierro points out.[61] It also assumes that the story of the escape from Egypt is an historical story, taking little account of the doubts of some biblical scholars on this point.

> Sometimes Gutierrez assumes the historical reliability of the Biblical narratives [of the exodus] without question; often he seems to know more about the episodes than any reliable historian would assert, and consistently he reshapes the details to fit the pre-established requirements of the theme of liberation.[62]

McCann makes much the same criticism of Sobrino's picture of Jesus. Despite Sobrino's self-imposed criterion of faithfulness to the history of Jesus, Sobrino, like Gutierrez, sees Jesus as acting from a class perspective, as somebody who lived in real poverty, as someone who was executed because ultimately he was identified by the Romans as a Zealot. Sobrino believes all this is historically true about Jesus. Of course Sobrino does not think that Jesus is the only leader to preach and act out socio-political liberation; but what makes the acts of Jesus theologically important is not that he is doing a unique thing, but that he is God. God in Jesus is thus incarnated in the liberation struggle.

But this takes no notice of the long debate about the logical propriety of claiming divinity for Jesus; it takes that belief for granted. It also assumes details about the historical Jesus which are, at best, very speculative. Even the Marxist writer Milan Machovec, who is strongly attracted to the person of Jesus while not professing Christian belief, does not think the picture of Jesus as poor, as politically conscious and active, as sympathetic in some degree to the Zealots, can be justified as being historically accurate.[63]

If liberation theologians wish to claim that in Moses or in Jesus God has acted in history to declare his option for the poor, it should be important that they base their argument on what can reasonably be claimed by historical scholarship.

> Critical history challenges theology to be intellectually honest in its use of Biblical narrative. If the events in the Bible cannot be verified, then theologians cannot present them as if they were historical fact.[64]

Thus McCann makes the valid point that

> The question is whether Gutierrez' salvation history is a religious myth about history or a dialectic analysis of real history.[65]

McCann thinks that it is the first of these options.

> What Gutierrez has actually done is to translate salvation history from one form of supernaturalism to another.[66]

apparently without even being aware that he is doing so.

When liberation theology speaks about events in the Bible like the Exodus or the historical life of Jesus, it needs to be much more clear whether its language is to be understood in a rhetorical, symbolic way or in a positivist historical sense.[67] This applies to the discussion not only of past history but of future expectations too. When liberation theology says that God will help the poor in the future, we need to know whether this means that God himself will directly intervene in history, or whether it means that if we believe in God's intentions and have hope, we shall then be enabled to turn our own history around.[68] Fierro believes that liberation theologians would do better if their language was interpreted in a symbolic, not a realist way. In his view, it does not really matter if we do not know very much of the actual history of the biblical events, or if Moses or Jesus were historically unaware of the socio-political dimension of their actions. There is a sufficiently strong historical basis for saying that their general attitude was in the direction of liberating action, even if historically they lacked the perspective to see this in explicitly socio-political terms. Thus he quotes Dorothee Sölle:

The point for us . . . is to come to know the basic direction of [Jesus'] behaviour and to turn his goals into a reality in a fresh way in our own world today.[69]

This is close to Segundo's approach. Segundo, as I suggested earlier, is far more aware and sophisticated in his use of scriptural material and does not think that Moses and Jesus can be seen as politically aware and active except in so far as they, and especially Jesus, provide the beginning of a new consciousness about authority and tradition. There is a historical core in the life and teaching of Jesus which is enough to provide a basis for a liberating consciousness through which we can interpret our own experience. Thus Jesus, or Moses, becomes the basis for a myth. They function as symbols – not totally divorced from their historical basis, but not tied to the limitations of that history or that context, triggering off the work of creative imagination.

Is this restatement more acceptable and more helpful? The main difficulty is that the interpretation now becomes no easy matter – or, perhaps, becomes all too easy and vulnerable to using the symbol in any way we please, with the consequent fading of specific meaning-fulness. The more detached the symbol is from history, the closer it comes to being an arbitrarily chosen attitude with no justification but that it suits me, my cause, or my class – though clearly this is what Segundo is anxious to guard against with the hermeneutic circle.

Segundo, realizing the need for a group which is both educated enough to make the reinterpretation and morally strong enough not to misuse the opportunity, is happy to accept the idea of an elite which is gifted with both intellectual and moral sensitivity and which will do the work of constant reinterpretation on behalf of the less able majority of the poor and the oppressed. If this move towards an elite within the mass is granted, however, it does change the nature of liberation theology. It is no longer the making of theology by the poor as they wrestle with finding help in the Christian tradition for themselves in their struggle, but the making of theology on behalf of the poor by an intellectual elite, those who are probably not themselves poor but bourgeois. Does this differ very strongly from the theology of which liberation theology is so critical, i.e. the theology of developmentalism, of people like Maritain and Nie-buhr, a theology which says the rich have a duty to share with the poor and to work for a just and harmonious society? Is the one more patronizing than the other? If a bourgeois elite is the key to enabling the poor to gain their place in the sun, is there any justification for assuming that the basic social reality is an antipathy between two social classes?

Liberation theology is surely justified in using a Marxian philosophy of sociological analysis. Most liberation theologians are at pains to say that they do not slavishly follow Marxism as a new gospel infallible in all its aspects, but that in their opinion and that of most theorists in our time the analysis of the economic and sociological divisions operating in society which Marxism offers is the most convincing and the most promising.

> Today Marxism is the broadest and most comprehensive of the theoretical approaches to human historical reality.[70]

Thus liberation theology and all political theology derive their *theology* from tradition and scripture but their *politics* from the best available political theory. Just as the church has used Platonism, Aristotelianism, and the philosophy of the Enlightenment at various stages in its history, so now, when Marxist political philosophy is dominant, theology uses this as a vehicle without losing its independent integrity.[71]

To those who claim that since Marxism is essentially atheist it is too incompatible with Christianity to be used as a vehicle in this way, we could counter that Marx's criticisms of Christianity were based on his own misunderstanding of Christianity; that there are many common features between Marxism and Christianity – a view of the present reality as fallen, as less than ideal, a hope for an eschatological utopia, etc.; and that Plato's philosophy was as uninterested in theology as Marxism and yet was used for centuries in the service of Christian theology.

I think we may grant all this, with some important provisos. If the Marxian model of socioanalysis is adopted as being currently the most convincing and the most useful, Christians need to be clear that this decision is, as Fierro says, a political and not a theological one. That is to say, Marxian socio-analysis should not be sacralized or turned into divine revelation. Especially the view that society basically comprises two hostile classes, rich and poor, powerful and powerless, is a human view. Christians who see society differently may be politically mistaken, may thus have a different and mistaken strategy for achieving justice, but are surely not to be condemned as un-Christian or as God's enemies because of that. Niebuhr in his earlier years was also convinced that Marxism 'has not been successfully challenged, and every event in contemporary history seems to multiply the proofs of its validity',[72] although he later modified his enthusiasm. But he warned that all political credos are partial and illusory.

> If the demonic enters life through the religious sanctification of partial and relative values, it can be exorcized from social life only by the worship of a God who transcends all partial and imperfect values.[73]

On the liberation theologians' own understanding of their task, their own theology must be transient and unfixed, not only because the situation which forms the context of the 'deutero-learning' is ever changing, but because when the poor are finally liberated, the option for the poor will no longer be available. If the Word of God is heard now in the voice of the poor, it will have to be heard in another way once liberation has come.[74]

This again carries the implication that the voice of God, or to use the other phrase, God's option, is not ultimately confined to the poor in any situation. But clearly it cannot be located in the words or claims of an oppressor. Perhaps therefore again the strict dichotomy into oppressed and oppressor is too simple and facile.

Another proviso to granting the right to liberation theology to use Marxism as its philosophic or analytic basis is that we must be convinced and shown that this *is* currently the best, most applicable, most useful model by which to interpret modern socio-political experience. This is a serious weakness in liberation theology. For the most part the correctness of this assumption is simply taken for granted. Liberation theologians do not actually demonstrate any detailed social analysis themselves of their situation, nor any reason for believing their claim that Marxism is the most useful method, leaving us to assume that someone else has made such an analysis of the causes for the Latin American situation – someone to whom theologians do not specifically refer.[75] It might very well be alleged that the liberation theologians, far from reaching conclusions for Latin American Christianity independently of the First World, have swallowed the line of the Frankfurt school but remained in ignorance of important opposing schools of thought such as that of Karl Popper and his 'methodological individualism'.[76]

> The fact is that political philosophy seems to be operating as if there were no line of reasoning but the Marxist one.[77]

It might further be alleged that liberation theologians are behind the times, that by and large Marxism is no longer seen as an attractive or helpful model in Latin America or Africa, that in China as well as the Soviet Union and its Eastern European satellites the strictly Marxist model is increasingly being abandoned, and that in fact countries like Japan or South Korea suggest that a developmental model rather than a revolutionary model of change is more effective. Since Latin America is not yet universally industrialized, the original Marxist model of the collapse of capitalism and the rise of the worker class needs considerable modification anyway. I am not suggesting that these allegations which I make so glibly are true: to back them up would require a great deal of detail, knowledge and skill. But such suggestions are made by some economists and political analysts, and liberation theologians show no more knowledge and ability to disprove such suggestions than I have offered to support them.

The model of a two-class conflict is central to liberation theology. It is a sort of kingpin around which many of the theological doctrines such as God's option for the poor, or interpreting the gospel from the perspective of the poor, revolve. If the kingpin is removed, the distinctive doctrines are significantly weakened. Yet the model is not proved or even argued, but taken for granted. At the same time there is at least some evidence in the world around us that a model of co-operation rather than conflict is one which has more potential for helping liberate the poor from the worst shackles of hunger, exploitation and lack of education, while admittedly no country is entirely free of these things.

The New Testament, it could be argued, assumes the co-operative rather than conflictual model, at least within the church. While the first generation of Christians were probably mostly poor, Jesus befriended the Pharisee Nicodemus, the rich Joseph of Arimathea, and Roman centurions. While it is clear that he is portrayed as cultivating unconventional disciples, the criterion of their unconventionality does not seem to have been poverty alone. Paul often assumes the goodwill of the Roman authorities. He assumes Philemon's goodwill towards his runaway slave Onesimus. Paul's description of the church as a society in which distinctions cease to matter[78] assumes a co-operative model as the ideal, even though in these passages he does not actually say that in Christ there is neither rich nor poor.

However, liberation theologians might argue that the church is not society. Of course Jesus and Paul wanted the body of disciples which would become the church to be harmonious, but the church and the world are not to be confused. In an ultimate sense this is true; the church is meant to be working towards the kingdom of God in the world, it is not itself the kingdom. But in a practical sense the boundaries between church and society are not easy to determine. In Latin America – or in South Africa – it is by and large the same people who belong to the church and to both the governing authorities and those governed. This does not mean that the state is the equivalent of 'Christendom', or that we should assume that the Constantinian ideal of Christendom is one to work for. State and church as entities may be regarded as quite distinct, with different natures and aims; but the individuals who make up both entities are the same individuals. If they can be expected to work in harmony in the church, they can be encouraged to work in harmony in the state, too.

I am suggesting that class conflict is not the only dynamic which operates in society. It is, of course, a reality; but it is not the whole reality. The expectations of inevitable conflict or of dependable harmony are both unlikely to be entirely true. Human society is not totally bad nor totally good, even in South Africa. It is not wholly conflictual, nor sufficiently co-operative. To lock our theological perspective and our hope for a better future entirely into a model of class conflict is an oversimplification, and one which closes off some possibly helpful avenues of endeavour.

On another tack, if liberation theology takes the truth of a Marxist class-analysis for granted, it also, paradoxically, takes the truth of much traditional theology for granted. Despite its much vaunted different starting point from traditional theology, it does not question many of the basic theological tenets. We have seen examples where conservative notions of the factual historicity of scriptural narratives are taken for granted with no apparent awareness of the fact that this historicity is now often questioned. So, too, the orthodox understanding of Jesus as God and human, and as second person of the Trinity, is assumed to be true. In fact, some important aspects of liberation theology – e.g. that because Jesus sided with the poor, this means that God sides with them too; that because Jesus suffered with the poor, God in Jesus suffers with them – would be very much weakened without a traditional christology. Since the human Jesus can hardly be said to have been victorious over the powers of oppression except as an individual who in the face of death remained true to his chosen lifestyle and stance on values, liberation theology could hardly be as confident in its hopes for liberation if it did not believe firmly in a resurrection, and in a very close, if not ontological, identity between Jesus and God.

The content of the core concepts of traditional theology are left unquestioned. To some extent this is justified: liberation theology has never claimed to be or wanted to be a new systematic theology. But in one important respect it is important that they give reasons for their assumptions about Jesus. Not only does liberation theology claim that salvation means primarily or at least initially socio-political liberation, but it also claims that Jesus is that saviour, that he was and is a political liberator.

It seems to me that there are no clear historical or empirical grounds for making that claim. It is not clear that Jesus' life changed the situation of the poor, or the slaves, or the oppressed, in his lifetime or in the early church. Indeed in John's eyes he does not seem to have expected to do so: 'The poor you always have with you.'[79] Despite the frequent quotation of Luke 4.18–21, there is no reference to Jesus actually liberating any who were literally in jail, or setting any downtrodden free. Liberation theology itself charges that in the history of the church, Christians have frequently themselves been the oppressor class. On the credit side we may legitimately claim that some Christians have been enabled through their Christian faith to throw off their own chains or help throw off the chains of others, but that claim could also be made for other religions and religious figures. Muslims point to the fact that the first muezzin was a black person, and claim with some justification that there is less race discrimination in Muslim society than in Christian society. Liberation theology, says Fierro, is aware that the destruction of human dignity makes it difficult to believe in God. It tends to assume that the restoration of human dignity, or the attempt to do so, puts God and Jesus back at the centre of things;[80] but perhaps if human dignity were to be restored by human effort, that would only go to show that a concept of God or of a divine Jesus is unnecessary. Liberation theologians assume that traditional theism and belief in the divinity of Jesus are true, and then go on to point to what they think are the socio-political consequences of that belief. They take no interest in the fact that for many people that faith is no longer tenable.

> It [i.e. liberation theology] fails to take note of the fact that the great theological problem of our day [in the West] does not concern the consequences of such a faith, a tradition or a dogma, but rather its presuppositions and the very possibility of holding the Christian outlook.[81]

If it is alleged that concern for the rationality of the faith is a bourgeois luxury for which embattled Third-World Christians do not have time, then liberation theology needs to show those whom it is trying to help that the faith which they are commending as an aid in the struggle is based on a reality, not a chimera, or else they may be selling us another false hope. In short, Western rational debates about Christian verities are not as irrelevant as they may seem. In order to convince us that their claims are valid, liberation theologians need in many cases to show us that they are aware of schools of biblical, political philosophical and theological scholarship to which they seem to pay no account.

Another general criticism that has been made about liberation theology is that its utopianism takes no account of human sinfulness. Gutierrez, for example, puts his Old Testament emphasis on the exodus, not the fall. This is the main area of difference between liberation theology and the Christian realist school of which Reinhold Niebuhr is the best known example. When the revolution has taken place, realists suggest, the poor are unlikely to find that their problems are over. A corrupt human society will be replaced by another corrupt human society. One of Edward Norman's major criticisms of liberation theology is that Christians need to be profoundly sceptical about any expectation of a better life here on earth.[82] I do not think the criticism is entirely valid. Certainly there is every reason to be sceptical about utopia on earth, as the result of various proletarian and peasant revolutions of this century show only too clearly. It is not true, however, that liberation theologians expect this utopia in any historical time, or that they identify utopia as a purely this-worldly hope. Sometimes liberation theology sounds as if it expects a utopia in this life:

> The term *Utopia* has been revised within the past few decades to refer to a historical plan for a qualitatively different society to express the aspiration to establish new social relations among men.[83]

But Miguez Bonino amongst others makes it clear that utopia is a mobilizing vision, an ideal in much the same way as in Niebuhr's theory, which is not expected to be fully realized in this world.[84] A more limited hope for a 'quantitatively better society' for the poor, even if not a perfect utopia, is surely a realistic and an achievable hope, leaving the obligation to continue to improve and perfect society under the prodding and inspiring influence of the idealist utopian vision.

When we try to draw all this together to say just how it is that liberation theology sees Jesus as helping us, the picture that emerges is a rather thin one.

1. Society, or at least Latin American society, we are told, is caught up in a conflict between the rich who have all the power, and the poor who have no power and are exploited by the rich. I am suggesting that this division of society into two classes is an oversimplification.

2. God is unequivocally on the side of the poor. He is opposed to the rich as a class, although not to rich persons as individuals. But if 1. is an oversimplification, so is 2.

3. The church and Christians cannot sit on the fence. They must choose sides, and must therefore obviously choose the side which God is on. However, if I am right about 1. and 2., then there are not just two sides to choose from, but a whole series of complicated choices to be made.

4. We know that God is on the side of the poor because he helped the Israelites in Egypt; or, more carefully expressed, he helped Moses to help the Israelites. We also know this because Jesus was poor, sided with the poor, was condemned by the rich and killed by the rich. Since Jesus is God incarnate, the actions of Jesus reveal the nature and attitude of God. But I have tried to show that the reasons given for endorsing God's option for the poor are not very convincing, involving a naive view of the biblical stories, a good deal of selection and distortion of those stories, and a dubious understanding of God's action in history. If on the other hand we follow Segundo or Croatto, and say that Moses and more especially Jesus are persons who with some historical justification can function as *symbols* for us of an ideal, of a hope for full humanness, and of suspicion towards the establishment and established theological traditions, then we need to ask whether our ideal is self-generated or comes from God. Does God reveal this ideal to us in Jesus, or did we already have it in our consciousness, and did we mould our concept of Jesus to fit that preconception? We also need to ask whether Jesus is the only or even the best symbol of that hope. I am not implying that liberation theology would be disqualified from our serious consideration if it did believe that the ideal was self-generated, and Jesus remodelled or reconceived to fit that ideal; but this would be a much milder claim than liberation theology makes for itself, and would imply that our socio-political stance is a humanly conceived, not divinely revealed, one.

5. Although salvation may be seen as covering much wider needs than the socio-political issues of adequate wealth, health, educa-

tion, security, freedom to make our own decisions, govern our own lives and control the fruits of our labour, these specific needs are primary in the sense that until they are met, other needs and issues cannot really be conceived of or taken seriously by the poor. Although this is a generalization to which a few people will prove to be remarkable exceptions, I fully agree with liberation theology on this point.

6. We are sure that these needs will be met. Our faith and hope is sure, partly because God is Lord of the historical process which must inevitably move on towards the socialist revolution, partly because Jesus endorsed these hopes and rose from the dead, thus confirming that God is Lord of history, and partly because Jesus will come again. Actually the reasons for our confidence are not very specifically spelled out in liberation theology. This is where traditional orthodox notions about the existence of a personal God, about the nature of Jesus and the fact that we are undoubtedly saved in him, supply the confidence that liberation theology largely takes for granted. To put it briefly, liberation theology assumes that Jesus is the Saviour and that we are saved. It then puts its whole energies into defining a concept of salvation that fits with the world and the experience of the poor as understood by socio-political analysis. Once having defined what salvation means in these terms, since we already know that Jesus saves, this must be what Jesus does!

I have given much more space to a general critique of the liberation model of salvation than to the older models because on the face of it it seems to be a model so close to the circumstances of Sipho. Let me finally turn more specifically to the question of what all this could mean for Sipho. As I asked of those earlier models, so I ask again, does this model fit his situation, and does it help him?

The most important way in which the liberation theology approach helps Sipho is in its definition of salvation. This is of more importance than it might appear to be. The church has for many centuries felt some responsibility to care for the poor, but frequently with a qualifying belief that God ordains the situation in which we find ourselves in life; and always as a somewhat peripheral responsibility alongside its real responsibility to care for the soul and to prepare the soul for its life in heaven. Political and liberation theology has brought out more strongly than ever before, I think, the scandalous problem for belief in God which the existence of poverty poses, and the commitment which must necessarily follow to change that situation. To this extent liberation and black theology mean that Sipho's situation is perceived by theologians in a different and clearer way than ever before, and commits the church more firmly than ever before to help Sipho. It defines salvation for Sipho very much in the terms that are needed. It makes it clear that a social relief programme which gives Sipho some comfort but does not give him *control* is not a true salvation. It also makes it clear that salvation in the more traditional and 'spiritual' sense cannot be a relevant salvation to the utterly poor like Sipho.

There are some ways, however, in which liberation theology could well be unhelpful to Sipho. This is especially true of the class-conflict model. Arguments about whether the conflict in South Africa is a racial one or a class one already consume energy that could better be given to the struggle. Sipho's life is affected not only by a rich/poor struggle, nor even by a black/white struggle. As I have described it, his life is also torn apart by struggles amongst the poor and black. There are degrees of poverty. Those who have a little money and security resent those who have none. Those with one political philosophy oppose to the death those with another. Certainly these inter-black conflicts are in part a reaction to the overall poverty and powerlessness amongst black people and a symptom of the frustration of a community unable to direct and control its destiny, hitting out at those in the immediate vicinity since the real target of their anger is beyond their reach. But when freedom comes, the conflicts will not disappear. Niebuhr's warning about the 'demonic' entering in when partial political truths are sacralized and absolutized is very relevant indeed.

The same danger is attached to the idea of the church as base community. If this is taken to mean that an adult Sipho and others like him will be greatly helped by getting together with fellow-believers who share their situation, for mutual support and encouragement in the light of a shared Christian faith, then clearly a base community could be of very great help. In the light of the study of scripture juxtaposed with an analysis of their situation, the base community could come up with useful, practical ways in which they could change their situation for the better. But if this base community is taken to mean that only those who share the situation of the group and the perception which the group has of that situation, are truly the church, then this can only weaken and divide the poor, the black people and the church more than they are already divided in South Africa, and increase the polarization betweeen the various black political groupings.

When the base community is further restricted to being not only an ideologically pure but also an intellectually and morally elite group, this poses greater dangers still to Sipho who is unlikely to be part of the elite, and who is therefore likely to be used and exploited, even if for the sake of the 'class', just as he is exploited and used now. As a contentious example, there are those who believe that international sanctions will eventually weaken the will and the power of the white ruling class in South Africa, and lead to liberation. Leaving aside the question of whether sanctions will have that effect or not, it is also widely realized that the immediate effect of sanctions will be to reduce the levels of employment and earnings of black people. It is extremely unlikely that Sipho or his mother or those like him will ever be consulted in the matter. Those opposed to sanctions will express concern for the Siphos of this world as grist to an argument which is really to their own advantage. Those in favour of sanctions will say that blacks accept these sufferings as part of the cause – but since these spokespeople are likely to be clergymen or trade union organizers or community leaders (or even white clergymen living overseas!), and thus will themselves, even if poor, hardly be close to Sipho's situation of desperation, they really mean that Sipho will suffer in order that their group can take over power from the present government. At least in the short and medium term, no elite black power base is likely to help Sipho.

If Sipho were to accept the picture of Jesus which liberation theology offers, and believed that Jesus in his earthly life espoused the struggle of the poor against the rich, and that Jesus, or God, will intervene in Sipho's own history to give his side or class the victory now, he would be creating his own myth about Jesus. That could be helpful to him, provided that he remembers that the myth is his own creation, and that the salvation/victory will have to be his own creation too. This does not at all rule out believing in God's grace. It does not have to be a modern form of deism. There is still room for God to be seen as enabler, as Spirit, as source of our energy, etc. But then the concept of Jesus which will be most helpful to Sipho – a concept to which liberation theology gives no attention – is a concept of Jesus as a human person not different in kind from Sipho, filled also with the grace-giving power of the Holy Spirit of God. This is a concept which we shall explore in the next chapter. Traditional Chalcedonian concepts of the divine/human Jesus are not the most helpful basis for making our own history or working for our own salvation.

In one important respect liberation theology could also be misleading to Sipho. Part of the result of the class-conflict model is that only the poor are seen as oppressed. Liberation theology is virtually silent with regard to the oppression of women, or homosexuals, or minority religious groups. In fact (although this may be the fault of the translators) anyone in the least sensitive to the use of exclusive language cannot help but notice that the writing of liberation theologians is peppered with words like 'man'. Yet in Sipho's black society, as in any other society, women are discriminated against. In a sense they are doubly oppressed, as blacks by whites, and as women by men, including black men. Sipho's own life is evidence of this – his mother is his sole support, his father being one who claimed as part of natural male privilege the right to move in with Claudia (at her expense), be fed by Claudia, make Claudia pregnant – for he did not want Claudia on contraception lest she should then be 'unfaithful' to him – and in a year or so move on from Claudia to another job, another city, and another woman. Her story and that of Sipho is not uncommon.

We have seen in other parts of Africa that once freedom comes, minority religious groups can still be discriminated against, although it is true that this is often coupled with racial or tribal prejudice: for example, the Ugandan expulsion of its Hindu and Moslem Asians, the persecution of the Dinka Christians in the southern Sudan. The threat of post-freedom persecution of Indians in South Africa is at least a possibility of which most South African Indians, who have not forgotten the 1949 or the 1987 attacks on themselves, are well aware. Religious toleration is an important and necessary quality in a land as religiously diverse as South Africa. As liberation theology works out how Jesus is the avenue to salvation, it needs to be aware, at least, of the potential for religious discrimination in a too-narrow model of how salvation is given us in Jesus. It needs to be aware, too, that liberation of the poor is not likely to mean that utopia has arrived. Edward Norman is surely right that no political system in this world will bring about the kingdom of God. When freedom comes for black people in South Africa, Sipho will still be at the bottom of the ladder.

There are, then, some aspects of liberation theology which could be truly helpful to Sipho, or to us as we ask how Jesus can 'save' Sipho. Especially, liberation theologians help us define what it is Sipho needs saving from, what it is that Jesus needs to be seen as doing for Sipho. There are some ways in which liberation theology seems to introduce unhelpful, even harmful, concepts seen from

Sipho's perspective. There are some aspects, particularly the question of just how it is that *Jesus* helps in liberating Sipho from that which shackles him, about which liberation theology does not seem sufficiently clear. There are quite a number of areas in which liberation theology does not provide a sufficiently firm foundation in logic and biblical exegesis for its model to be entirely trustworthy.

3

Black Theology

We need to consider whether black theology, which began in North America but is now an increasingly strong force in South Africa, has different insights to offer for Sipho's situation from those of Latin American liberation theology. James Cone tells us that while he is now very aware of liberation theology from Latin America, he was not aware of it when he first wrote of black theology.[85] Similarly there is little if any evidence of Latin American influence in the first serious book on black theology in South Africa[86] – though much evidence of influence by Cone and Willmore. Boesak's *Farewell to Innocence*,[87] the first extended piece of black theology in South Africa, is very much a response to Cone.

South African black theologians are naturally not insensitive to the questions raised for theology and for soteriology in particular by the situation of children like Sipho. The emergence of the *Kairos Document*, in so far as it can be said to be representative of black theology, was largely prompted by the plight of the children in Soweto in 1985.[88] However, the question for us is whether we can learn from black theology things that we cannot learn from Latin American liberation theology.

It is not easy to categorize South African black theology at this stage. Not all theologians who happen to be black necessarily share the same views or belong to the same school of thought. In that respect they are much less heterogeneous than Latin American liberation theologians. While black theology in North America is represented by quite an extensive library, black theology in South Africa is much smaller in volume, partly because it is really only since Boesak's *Farewell to Innocence* that South African black theology came into the limelight, partly because local publishers place themselves at risk in publishing black theology, and partly because black theologians remember all too well what happened to Steve Biko, Albert Luthuli and other martyrs to the cause. We should respect deeply the courage of those who are still writing.

It would not be true to say that black theology is just another version of Latin American liberation theology, although we shall see that there are many similarities, and the more recent writings show a clear trend towards the Latin American model. If black theology means a theology of black people reflecting on their experience of rejection and discrimination, one could say that the roots of South African black theology go back to the prophetess Donna Beatrice in Angola in the early eighteenth century,[89] or to the separatist movements of the late nineteenth century away from missionary paternalism and white control (e.g. Nehemiah Tile, J. W. Dwane, etc.), or to the Zionist type of movements which developed as a curious combination of American pentecostalism and African traditionalism. The concerns of black theology are certainly at the heart of the *Nkosi sikelele 'Afrika*, dating from early this century. Thus the perspectives of modern black theology go back to roots existing long before liberation theology became well known, and it does have its own distinctive features.

The features shared in common with liberation theology are those of starting from the situation of the oppressed – in this case a black oppressed – as the basis of one's theology; an insistence that salvation has to do with this world as well as the next, and that political history and salvation history are not two different things. It therefore has an emphasis on orthopraxis rather than orthodoxy, and on the need to analyse the reasons for the situation of oppression and to address the full energy of the church in combatting that situation. I shall look at these similarities in a little more detail below.

The differences with liberation theology in its Latin American form are the possible combination with political theology of traditional African religious concepts; a greater suspicion that perhaps even a reconstituted theology will still prove to be enslaving rather than liberating; a blurring of the class conflict model; a rather greater willingness amongst some to work with other theologies, other races and classes; a much more explicit grappling with the question of whether or not violence is to be espoused; and in particular a greater emphasis on the Bible rather than on experience as a basis or norm of theology. However, as we shall see, virtually all of these different features will be energetically rejected by some, as an illustration of my rueful comment that South African black theology does not easily fit into categories.

South African black theology is a remarkable, resilient phenomenon which deserves the full-scale study that so far no one has provided. This book is not that study! I shall not attempt here to discuss every aspect of black theology, but only to try to point to those features which have to do with our discussion of christology and soteriology. A thumbnail sketch of the origins of black theology helps us to get an idea about this. Although I have suggested that in some ways its origins lie back in the nineteenth century or earlier, modern black theology in South Africa emerged as part of the black consciousness movement that arose to fill the vacuum left after the banning of the African National Congress and the Pan African Congress in 1960.

> Black consciousness has provided a very important context for developing a theological hermeneutic. It has challenged black theologians to take seriously the particularity of black experience.[90]

There seem to have been two distinct and simultaneous initiatives which gave birth to modern South African black theology. One came from the University Christian Movement, a multi-racial student organization with Basil Moore, a white Methodist minister, as its energetic secretary. Moore organized a series of conferences as part of a black theology project, culminating in a conference in 1971 in Roodepoort which produced a number of papers, many of them greatly influenced by the work of James Cone.[91]

The other initiative came from a black student group which had split off from the multi-racial University Christian Movement to form the purely black South African Students Organization, with Steve Biko as president. The organization convened a conference in 1971 which gave rise to the Black People's Convention. The BPC in turn developed a number of projects, among them a black theology project.

Thus there are some outside influences behind the development of black theology in South Africa: the early work of James Cone and his emphasis on the gospel for oppressed blacks being a different gospel from that preached in white churches, and also paradoxically the work of a white liberal in bringing Cone's work to the notice of black theologians who were still heavily influenced by their

Westernized seminary training. But within South Africa there was also the growing awareness amongst young black people of the need to part company from whites, even liberal, well-intentioned whites, in order to discover their own identity and develop a pride in that black identity.

I am inclined to say that South African black theology, at least in its earlier 1970's form, was more the result of church people reflecting on the gospel in the light of experience of oppression and the need for liberation and less the result of input from professional theologians versed in sophisticated Western political theory than is the case with Latin American liberation theology. Whether there is also an influence from traditional African religious ideas is a disputed point. Gabriel Setiloane would say this is the case;[92] Manas Buthelezi denies this[93] and draws a distinction between African theology and black theology; Desmond Tutu takes a middle line.[94] There is little evidence of any such influence in the writing. Not all supporters of black theology are African, and they therefore do not all share such an influence if it exists. It may be (though some would disagree) that traditional African religious ideas have now become so blurred with Christianity that a speculative reconstruction of their original form is only a romantic recreation of a lost past. It is probably more accurate to say that while traditional African beliefs no longer exist in pristine form, they have become merged with more recent experience and with Western concepts to forge a living black culture which while rooted in history is not the same as the pre-Christian culture but which, nevertheless, is still a distinctive factor in the formation of black theology.[95]

The University Christian Movement and the South African Student Organization were declared banned organizations: Basil Moore fled to England; Steve Biko was killed. Black theology thus did not advance very fast for another five or six years until the publication of Boesak's *Farewell to Innocence*. Boesak continued to build on the work of Cone rather than on Latin American liberation theology. Desmond Tutu's star was rising in the mid-1970s. His ideas must be gleaned from sermons and a few journal articles, since (as with some other South African black theologians) ecclesiastical administration inevitably takes most of his time. He seemed to build on a different foundation, that of Anglican Catholic social teaching in the Frank Weston and William Temple style. Both Manas Buthelezi and Simon Maimela write in part out of a Lutheran background. But by the 1980s the new theologians were and are much more closely and consciously influenced by Latin America –

or, to be more precise, by the same sources that inform Latin American liberation theology, that is, Marxist social analysis, the Frankfurt school, Paul Ricoeur, and Paulo Freire. For all these reasons it is a mistake to think that the views of the earlier black theologians like Boesak, Tutu, Buthelezi or Maimela are the same as the newer writers like Chikane, Mosala, Tlhagale or Mofokeng.

What they all have in common with liberation theology, however, is an insistence that God has a special concern for the oppressed, and that since salvation is concerned with the wholeness of life, salvation must include (though not be confined to) liberation from oppression. The demands of the Christian gospel 'are incompatible with unjust, alienating, and polarizing social arrangements'.[96] A purely spiritual gospel is alien to an African idea of the wholeness of life.[97]

Thus since the gospel has practical implications, and since the South African black theologians are much more concerned about practical issues than about metaphysical truth, they too can be said to start their theology with praxis.

> Black theologians because of black consciousness have had to wrestle with the challenge of how they can meaningfully participate in the ongoing struggle for liberation.[98]

Or, in words which reflect the language of Latin American influence:

> Action precedes knowledge, praxis precedes theory, involvement (commitment) precedes theologizing.[99]

Together with concern for the practical, liberative implications of the gospel goes an insistence on recognizing the true causes of oppression, on socio-political analysis, and on seeing that sin is structural or societal as well as individual.

> As any theology has to relate to its particular context, the need to discuss the political situation as it affects blacks will be very crucial. This will require a socio-political analysis of the situation.[100]

More recent writers[101] are suggesting that this analysis needs to be of a Marxian type, though this is a matter of some dispute.

This links with the idea of conscientization, enabling black people to see that they are oppressed and why they are oppressed.[102] It also means that black theology like liberation theology sees the hermeneutical implications of this: that black people come to the Bible and to the received tradition from their own history, culture and situation, and interpret the Bible and tradition in the light of that, while at the same time allowing the Bible to be a normative reference point in understanding how to find liberation from the confines of that situation – thus the hermeneutic circle.

Thus there are many similarities with liberation theology, and in recent years much conscious modelling of black theology into that pattern. There are also a number of distinct and different features. South African black theology is somewhat divided in itself about the class-conflict model of Marxism. These divisions sometimes become bitter ones. It is clear to all that they suffer because they are black, and that most black people are poor people. Thus, to be black means to be poor and oppressed. But are all poor people black? And what of the few Africans and rather more Indian people who become relatively wealthy? Is the struggle in South Africa one of white versus black or bourgeois versus workers and peasants? Should the black church welcome liberally-minded whites as allies? Are bourgeois African, Indian or mixed-race people black? Race analysts are wary of collaboration with whites in the struggle;[103] class analysts are wary of collaboration with bourgeois black businessmen or doctors, etc. This difference of opinion parallels divisions between the African National Congress and the Pan-African Congress, between the South African Students Organization and the United Democratic Front, etc.

More recently some have suggested that the oppression in South Africa began as a class struggle but, since the working class were virtually all black, racial discrimination began to have a life and validity of its own. It would seem to me that the dispute is one in which everybody is partly right, and would not be worth trying to adjudicate except that it seems to be at the heart of much of the killing taking place in Sipho's home town.

Whether one chooses class or race as the basis of the analysis, perhaps the basic point is that for black theology, God is on the side of the weak, whether black or worker. But in fact, at least for some black theologians, the conflict model is not used as strongly. Thus Mpunzi says

Although it [black theology] directs its voice to black people, it nonetheless hoped that white people will hear and be saved.[104]

Thus, too, Boesak rejects any identification of the gospel with sectional black nationalism.

Christian faith transcends all ideologies and all nationalistic ideals. It transcends specific groups and nations with their specific ideals and interests.[105]

Dwane argues that black theology, unlike liberation theology, does not see itself as the whole of the theological endeavour, or even the whole relevant truth for black people, but as only a part of the whole.[106] This point cannot be stretched too far. There are other voices in black theology which do stress the conflict model and the need for black theology to distance itself from other groups and other theologies. More recent black theology also tends to stress that there can be no meeting or reconciliation between the oppressors and the oppressed until the former have repented and amended their ways.[107]

South African black theology often differs from liberation theology in the degree of normativeness which it attaches to the Bible. It also differs from James Cone, sometimes quite strongly, in this respect. Where Cone seems sometimes to allow the black experience of oppression to govern one's interpretation of the Bible in the hermeneutic discipline,[108] Mgojo on the other hand says quite clearly that biblical revelation is 'the first and most important source of knowledge in theology'.[109] and Boesak says

> We fear that Cone attaches too much theological import to the black experience and the black situation, as if these realities *within themselves* have revelation value on a par with scripture,[110]

although Goba criticizes Boesak strongly on this point.[111] Some South African black theologies therefore distinguish between the *sources* of black theology, that is, the agenda with which it has to deal, the experience of oppression, the culture and history in which black people live, and the *theological norms* which govern it, the revelation of God in scripture and in worship and sacraments.

However, again we must be aware that not all black theologians would agree with this. Mosala, for example, criticizes black theologians who talk about black theology being governed by biblical norms. He is as wary of biblical normativeness and of the intentions of biblical criticism as any of the more radical recent Latin American liberation theologians.[112]

As far as christology is concerned, South African black theology takes the same approach as liberation theology. It claims to start not from scripture or traditional theology but from the problem. The problem is the experience of oppression, and to ask who Jesus is for us in this situation. South African black theology commends its christology, not to rational sceptics as in the post-Enlightenment West, but to those disillusioned people who are prevented from growth into fullness. It sees the salvation which Jesus brings in primarily political terms. Like liberation theology, it sees Jesus as committed to social liberation, for example on the basis of Luke 4.18–21. It sees Jesus as identifying himself with the poor and marginalized; and, because Jesus is thus identified, God incarnate in Jesus is identified with these groups too.

> Incarnation means identifying with humanity. It means identify-
> ing with humanity's weakness, suffering and pain. It means
> identifying with the struggles of the people.[113]

Thus the idea of incarnation is very important. In the one who was born in a manger as an apparently unimportant and marginalized person, who died on the cross as a victim of an alien political power, God was present, identified with the poor.

Like liberation theology, it also sees the exodus as an important paradigm for God's relationship with the poor. This is a favourite theme of Desmond Tutu.

> God is God who is always on the side of the oppressed to lead
> them out of all that enslaves them and makes them less than what
> he intends them to be, into the glorious liberty of the sons of
> God.[114]

However, Tutu does not make the distinction that Segundo does between God leading the people of Israel out of Egypt and God enabling Moses to lead the people. It is not clear whether Tutu envisages God intervening directly, and this is not really clarified by many other black South African writers either.

It is not clear, to me at least, how Jesus fits into the exodus paradigm in this theology. There is much emphasis on his identifica-tion with the poor; but if he is one of the poor, how is he also a Moses? In fact, since the black people are still oppressed, the liberation into the promised land is something that lies in the future rather than something which Jesus has already accomplished. For this reason, Buthelezi seems to suggest that Good Friday is an event with which blacks feel more identified than with Easter.[115] Just as Jesus died an undeserved death, so black people see themselves as enduring like him a suffering which they have not provoked or deserved.

They suffer 'innocently' without having actively provoked any-
body, they suffer simply because they are black people.[116]

But the innocent suffering of Jesus is understood to have been
turned by God into a medium of divine love and restoration. Where
suffering is oppressive God turns it, in the cross, into a means of
redemption.

> The violence of the cross thus became the foil of God's love. The
> brilliance of God's love shone through the violent cloud of death.
> It is not the violence of the cross that saved us but the love of God
> that endured it.[117]

Buthelezi seems here to be saying something very similar to
Moltmann: God also endured suffering on the cross, and thus
showed us his love. Goba makes the same point.

> God not only shares our suffering in the death of Jesus, but
> becomes the source of hope and liberation.[118]

We find then in South African black theology themes which we
have also found in Latin American liberation theology and in
European political theology. At the same time, these theologians
also still hold to most of the traditional christological and trinitarian
doctrines of orthodox Christianity. They do not much discuss, but
nor do they deny, the truth of notions of redemption through
substitutionary atonement.

Yet it seems to me that, while it would be unfair and inaccurate to
force all South African black theology into any single pattern, the
most important way in which Jesus is seen to liberate black people is
by showing them in the incarnation that God cares about and
identifies with black people. Black people in South Africa have
reason to feel utterly humiliated and devalued. They have grown up
having to use separate entrances into public buildings, being
refused access to most normal amenities. They know that if they
come to a white person's home they must often come to the back
door. They know that their education, their salary, their pension,
will be determined by their race. Even if the laws have changed in
some of these matters, the changes are recent, and the patterns of
behaviour have not changed. The efforts of well-meaning white
people are perceived as paternalistic, as reaching down from
positions of power and self-confidence to help those whom they
consider to be less fortunate – and less able – than themselves.

Thus the theme of black consciousness is a very powerful one. Steve Biko stands out especially as one who encouraged black people to take pride in their culture and their identity, to seek help from no outside groups but to liberate themselves, to develop a sense of anger at their treatment rather than passively accept it. The essence of black consciousness is

> . . . the realization by the black man of the need to rally together with his brothers around the cause of their oppression – the blackness of their skin – and to operate as a group to rid themselves of the shackles that bind them to perpetual servitude. It is based on a self-examination which has ultimately led them to believe that by seeking to run away from themselves and to emulate the white man they are insulting the intelligence of whoever created them black.[119]

Apartheid, in effect if no longer in official theory, evaluates a person in terms of race. It says that black human beings are not as human as whites.

In order to be liberated from this mind set, black theology points to creation, to God creating all people in his own image. It points even more strongly to the incarnation. In Jesus, marginalized because of his race, also poor, also depersonalized, also pushed around, and eventually killed, black people can see a reflection of themselves. But God was in Jesus! In Jesus, God came right alongside with, was totally identified with, a poor person like themselves.

In fact most black theologians go further, and say, along with Chalcedon, that Jesus was God. 'Jesus emerges in the final analysis as *vere homo, vere deus*.'[120] As God he is not one who passively accepts evil. Black theology 'wants to describe Christ as a fighting God and not a passive God who accepts a lie to exist unchallenged.'[121] Thus a fully incarnational theology seems to be very important to them, not so that Jesus as God can pay for their sins, but so that Jesus as God can be alongside them, suffer with them, as a demonstration of his love. Here surely is the classic exemplarist theory, not in the literal sense of Jesus setting a good example for us to follow, but in what I described earlier when discussing Rashdall: the sense that a fully divine Jesus exemplifies God's love for us. If we ask of this theology the question Denny asked Rashdall – how does this identification save us? – the answer is somewhat different, though. It is not God showing sinners his love so that they may repent. It is God showing those sinned against his love so that they may know they are loved and lovable, that they are invested with dignity and value and preciousness as God assures them of his love, as a *riposte* to the indignity, devaluing and insult that the South African situation pours upon them. There is no doubt that this is a very powerful message.

4

A Critique

There are problems with some aspects of black theology for all its power. There are all the rational problems associated with incarnational christology which we looked at in an earlier section, so that black theology may be forced into saying that incarnational language is powerful in its symbolic rather than its realist import. Moreover, a rediscovery of black dignity does not in itself change the situation. Black theologians look back to the Incarnation to find assurance of their dignity and value – and also forward to the hope of liberation. There are two rather different ways in which this hope is expressed. There is the hope that in the near future God will intervene and save his people in a new exodus-style deliverance. This hope is difficult to maintain.[122] As symbolic language it has undoubted power. If it is intended in a realist way, it encourages passivism and is also perhaps a false hope.

But there is also the somewhat different hope that black people, having rediscovered their inherent worth, will create their own liberation, which is God's plan for them.

> Black theology of liberation thus shares the fundamental biblical conviction which holds that the world and humanity are not given, finished and static realities but they are dynamic realities which are undergoing continual change and development in response to God, who leads them towards their completion in the eschaton.[123]

> Black theology of liberation calls men and women to play their part and to be on the cutting edge of human liberation from all

forms of social and spiritual oppression, thus becoming partners with their creator in the refashioning of this unjust world into one in which they will find fulfilment.[124]

Buthelezi says that since Christ is Lord over every situation, we must build hope in the community by ministering to social conditions, not with charitable giving but by providing skills to enable persons to have self-respect and make their own contribution to the rebuilding of the community.[125]

There seems to be an unnoticed shift here in how what Jesus does for us is perceived. Jesus is the expression of God's love for the poor, the figure of traditional incarnation doctrine. He is the Messiah to black people, telling them that God has a different purpose and intention for them. But more important, Jesus *is* the poor person. As a poor person he is beloved by God. As a poor person he nevertheless has power over his own situation. Even though his stand leads to his death, death does not obliterate his cause. He is the New Man, the New Adam, the one who shows us how a poor person is still, by the power of God in him, victorious over the 'powers' of this world and able to retain his conviction, his commitment, and refuse to accept that he is a non-person.

The incarnation means that we must insert divinity into our humanity.[126]

God in Christ has demonstrated that healing and renewal of human situations are within the divine ability to bring about.[127]

From this perspective, traditional Chalcedonian incarnational theory does not seem to fit as well as a concept which sees Jesus as like us in kind, that is, as human yet approved by God – so that we may see how we ourselves, with God's power, can be and can act.

To the extent that black theology is like liberation theology, the same critical remarks would apply, for instance the conviction of black theologians that on the basis of Luke 4 Jesus can be seen as a liberator of the poor, a liberator from prison chains, etc. There is sometimes the same *naiveté* about the historical Jesus, about the model of the exodus, etc., that we noted in Sobrino and Gutierrez. To the extent that black theology adopts a class-conflict model, the criticisms that we made of liberation theology as far as Sipho's plight is concerned apply even more sharply, since it is this model which is at least partly the very real present cause of Sipho's tragedy. But not all black theology does accept this model.

The most significant thing for Sipho in black theology is the emphasis on black consciousness, and on Jesus as a liberator from negative self-devaluation amongst black people. Here really lies the key for Sipho's liberation. Black people may interpret Jesus as a messiah promising God's intervention and aid; but no such intervention has come. We make our own history. They may interpret Jesus as God, who came to live among the poor in his *kenosis*; and that will indeed plant some seeds of self-worth in their consciousness. But the more Jesus differs from us in kind, or the more 'divine' he is, the less able we will be to see him as a model of hope for us as we make our own history. We may know we are loved, but we do not know we are able. It seems to me that it is in seeing Jesus as human, yet as one who knew that God loved him and had a profound destiny for him, that the needs for black consciousness are most powerfully met. This Jesus provides hope and evidence that black people can be victors, not victims.

IV

Conclusions

Drawing the Threads Together

It is time to attempt to draw together some of the loose strings. I have said that in my opinion christological questions come after soteriological ones.

> Almost all Christological conceptions have had soteriological motifs. Changes in the soteriological interest in man's understanding of salvation, explain, at least in part, the different form Christology has taken at different times.[1]

We do not begin with a philosophical or ontological account of the nature of Jesus and then work out the implications of that as far as salvation is concerned: or at least, we may do so, but with the risk that this Jesus will be irrelevant to our needs. The early church and indeed the Chalcedonian Definition itself, believed that our definition of the nature of Jesus arose out of the experience of salvation. This is not very different from what the liberation theologians say in our own time. We come to Jesus out of the background of our own experience, our own needs – and in the case of liberation and black theology, out of the context of our own situation of oppression. We read the scriptures and the tradition concerning Jesus from that perspective: we can do no other. We come to christology out of a value-laden experience.[2] There is no *tabula rasa*.

I am not going so far as to say that an ontological account of the nature of the person of Jesus is ruled out. I think it appropriate for us to attempt that, as far as we can. But the ontology arises out of primarily functional concerns, if what we are concerned with is a living faith in God and not only with speculative philosophy.

Furthermore, the initial soteriological concerns will be to do with this world and present realities. That is to say, from a South African perspective issues such as salvation from guilt, salvation from death, salvation from the 'wrath of God', have to be seen initially at least in the context of salvation from oppression. This is true partly because it is the condition of oppression which gives rise to the sin, the guilt and the death in the oppressed people. The poor housing and economic conditions cause various kinds of anti-social behaviour. The other part of the truth is that while people live under such very poor conditions, other less immediate aspects of salvation and of religion generally, such as alienation from God, fear of hell and damnation, Jesus dying for our sins, initiation into a life of prayer and meditation, are often inconceivable, inappropriate and insensitive. The bread-and-butter issues must take precedence.[3]

I have tried to show that none of the traditional ways of understanding the atonement really answer Sipho's most urgent problems nor those who share his situation in South Africa. It may be that if Sipho's present problems were solved and he were able to live in relative security, with adequate material provision, with access to better education, with more control over and responsibility for his own life, many of the traditional atonement theories could become more sharply relevant for him again, particularly those theories which deal with human feelings of guilt. Greater personal power means greater personal and individual responsibility and the consequent risk of alienation from God through the misuse of that responsibility.

I have tried to show, too, that the strong distinction made by older theologies between 'objective' and 'subjective' theories of atonement,[4] is an unwise distinction, given the fact that there is no evidence of any objective change in Sipho's situation. God has not intervened, as far as we can judge, to change the course of his history – and if he does it will be too late. Nor has God brought about sufficient change in the outlook and behaviour of those white Christians who are responsible for Sipho's oppression. If we are to retain belief in God, we can only explain this by placing much more emphasis on the subjective aspects of atonement:[5] we must argue that while God provides the opportunity, the guidance, the grace, for salvation, humans must appropriate this for themselves, and the effectiveness of salvation depends on human responsiveness.

I shall be suggesting that the saving work of Jesus is to encourage and enable us to make our own history. He is a catalyst in a process of 'autosoteriology', of self-salvation. This process is not one we can follow alone, without the aid of others, especially without the grace of God; but given this help, we have to then save ourselves. I am thus opting plainly for a 'subjective' salvation theory, and in a sense for an 'auto'-salvation theory.

This means that our salvation is not certain, at least in any immediate or even mid-term sense. Dismayed Christians who find this a problem may be mollified by Paul's admission that even he was not certain of attaining the prize.[6] It is because humans are sinful, weak and fallible that Quick wanted an 'objective' atonement theory, since only an objective atonement would be reliable; but we have seen that whatever theory we may choose to hold, the plain historical truth of the matter is that many people, even many Christians, are not saved from lives of degradation, moral collapse and brutality. Human attitudes, decisions and lack of decisions are the key factors. Sipho's salvation appears to depend in part on a change of heart in those who have created his chains. Many of those who imprison him in poverty are themselves Christians, genuinely seeking to obey God, sincerely wishing to serve God and to be saved themselves. This has not prevented their moral blindness to the effects of their actions. God has not changed their hearts, nor confounded their actions. Those who wish to change may find guidance and grace from God to do so. But the initiative, it would seem, has to come from the human individual. This surely rules out purely objective theories.

Sipho's salvation depends on being prepared to do something about his salvation for himself. Again, traditional atonement theories have not encouraged this initiative. If Sipho and his people are to gain the self-determination and power which is necessary to direct their own lives, then since some 180 years and more of South African colonial history suggests that no such power will be given to them voluntarily by the whites, self-determination will be achieved by taking that power, not waiting for God or the President to give it to them. I do not mean to imply here that such taking of power will have to be violent or even by revolution; that is another issue. There are conceivably non-violent means of taking power, as Gandhi and his *satyagraha* demonstrated.[7] I certainly do not mean to imply here what is normally meant by Pelagianism, that is, that God's grace is not necessary for salvation. I hope to show in this chapter that taking power and responsibility over our lives is something that we do by God's grace, with God's strength. There are examples in South African history of black people who have done just this. There are also, however, many who have not known how to, or

been able to, commit themselves to this step. A Christian soteriology must be shown to relate to this need, or it is no salvation.

Salvation for Sipho, while it may ultimately include eschatological aspects, must be primarily salvation from his socio-political
situation, from the social structures which so severely handicap his
humanness and his potential. We have noted that in Christian
thought, possibly even beginning with the New Testament, the
broader concept of salvation became narrowed down and spiritual-
ized into theories of atonement for personal sin. But it is impossible
for us now to separate out atonement and salvation. Until the
socio-political situation has changed, it is rather unlikely that
children like Sipho can grow up familiar with 'whatever is true,
whatever is honourable, whatever is just, whatever is pure,
whatever is lovely, whatever is gracious'.[8] As long as black people
are humiliated and rendered unable to love and respect themselves,
they are less able to love and respect God. Reconciliation with God,
atonement in that sense, may follow, but cannot normally precede,
salvation from this degradation and devaluation.

What then do we mean by salvation for Sipho?

1. It must mean a discovery of his personal inherent worth and
value as a human person. Those having power in the community
need to make this discovery concerning Sipho, and Sipho needs in
due course to make the discovery about himself. As a human person
he has certain inherent rights. He has a right to community concern
for his health. He has a right to an adequate education. We leave
aside the difficult truth that nowhere are such rights equally
available to all people in the community, and make the lesser point
that unless these rights are granted at least to an adequate extent,
Sipho cannot be saved. The community needs to recognize that
Sipho counts as an individual. Sipho needs to learn how to demand
these rights from the community, for if he does not know he is worth
these rights, then he will acquiesce in all that happens to him. *Thus,
if Jesus is to be of saving help to Sipho, his work must be in part to
teach the community and Sipho that individuals matter, and have
worth.*

2. If the belief in his own worth is to be more than a merely
arbitrary belief, or one granted by a merely convenient human
social contract as being likely to produce the best social results, then
Sipho will need to believe that as an individual he is valuable in the
eyes of God, that he is loved because God has created him and
decreed him to be of value. To use a different metaphor, his self
worth must be ratified by what is held to be ultimately true and real.

If Jesus is to be of saving help to Sipho, his work must be to show that God gives this value to individuals.

3. For that belief to extend beyond a theoretical level, Sipho will need to believe that God has a purpose or destiny for all creation, and that Sipho's own life is part of that purpose. This need not entail believing that God has mapped out every detail of either the world's or of Sipho's future, but if God loves his creation which is so manifestly incomplete and unsatisfactory in so many respects, he must intend that there is some process of development and improvement, and there must be some way in which Sipho can be part of that process. *There must be in Jesus some revealing of that process and of Sipho's potential part in it.*

4. While believing in his own worth, Sipho will also need to believe in the worth and corresponding rights of others, for it will only be when society in general recognizes these rights that Sipho's own rights will be more or less secure. He will need, therefore, to be a 'man for others' as well as a man for himself. Once freedom has been won, then mercy for the defeated, sensitivity to the rights of black and white minority groups, the Indian people, the members of smaller tribes or social groupings, will be very important. Africa has provided many recent examples of freedom which has turned to new tyranny. *Jesus will need to be for us one who encourages and enables us to be for 'others'.*

5. Sipho lives in a community which is at present deeply and violently split in many ways, not only racial but also ideological. In addition to all the major divisions in South African life, Sipho's community is split too because of quarrels over land, feuds between 'factions' which have been going on for a generation. While the causes of these divisions are rooted in poverty and powerlessness, it is still true that salvation must include a rebuilding of a divided community into one community where racial, tribal and ideological differences are seen as enrichments, not as reasons to exclude or devalue people. *A saving Jesus will need to be one who creates such a community, and who calls Sipho to be not only a member but in some degree an initiator of such a community.*

6. When, as must inevitably happen, Sipho fails from time to time to live according to what he believes are God's purposes for himself or others, he will need to know that God is a forgiving God and that a new start is possible. He needs to believe in a God who calls us to the highest standards of integrity and love, and who unreservedly forgives us when we fall short and turn to him in penitence – unreservedly, because otherwise our load of guilt and

anxiety must become decapacitating. *Jesus, to be a saving figure, will need to be one who enables us to perceive that God is indeed a forgiving God.*

7. Since the humiliation, powerlessness, brokenness existing in Sipho and his community are the products of the social and economic structure of the society in which they live, the work of Jesus must also have some effect on the structure. Here, however, there is a difficulty. Jesus lived in a society structured quite differently from our own. The world has changed in countless ways since Jesus lived on earth. There will be those who think we can draw blueprints for a better structure of society from the Bible because the Bible is the Word of God for all time, or because the essential structural and economic elements in society are constant and unchanging. It is true that if Jesus offered such guidelines and they were correct guidelines he would be of the utmost importance and relevance. However, I do not think detailed guidelines of this kind can be found in the Bible. I do not think that the Bible or the New Testament endorse socialism or communism or capitalism. Nor do I think that if such guidelines were found to be offered, they would prove relevant in the twentieth century. Since Jesus' time we have seen tribes become nations, and are now seeing nations disappear into larger global components. Our society is so different from the society in which Jesus lived that we cannot hope to find more than occasional pointers from so long ago. I do not think that Jesus saves us by showing us the shape of an ideal societal structure except in the broadest generalities.

This need not dismay us. I do not think we can deny that Sipho's issues are caused by societal structures; but I do think that the changing of these structures can only be initiated by individuals and groups of individuals working together to develop relevant structures. Society will not change of itself but through individuals who collectively change it. Although the work of Jesus will be to call individuals to a new lifestyle with new values, and not to provide a primer in applied political science, it will be from renewed individuals that the structures of society change. Even in Marxism there is an ambiguity between the idea that the collapse of capitalism happens because of the inevitable economic process, and the idea that the efforts of the workers achieve the revolution. Thus neo-Marxists come close themselves to saying that salvation begins with conscientized individuals who give their lives on behalf of others. *Jesus, if he is Saviour, must be a conscientizer of individuals.*

Let me recapitulate to draw together the statements I have made so far about what kind of work Jesus will need to do if he is to be of saving relevance to Sipho. He will need to be one who bears witness in his life and teaching that individuals matter, that they not only have an inherent worth in Jesus' eyes but are valued thus by God. He will need to be one who shows us that God has a purpose for his creation and for each human individual within it. He will need to be one who teaches, and enables us to care about, the rights of others, to love our fellows, and to allow them to grow into their God-intended potential. He will need to have been a builder in his own era of a new, undivided community or family of humans, and to enable us to build such a community in our era. He will need to be one who not only motivates and enables us to fulfil these ideals, but also shows us that when we fail to do so we can be forgiven and can make a new start.

Words which have cropped up frequently as I discuss what salvation needs to comprise are those such as 'show', 'motivate', 'enable'. We frequently do not know our human potential or purpose. We do not know what kind of people we can be, nor what kind of world God wants us to live in. We do not believe we are able to build a better world, nor know how to do it; we have no goals to work for. In fact we are often not able, without help from outside, to achieve these goals. Jesus will need to be a 'revealer', a 'motivator', a 'transformer'. I believe that we can show he was all of these things in his own time, and will give attention to that presently. Despite the difficulties of recreating a picture of the historical Jesus, I believe that there is abundant evidence that he performed these functions.

Yet we shall also have to admit that the ways in which the New Testament and early church understood the salvation which Jesus brought will be in some respects very different from our own perception. We live in a very different world. The early church believed that they needed a divine rescuer, that God himself would intervene to put right the troubles of his people. They believed that Jesus was the Messiah, the Son of Man, who in traditional Jewish expectations would usher in the new era; and that the new era, with the end of the world, would happen soon. They were mistaken. Perhaps Schweitzer is right, and the human Jesus also understood his work in this way and was mistaken too.[9] If we hold out hopes of imminent divine intervention in our own lives, we are flying in the face of history. We shall have to find a way of understanding Jesus as Saviour which is not dependent on the direct intervention of God, for all the reasons we have looked at earlier.

What makes our task more difficult is that we shall have to show that our own understanding of the saving work of Jesus grows out of what we know of his historical person and nature, and that it is an understanding which is significant enough to count, and yet not so final and exclusive as to lead to the sort of dangers we have looked at earlier in association with exclusivist theories of Christian salvation. That is, we shall have to find some credible middle ground between saying that Jesus made some potentially helpful remarks along with other great people in human history (in which case he is hardly our 'saviour' any more than Tolstoy or Emily Dickenson are saviours) and saying that the work of Jesus is so utterly unique that only those who explicitly accept Jesus as saviour have any worth or hope in their lives at all.

I must therefore add two further aspects to the salvation which we need from Jesus.

8. The model of salvation which we use must be one which is still credible even when we do not succeed in our aim, except on a purely individual level. The salvation which Jesus brings must be one which enables us to save ourselves with the help of God through Jesus – for that is what is implied if we no longer expect a direct divine intervention. But since we and our fellow humans are fallible, weak and free, we shall sometimes fail to save ourselves or be prevented by others from saving ourselves, and God's purposes will often be thwarted. It will be necessary for our model of salvation in Jesus to show that God's purposes are worth striving for, for the sake of the striving itself, with little expectation of achievement of these purposes outside our own personal obedience and integrity. I am thus in the somewhat difficult position of agreeing with liberation theology that individual salvation depends on change in societal structure – and yet agnostic about whether societal structures will necessarily be changed, at least in the lifetime of the individual concerned. All that we can be sure of is that it is possible for individuals to free themselves from being cowed and enslaved by those structures, and we are left with individual salvation after all.

9. Yet if God is to be God, there must still be the belief that ultimately, in however long a term, God's purposes for society will be achieved; that 'sin is necessary, but all shall be well, and all shall be well, and all manner of thing shall be well',[10] to quote the Lady Julian of Norwich who lived through times as bleak politically and ecclesiastically as in South Africa now. There must be hope, or else salvation in Jesus will be no more than the Stoic belief that we do

our duty without any expectation at all that it will make any difference. The likelihood is that in South Africa God's purposes will be refused in the short term; but there must be hope in a long-term victory. Hope enables perseverance. To the extent that Sipho and his peers cease to accept that only the *status quo* is possible and begin to believe that another kind of world and society is possible, and to work for that society, then whether or not he and others succeed in their lifetime in establishing that new world universally, they themselves will have begun to live in that new world, and their lives will have purpose, meaning, dignity and self-directedness.

I believe that despite all the difficulties surrounding the historical picture of Jesus, it is clear enough that by the time the Gospels were written Jesus was seen as fulfilling all these needs. We cannot know how far the Gospels have idealized the historical Jesus of Nazareth. There must, however, have been some basis in history upon which the idealized account came to be written. It is enough, in any case, that the Gospel story about Jesus shows him to be one whom the tellers of the story – the evangelists, the early church whose oral tradition the evangelists drew upon – believed to meet those needs for themselves. It is the story of Jesus, the picture of Jesus which the Gospels pass on to us, which must be of saving power for us if the figure of Jesus is to be of help, since we do not possess the detailed history.

If, hypothetically, someone should show that the historical Jesus was utterly different from the Jesus of the story, we should have to cease claiming that Jesus is a saviour. The hypothesis is unlikely to be true. The historical Jesus must have been similar enough to the Gospel Jesus for the story to have been formed.

The overriding concern of the Jesus of the Gospels was the kingdom of God. The kingdom of God means, as Newman points out,[11] the acknowledgment and acceptance by all people of God's purposes for the world. Jesus called on all his hearers to make that acknowledgment.[12] Jesus also taught that God welcomed into his kingdom those whom the society of Jesus' time thought to be excluded: different race groups, like Samaritans and Gentiles of all kinds; the supposedly inferior feminine sex; different political and ideological groups like Jewish quisling tax-collectors or Roman centurions. Jesus welcomed them all.

This was largely the content of his teaching. It brought him to the cross. John Howard Yoder,[13] arguing against the charge that Jesus' preaching was either apolitical or irrelevant to modern social issues, says that the Gospels show that Jesus' life and teaching were very much concerned with political issues. Yoder illustrates this from the Gospel of Luke, but claims that 'any other gospel . . . could equally well have been used'.[14] Jesus' deeds 'show a coherent, conscious, socio-political character and direction and . . . his words are inseparable therefrom'.[15] I quote Yoder because it goes beyond my scope here to examine the Gospels in detail to demonstrate my point, and I believe Yoder has demonstrated very convincingly from scripture the claims I am making.

Yoder suggests that Jesus was concerned particularly with the plight of the poor, and with the inauguration of a biblical 'year of jubilee' entailing the remission of all debts, the liberation of all slaves,[16] and the redistribution of all capital, not in any institution-alized enforced way – 'Collectivism was contrary to the spirit of Moses'[17] – but as a one-off jubilee ordinance to make it possible for the poor and indebted to start off afresh. Yoder's thesis is supported by Harvey Falk, who suggests that Jesus' concern was to convert Gentiles to the Noachic law, which would have entailed acknowledging that the promises of the year of jubilee were still in force.[18]

Yoder has adopted the idea of the year of jubilee from André Trocmé, and in order to convince us probably needed to provide a more detailed argument, though certainly the framework of jubilee teaching does help make sense of many of the Lukan hard sayings and difficult parables such as that of the unfaithful steward.[19] Yoder establishes very convincingly, however, that Jesus did not die on the cross because he decided to be a ritual sacrifice or make a penal offering for sin, but because he adopted an ethical, socio-political and economic stance which was so unacceptable to both Jewish and Roman authorities that they had to kill him in order to silence him.

Where traditional atonement teaching has been that Jesus had to die in order to pay for the sin of the world; that his death was thus predicted by the Old Testament; and that therefore the social and circumstantial factors leading to his condemnation are not import-ant, Yoder emphasizes that Jesus died because of his social and political teaching and his commitment to the poor and disadvan-taged.

This is really the same point that we have noted in Moltmann,[20] and for that matter even in Rashdall[21], both of whom also showed us that in human terms Jesus died because his message was an unpopular one with Jewish and Roman authorities. Yoder makes two additional points. Not only did Jesus teach about and live out a kingdom of God in which concern for marginalized people would be emphasized, poor people loved, and rich people encouraged to share their wealth – which is likely already to be an unpopular message with those in power. He also taught that this kingdom was to be worked for without violence. In fact Yoder sees the temptation of Jesus in the wilderness and throughout his human life as being largely concerned with the temptation to become a violent crusader.

> The one temptation the man Jesus faced – and faced again and again – as a constitutive element of his public ministry, was the temptation to exercise social responsibility, in the interest of justified revolution, through the use of available violent methods.[22]

Thus Jesus condemned the *status quo* of his own time, and rejected the overthrowing of the *status quo* through violence.

> Because Jesus' particular way of rejecting the sword and at the same time condemning those who wielded it was politically relevant, both the Sanhedrin and the Procurator had to deny him the right to live.[23]

As a Mennonite, perhaps Yoder has a special axe to grind in the question of non-violence, and whether or not a just war or a just revolution theory can be held by the followers of Jesus could be debated. Nevertheless, whatever may be said about the larger issue of whether or not war and revolution are ever justified in a fallen world, it seems clear that with regard to the personal choices open to him, Jesus made no attempt to rouse any forces of resistance to protect himself in his hour of danger. He perceived his own call to be one of bearing faithful witness to the kingdom of God, to the need for caring for the outcast and the poor, and of accepting the consequences of that call, which is the probable rejection by the rulers of society. The passion narratives make clear that his persecutors were forgiven, and their violence and hatred were unable to turn either his obedience or his love.

Yoder's other additional point is that not only did Jesus accept this kind of cross, but that his disciples must do so too. We have learned to recognize that the emphasis in Mark's Gospel, echoed in Matthew, upon the disciples taking up their own cross,[24] is probably evidence that the first persecutions were looming on the horizon for Gentile Christians when Mark's Gospel was written. We have come to see that Luke's subtle change from 'taking up one's cross' to 'taking up one's cross *daily*' changes the original meaning of the *pericope*.[25] Yoder picks up this point with reference to Paul, who urges the disciples to 'suffer' for Christ.[26] There is no New Testament suggestion that we should imitate other aspects of Jesus' life: his occupation as a carpenter, his celibacy.

> Only at one point, only on one subject – but then consistently, universally – is Jesus our example: in his cross.[27]

And then:

> The believer's cross is no longer any and every kind of suffering, sickness or tension, the bearing of which is demanded. The believer's cross must be, like his Lord's, the price of his social non-conformity. It is not, like sickness or catastrophe, an inexplicable, unpredictable suffering; it is the end of a path freely chosen after counting the cost. It is not, like Luther's or Thomas Müntzer's or Zinzendorf's or Kierkegaard's was . . . an inward wrestling of the sensitive soul with self and sin; it is the social responsibility of representing in an unwilling world the order to come.[28]

Walter Wink has explicitly examined the situation in South Africa from the same point of view. He takes issue with Buti Tlhagale's argument that a just revolution can be justified on the same Christian grounds as a just war. Wink argues that Jesus encouraged the use of all sorts of ways of subverting and dispowering an oppressive regime as a constructive non-violent strategy, but never countenanced the use of violence.[29] In brief, Wink sets out to show that Jesus' method was to embarrass his opponents, or shame them into changing their approach, or use humour, while at the same time retaining a recognition of the humanness and of some latent good in his opponents.

> No one can show others the error that is within them . . . unless the others are convinced that their critic first sees and loves the good that is within them.[30]

I do not doubt that this remark is true. I think the Gospel picture of Jesus also fits with Wink's description of his 'third way'. But it is also sadly true that there are times when there seems to be *no* good within the enemy. As people said of Gandhi's methods; they worked against the British, but might not have against Stalin or Hitler! It is not proper for me as a sympathetic but privileged white person who does not suffer the brunt of apartheid to say to black people that they should see and love the good in their enemy. Nor does the South African government, or popular white opinion, see any good in the African National Congress and its like. Thus whatever truth there may be in Wink's approach, it is not a truth which white people can offer to suffering black people who are already at the mercy of a government which does not use polite tactics of humour, embarrassment or sharp and witty debate, but sends in security forces armed not with satire but machine guns, whips and pick handles.

The difficulties about a pacifist approach in the South African context are very clear. If it is true that Sipho's woes are largely caused by political structures, those political structures have to be changed. The African National Congress claims, with historical justification, that they have tried since the beginning of the century to change these structures through non-violent methods, without success. Many blacks, including Christians, feel therefore that there are no options left but violent revolution or guerrilla attacks. Many churches appear to agree with them, or at least to concede that violence in South Africa cannot be rejected out of hand.[31] If Yoder and Wink are right about Jesus' own stance – and I think it would be very difficult to refute that – is this not yet another instance of a New Testament perception which cannot work in our own time?

I fear that my own answer is a very Anglican 'both . . . and' one. I cannot comment on the question of whether at present the approach of revolutionary violence is strategically correct in South Africa. I also cannot deny that in principle there are times when war and revolution are the only options left. Thus revolution may be justified in South Africa, now or at some future point, and if justified, then Christians may have a duty at that time to engage in it. In a sense the fulfilment of that duty will be part of the establishment of God's kingdom – but only in a partial way. If the decision for a revolution were strategically correct, then the result after the revolution would be the creation of a different set of circumstances in which the kingdom of God, so long stifled, may begin to grow. Violence may remove certain obstacles, like a plough turning over the baked rocky soil. It cannot in itself establish the kingdom, any more than ploughing creates a garden. Violent revolution may push away some barriers. However, it will also create hatred, resentment and bitterness. Christians may as a last resort have to participate in violence; but that will not be their distinctively Christian contribution. It is the old story of living in both the old and new aeons at the same time.[32] Revolution may, tragically, be necessary. If the result of the revolution is not to be tragedy alone, then there will need to be a gospel, a good news, of forgiveness and peace, and in this the kingdom of God will begin to be planted.

Jesus seems to have befriended representatives from almost every group: tax collectors like Levi, Zealots like Simon, Pharisees like Nicodemus; working-class people, rich people like Joseph of Arimathea, Greeks like Philip, women like Mary and Martha. All seem to have united with him regardless of social status. This was no casual kindliness, since it cost him deeply in terms of popularity and acceptableness. Individuals counted for him. There seem to me no reasons to doubt the historicity of this picture. It is possible that the historical Jesus was not always so accepting; for instance we have commented on his recorded criticisms of the Pharisees. It is likely, though, that much of the anti-Pharisaic material has been expanded by the evangelists in the light of the early church's own battle with the Pharisaic party, especially after the fall of Jerusalem. Where Jesus' first human instinct may have been to reject some people in some circumstances, this was not his final or considered stance.

Jesus, then, is indeed the one who came bearing witness in his life that individuals matter, that the poor and marginalized matter most of all. He not only taught this of himself, but with the passionate conviction that this was what the kingdom of God meant, that this was the will and purpose of God. In loving his 'little ones',[33] Jesus believed that he was loving them for God. The poor, and indeed everybody, are not only loved after Jesus has died for them to pay for their sins. They not only have an importance in Jesus; they have an importance because God wills it so.

It might be argued that a doctrine of the incarnation of God in Jesus is a guarantee of the doctrine that the poor matter. We have noted the tendency in some liberation theology to say that as Jesus was poor, so God identifies himself with the poor. I would argue two things that count against it. It is not at all clear, in the New Testament, that Jesus was born literally poor. A carpenter's son was not necessarily poor, even then. It would appear that he voluntarily became poor in the sense of having no home,[34] but a peripatetic teacher although without fixed address is not necessarily poor either, and there is no suggestion that Jesus lacked food, clothing, or any of the basic needs to which Sipho's family cling so precariously.

Secondly, if the poor only become valued because Jesus has come to them, we are at least potentially back in the dangerous shoals of exclusivism. Jesus did not encounter and enrich all the poor in his own time. He is certainly unknown to many of the poor today, in Asia if not in South Africa. Jesus is important not because as God he came to the poor but because he announced that God already loves and is identified with the poor and marginalized.

And Jesus encouraged those who follow him to love the poor for his sake; indeed, he taught that any service done to the poor was service done to him. This idea finds its way into South African thinking not only through Matthew 25, but through a speech well known to the Catholic-minded wing of the Anglican church made by Frank Weston, then Bishop of Zanzibar, to the Anglo-Catholic Congress of 1923 after the battle for recognition for Catholic ceremonial in the Church of England had been won.

> You have your Mass, you have your altars, you have begun to get your tabernacles. Now go out into the highways and hedges, and look for Jesus in the ragged and the naked, in the oppressed and the sweated, in those who have lost hope, and in those who are struggling to make good. Look for Jesus in them: and when you have found him, gird yourself with his towel of fellowship and wash his feet in the person of his brethren.[35]

The speech is close enough to Tutu's approach for him to have quoted from it at length in his enthronement sermon as Archbishop of Cape Town in 1986. Surely, as black consciousness theologians have pointed out, here is a very powerful message indeed for Sipho, a message which has the potential to enable him to take pride in himself as a poor, black, rejected person who is not only worthy of God's love but who is to be loved as the 'substitute' for Jesus. As Tutu has said, this belief is one which arises out of our doctrine of creation. It does not need a Chalcedonian doctrine of incarnation to establish it.

> Jesus teaches me that God loves me: in his concern for individual, Jesus shows me that God loves individuals.[36]

This belief also does not need a doctrine of substitutionary atonement in which the poor are only loved because Jesus has died for their sins. Jesus is not a substitute for the sinner; rather, in this view, the poor and sinned-against are substitutes for Jesus, people to be loved in the here-and-now as an extension of the disciple's love for Jesus.

But surely, we may ask, this does not make Jesus unique? Are there not many who have taught the same doctrine? That may be so, although perhaps there are not many who have taught this unlearned from the Christian tradition. For most black African people of South Africa, who have already learned of Jesus, he is the significant one who teaches them this. Hypothetically they might have learned it from Tamil poets or Gandhi or a *bodhisattva*; in fact, it is the story of Jesus which is known to them and which in its power and drama can affect and change their self-perception.

This is not true of all black South Africans. Most Indian people and many people of Indonesian ancestry (the Cape 'Malays') have other significant figures who for them teach and exemplify the love of the poor and outcast. It might be possible in a comparative way to ask whether these figures exemplify this as well as Jesus; it seems more important to recognize that there are other teachers, other exemplifications of the love of God, rather than divide black people still further into unnecessary religious competition. The point i am making is that for most South Africans, black and white, Jesus is the figure who is known and revered, and to whom people most easily look for salvation.

In his chapter in *The Myth of God Incarnate*, Dennis Nineham raises an important worry about interpretations of the significance of Jesus along the lines I have been suggesting.[37] There is a tendency, he says, for those who no longer hold to an ontological uniqueness in Jesus, to suggest that he is morally unique: he quotes John Robinson as a typical example.

> It is in Jesus, and Jesus alone, that there is nothing of self to be seen, but solely the ultimate, unconditional love of God.[38]

Nineham reminds us that the historical grounds for making this claim for moral uniqueness are shaky.

I hope that I have made it clear that I am not claiming that Jesus was necessarily morally perfect in his life on earth, nor that he is unique in the degree of selflessness by which he lived. We cannot know that this was true of Jesus; we cannot know that it is not true of some other individual. I am claiming that we have sufficient historical grounds for saying that the story of Jesus points to new hope for humans.

Nineham asks:

> Is it necessary to 'believe in Jesus' in any sense beyond that which sees him as the main figure through whom God launched men into a relationship with himself so rich and fulfilling that, under various understandings and formulations of it, it has been, and

continues to be, the salvation of a large proportion of the human race.[39]

I am suggesting something parallel: that Jesus is the main figure (not the only one) in the culture and consciousness of very many black people in South Africa, through whom God can launch people into a relationship *with each other*. The story of Jesus has that power.

There are many in the world and in South Africa who are committed to justice without being Christian, and they should be honoured for that. It is hard, however, to be committed to 'justice' as a cause. One is committed to people. One works the more passionately for justice because one is indignant on behalf of individuals whom one knows or hears about, who suffer under injustice – or because one is inspired to follow the example of a significant other who has deeply impressed us. Because Jesus was who he was and because the story about him captures our imagination and excites our devotion, he becomes for many the focus for a commitment to abstractions like justice and love. In him they cease to be abstractions and become real and 'incarnated'. We may learn to love him as the personification of that which is impersonal, the incarnation and concretization of that which is abstract.

The story is all the more powerful because Jesus not only taught this love, but manifested it. This is of crucial importance. Jesus did not only teach as theory that individuals are worthy of love, but manifested it as fact. As Dorothee Sölle points out, he is not just a teacher in the Enlightenment sense of one who is 'a model of virtue and purveyor of knowledge'[40] but one who gives himself to those whom he teaches:

A teacher who does not give himself – in, with and under the facts that he conveys – is not a genuine teacher.[41]

He was not just a teacher of an impossible dreamy ideal, but one who to a remarkable degree must have incarnated it. We may allow for some evangelistic hyperbole and hagiography, but the impact of Jesus' life was sufficiently strong for the theme of love to dominate not only the Gospels but the Pauline and Johannine corpus. Yoder sums it up well.

Jesus was not just a moralist whose teaching had some political implications; he was not primarily a teacher of spirituality whose public ministry unfortunately was seen in a political light; he was not just a sacrificial lamb preparing for his immolation, or a God-

Man whose status calls us to disregard his humanity. Jesus was, in his divinely mandated (i.e. promised, anointed, messianic) prophethood, priesthood and kingship, the bearer of a new possibility of human, social and therefore political relationships.[42]

The point of this is surely not that as God Jesus shows us that he loves humans, but that as a human he shows us that a life of concern and love for others is possible. Sipho learns from Jesus not only that he is worthy of love, but that he is capable of love. A Chalcedonian incarnationalism weakens this witness considerably. If Jesus is different from us in kind, his example carries no potential hope for human nature.

If Jesus were not human it would cast into doubt the question whether other human beings could participate in the reign of God, which is the life of the Spirit, as Jesus did.[43]

It is true that Chalcedon said that Jesus was human, and it is true that it is possible, with ingenuity, to conceive of the divine-human Jesus having a genuinely human consciousness;[44] but for Chalcedon Jesus is not merely human. The Chalcedonian Jesus is *sui generis*, perhaps tempted liked us, but at base one who because he is different in kind from us cannot sin, cannot fail, since he is God. This Jesus does not convey the same sense of hope for human potential. But if he is not different from us in kind, if the difference is only one of degree, then his life does bear out real hope for us.

Luther distrusted the concept of *imitatio Christi* because, he held, such imitation was impossible for sinful human beings, and would encourage a gospel of salvation by works.[45] For different reasons Tom Driver, too, rather more recently expresses some reservations about the idea of imitating Jesus.[46] In some ways his warning is correct. Driver contends that to take the historical Jesus as our model is to fix upon a time- and culture-conditioned human person as an unchangeable ideal. We cannot imitate Jesus in his views about demons, or about an expected early second coming. Yoder has said that we do not imitate everything about Jesus. He is not a platen into whose features we must, Procrustean-like, be forced. In that sense Jesus is not an example. But in the sense that he shows human potential stretched towards the ideal, he is the bearer of new hope for us. He is the revelation for us. There may be other revelations in other societies, but he is the revelation for us and for Sipho of the new humanity. He is the one who teaches us and enables us to care about the rights of others. He enables by showing us that it is possible. In that sense, he is a model with whom we need to identify, whose vocation and destiny we need to reproduce.

> In the synoptic gospels we have a relatively small but important group of sayings about discipleship which in general stress the continuity of purpose, method and even lifestyle that is to obtain between Jesus and those whom he chooses to become his representatives (imitation is not the best word to describe what is really a reproduction in the disciple both of the destiny and also the moral character of his Master).[47]

Here Colin Hickling is suggesting something very close to the heart of what I believe salvation in Jesus really means. It is not rescue from the powers of evil, or rescue from our economic plight or our poverty, though it is true that all of these things may prevent us from being saved. Salvation is essentially to be 'in Christ'; it is the reproduction of the character of Jesus in his disciples.

> This, in the fundamental language of human personality develop-ment, is what salvation means. It is both a more exact and a more demanding conception than the one implied in the irreducibly mythological and dualistic conceptuality of deliverance from the present dominion, and ultimate overthrow, of the powers of evil.[48]

For Hickling, this is not just a matter of each individual following Jesus' example, though the conscious effort of the disciple to model his or her life on that of Jesus is part of it. Hickling also believes that membership of the church, sharing in liturgy and sacraments, being part of the interrelatedness of Christians to each other, is part and parcel of the development process whereby each individual is moulded into the pattern of Jesus.

But the process is aimed at each individual Christian. This is a different emphasis from that in much liberation theology, which tends to stress the poor as a group and Jesus' identification with the group. In the view I am describing, social issues and responsibilities and the structural nature of oppression are taken just as seriously, but the starting point for salvation is not the group to be rescued by God or by inevitable economic processes but the individual who, becoming more and more 'in Christ', becomes at the same time more and more socially committed. He or she takes on Jesus' burden for the poor, and does so in love of Jesus and in Jesus' name in love of the poor, not in order to achieve self-liberation but to

work for the social liberation of others. Yet in that very commitment such individuals are also liberated or saved themselves.
Liberation, then, is not only setting free the poor from their bonds,
but setting free the disciple from self-denigration, poverty, helplessness and indifference. Individual liberation is really where it all
begins. This fits, I suggest, with the Gospel story of Jesus, whose
parabolic way of teaching is one which challenges individuals to
come off the fence and make a commitment.

But does it fit with the case of Sipho? I have argued all along that
the sufferings which Sipho endures render him incapable of
achieving his potential – yet apparently liberation means to live up
to one's heroic potential even in circumstances of oppression and
adversity.

This is a real problem. My argument that his situation means that
much traditional language about salvation simply does not fit his
case until his situation has improved to the point of being able to
take some responsibility for himself was an argument intended to
show that salvation from guilt and wrath and the consequences of
Sipho's sin were not appropriate; but it seems to rule out this
exemplarist approach as well.

In a sense I think that this is so. There may be some shining
exceptions, but most 'Siphos' in this world will not be able to
respond to and follow the example and call of Jesus until their
situation of degradation is ameliorated. Therefore those who are
less weighted down than Sipho are responsible for making Sipho's
salvation possible, too. Salvation begins with individuals, but those
individuals make it possible for other individuals also to be saved –
by working with them and working on their behalf to improve their
lot. We live in interdependence upon one another. I am saved, I find
meaning and purpose in my life, I enter the kingdom of God, when
I begin to work for the salvation of others. They are saved by
my efforts, I through theirs. Jesus is the catalyst for this process to
begin.

As we seek to follow the example of Jesus, we need to remember
that the example leads to the cross. There is no guarantee that the
work of the committed individual for the deliverance of the poor
will be successful. At this point I part company again with at least
some of the voices in liberation and black theology. There is no
certain victory for the poor in the short term. All that is certain is
that the individual who follows Jesus can, like him, refuse to be
cowed into inaction and silence. Whether the fight of committed
individuals for the sake of the poor is a successful fight is another

and uncertain matter. David Nicholls warns of an over-optimistic incarnationalism. He quotes Henry Scott Holland as an example of the sort of liberal who believes that the Kingdom of God's 'gradual conquest of the world would be marked by the line of its visible success. Step by step it would press that line forward'.[49] The reality is not like that. There is no guarantee that the path of discipleship will lead to victory for the victims in society. Yoder refers us to the Pauline teaching about modelling ourselves on Christ. In baptism, says Paul, the Christian takes on what is *essentially* relevant about the imitation of Christ; that is, to share in the concerns, the priorities and especially the sufferings of Jesus.

This model of christology is not within the sort of liberal category which says that provided people are pointed in the right direction with an adequate education and income, all will be well. It is impossible to be that sort of liberal in South Africa. Education, money and power have not stopped the white minority from being suicidally blind and selfish, nor is there any guarantee that a free black society will be very different.

In a world in which God does not directly intervene, in a world in which we make our own salvation with the help of God, there can be no certain outcome. A life lived for the kingdom of God will often meet with resistance, and there is no guarantee that the faithful servant will not be prevented from accomplishing his or her goals. This seems to me to raise the issue of duty. We are called, by the example of Jesus, to be concerned about the needs of others, to love them. If we only heed that call when there is reasonable certainty that we will be understood, that our caring outreach will be respected, that our efforts will be successful, we are unlikely ever to begin. I do not think that Jesus had that certainty.

I have in mind the Jesus as portrayed in Mark's Gospel, who after beginning his ministry of teaching and healing in Galilee found that the authorities opposed him. He realized, and in the three great prophecies of his coming passion[50] warned his disciples, that 'the Son of Man was destined to suffer grievously'. He set his face to go to meet that destiny in Jerusalem. He continued to teach his message in the face of official hostility. He sought to live out his life of obedience to his calling, regardless of the consequences.

The details in the Markan prophecies, the very exact foretelling of the events of his passion and of his resurrection, are surely evangelistic additions made with hindsight. A truly human Jesus would not have *known* for certain what would happen to him, or even that he would rise again. What he must have known, from the growing evidence around him, was that his chosen course would lead him into danger and possible death. What he must have believed was that nevertheless this was the path to which the Father called him and in which the Father would sustain him. So he set his face to Jerusalem and did his duty.

That last phrase recalls what many will think is a dead-end Kantianism. There are many difficulties associated with Kant's 'moral imperative', but there are several aspects of Kant's teaching on duty which seem to be relevant in our situation as well as being consistent with the life and example of Jesus. Kant recognized that to do one's duty is neither easy nor automatic. It involves overcoming the 'sensual' – for our purposes we might say the 'selfish' – part of our nature. We choose a path of duty auto-nomously, i.e. not because anyone forces us to or because it is easy or instinctive but because reason tells us that this choice is right.

The chosen action will not necessarily be effective or useful. The virtue of a right action, for Kant, does not depend on its results but on whether it is in accordance with the 'categorical imperative', with what our rational conscience tells us is right. Duty for Kant is unconditional. We do it regardless of conditioning factors. The moral worth of an action depends not on its results but on its intentions.

This has some considerable relevance to our situation and to a praxis-orientated soteriology. Liberation of the oppressed is surely a categorical imperative, i.e. right for all people at all times. Love of others is a categorical imperative. Regardless of the admitted difficulties in identifying the categorical imperative in Kant's own work, these duties stand out clearly from scripture, from the life of Jesus, and from our experience of oppression around us. Thus I choose to commit myself to love and liberation on the basis of reason enlightened by the biblical witness. It is easy to show that the example and teaching of Jesus is a major inspirational and motivational factor in this choice. Thus Jesus is of soteriological significance.

However, I follow Kant in this matter and commit myself to the cause of liberation because I think it is right, not because I am necessarily confident of success. I cannot be confident of victory, except that in the very long term God's purposes must prevail. Perhaps there will never be a just society in South Africa. But if one were possible, it would be right. Jesus did not establish a just society or a loving world. In that respect he was not victorious. But he committed himself without reservation to the struggle for justice and love; and the only victory he guarantees is that if we trust in God and follow Jesus we will be enabled to commit ourselves to that struggle too.

O. C. Quick would have disagreed. He condemned this point of view (which he associates with Stoicism) on the grounds that

> It is impossible for a man to sacrifice himself wholly in a great cause unless he believes that the sacrifice will not be in vain . . . In giving his life as a ransom for many, Jesus believed that God would provide that the life so given would not be thrown away.[51]

If God would not 'throw away' the life of Jesus without some tangible result following, then he seems to have been ready to throw away the lives of many subsequent martyrs. Many black lives have been thrown away, many children have died of malnutrition, many people have been killed in township fighting, and most of them have by now been forgotten. Perhaps cumulatively their deaths may result in change, but that is not obvious yet. All we are left with is the conviction that people should risk their lives in the struggle for justice if only for their own integrity, the hope that others may follow their example, and the conviction that this is what life is all about.

Here we pick up again on the theme of sacrifice, in neither a propitiatory nor an expiatory sense but as the likely cost of duty. There is a principle or ideal of sacrifice in human life, in obediently following along the road of duty, which sustains us and which Jesus personifies. To quote Sobrino:

> The content of this faith . . . is instead of a victorious struggle against the conflicts to be found in real life experience. So faith becomes fidelity, not an idealistic fidelity but a fidelity lived in and through suffering.[52]

I have said that the model I am building of salvation in Jesus is not meant to be Pelagian, or even semi-Pelagian, although my remarks about our having to save ourselves may already have incriminated me. I do not suggest that even our initial steps towards salvation are taken without the grace of God, which is what Pelagianism really means. I am suggesting that Jesus, revealing to us the potential of the new humanity, does so precisely because he was open to the grace of God to an unprecedented degree.

Paul Newman argues, as I do, that our present context and experience make it necessary to have a 'paradigm shift' (to use Kuhn's overworked phrase) in our christological model, and offers instead of the Chalcedonian two-nature model one which sees Jesus filled with God's Spirit. He outlines what he regards as the activities of the Spirit of God in the world.[53] Much like John Taylor,[54] whose work he summarizes, Newman's understanding of the Spirit of God is as a power operating in the world enabling created things to be fully themselves, urging creatures to higher consciousness, creating occasions for responsible choice, calling forth a willingness to sacrifice self, releasing springs of creativity. He sees the work of the Spirit as analagous to Einstein's energy, or as a sort of organizing pattern implanted in the world to bring order out of chaos.

In fact, as he remarks, his concept of Spirit is not very different from the concept of Logos in neo-Platonism and in early Christianity. One might ask, therefore, whether his christological model is really very different from the Chalcedonian one, merely replacing Logos with Spirit. But in neo-Platonism the Logos was obviously not seen as confined to Jesus. The Logos is God's immanence in all creation. The *logos endiathetos* and *logos prophorikos* (the word immanent and the word spread forth) were seen to work in all creation, but since the emphasis was on reason and understanding, the Logos was especially present to the human mind. This is a doctrine of panentheism, not of incarnation.

Thus although Newman doesn't say so, he is perhaps going back behind the roots of Chalcedon to use the Logos concept in a different way, with less emphasis on reason than on energy and creativity; and in this model Jesus is not 'the Logos' but is filled with the Logos or, in Newman's preferred terminology, filled with the Spirit. In his human life Jesus exemplified all of the qualities which the Spirit of God, working in humans, makes possible.

Newman takes the scriptural record of Jesus' life very seriously, and like Yoder believes that with the aid of modern scholarship a sufficient picture of the historical Jesus can be built up to say with some certainty that Jesus exemplifies the work and power of the Spirit in a unique and special way. By the power of the Spirit, Jesus lived the kingdom of God; he embodied it in his own person. To quote Yoder on the same point; in Jesus, '. . . we find an utterly precise and practical instruction, practicable because in him the kingdom has actually come within reach. In him the sovereignty of Jahweh has become human history'.[55] Jesus allowed God to reign in his life, so that in his life the will and purpose of God were made manifest. Because he was obedient to God, he lived out God's love for the poor. The kingdom comes within reach, as Yoder says, not because God intervenes directly, but because Jesus came among us to speak and act on God's behalf, proclaiming the kingdom and inviting us to live according to kingdom ethics.

But in all of this the Spirit is present in Jesus in no different a way from that in which the Spirit is present in us, except in the degree of Jesus' openness and obedience. Jesus reveals what human life, once truly open to the Spirit, can be. This is his saving significance. Thus our picture of human life is changed by Jesus. Our deep pessimism about human potential is lifted, for here was a man who was faithful. Jesus restores hope for humankind. He gives the lie to those, like the South African government, who believe that it is impossible for humans to love across racial boundaries. Where apartheid assumes the worst of humans,[56] and assumes that human selfishness and xenophobia is so great and so intractable that races must be kept apart, Jesus shows us a different kind of humanity.

To say this is, of course, to side with theological liberalism. But the alternative, to say that humans are inherently and predominantly evil unless specifically redeemed in an objective, transactional, almost mechanical way by redemption in Jesus, must mean that actually apartheid is correct. Inherently evil humans must indeed be kept apart like dangerous beasts in separate cages. Provided we see Jesus as human and not as a God-man, he shows us that humans are not necessarily and inherently evil. This is not to deny human sinfulness: it is to argue that Jesus shows us that one who is 'engraced' by God can overcome the conditioning of generations within society. The grace of God can enable us to change. Jesus is the evidence that this is so. He is Saviour, not because in his death a transaction is made between God and himself as a once-for-all sacrifice for sin, but because he enables us to live in the power of the Spirit. He does this, in Newman's view, in four ways.[57] He calls us to return to obedience to God; that is, to conversion. He calls us to continue to grow in the Spirit after conversion, since growth into a Christian life-style is not a sudden thing. He speaks prophetically or judgingly to the authorities reigning in his own time, recalling them to their proper function in obedience to God. He affirms that social structures, law and human wisdom have to be renewed, not destroyed.

To reinterpret this slightly to fit the situation of Sipho, Jesus calls Sipho to recognize that he is welcomed into God's kingdom but also called to obedience to carry out the purposes of God in his life and that of his people. Thus Jesus *teaches* Sipho. Jesus gives evidence in his own life that living in the power of God's Spirit is possible, and thus *encourages* Sipho to do the same. Jesus challenges those at present in authority over Sipho, who in this case are themselves Christian, at least in intention. This will not always be the case in every situation of oppression. In Sipho's circumstances it means that the disciples of Jesus who now wield unjust power over Sipho may be challenged and brought to repentance by Jesus. There are in fact glimmerings of hope that the Dutch Reformed Churches may yet fulfil the role of rebuking and recalling to proper obedience the secular powers who are members of these churches. Thus Jesus *supports* Sipho. Jesus affirms to Sipho and his peers that what is required for his kingdom to prevail is not anarchical destruction but the building of a new and better social structure.

All of this is very important for Sipho. In the new South Africa there will need to be authority, and social structure, and restraining forces of law and order. Jesus does not call for the destruction of the 'powers'. We have learned from Paul that the 'powers' and 'authorities' have a proper place within God's purposes. They do not need to be destroyed but to be called back to a proper obedience to God's purposes.

However, a consequence of such a view is that Jesus' relevance to Sipho is a reaching out from the past. If we think that Jesus saves because he died for our sins, then since the sacrifice on the cross was sufficient for all time, it has as much effect now as when the human Jesus went to the cross. If, however, we think that Jesus saves by being a teacher and, more important, a model, a revelation that a fully humanized life is possible, then the problem that he did this in another time and in very different circumstances is more acute. His example and encouragement become potentially less relevant. Newman is quite honest about this.

> The risen and ascended Jesus is no longer himself an active agent in human history except inasmuch as God as Spirit continues to encounter people in and through the remembrance of Jesus.[58]

At this point the doctrine of the church becomes very important. Black working-class and rural peasant Christians do not, for the most part, have access to Jesus primarily through reading the scriptures, let alone through following scholarly research and criticism. They hear about Jesus in sermons; they meet Jesus in the church. For many people the church is the most important social community to which they belong. In the church and the church alone they may sometimes (not always, alas) find recognition of themselves as individuals and persons who matter and who belong. A new twist is given to Cyril's *extra ecclesiam nulla salus*. In the church, or the Thursday afternoon church womens' group,[59] they will be prayed for in their troubles. The church is where they come to express their needs, and even their anger against the oppressor. Since these people have little access to other large buildings, church buildings often serve as focal points for community meetings to express grievances, or show solidarity. But in theory any organization with wide community membership and with buildings in which to meet could fulfil these more practical needs. If we are asking if and how Jesus saves, there must be some way in which we locate him in the church.

Tom Driver describes Christ as a 'presence within the ritual community'[60] and even goes so far in one place as to say that Christ is only to be found in the eucharistic ritual community.[61] Driver is certainly not speaking of a 'real presence' in the bread and wine, though I would argue that in fact the bread and wine do become the effective symbols for what Driver is talking about. But he means that as I develop a relationship with those with whom I break bread in the eucharist, so I find Christ. Christ is, for Driver, the expression of a *communitas*, the human form of the encounter between God and the world, and is not confined to the historical person of Jesus. In the church the sense of *communitas* can potentially be experienced; and having experienced *communitas* in the church, I will feel more painfully the lack of community in society. Thus conscience and the urge to change the evil *status quo* is born.

This depends, of course, on whether *communitas* is built up in the church. Newman says that one of the gifts of the Spirit of God is to create an 'ethos', a vocational principle operating not just in an individual but in a whole community, and that part of the evidence that Jesus is indeed saviour is that the encounter with Jesus did create amongst his disciples the ethos of a community committed to living out the kingdom of God in the world.[62]

Sipho lives in a community where normal community links and values have largely broken down. There can only be hope for Sipho if a new community is raised up. The church cannot be the whole community; if the church and the nation, or the church and the class, become the same thing, then the church has become 'Christendom'. Such a church has become identified with the secular and imperfect community and can no longer bear witness to anything beyond. (This is a strange irony that liberation theologians do not always appear to appreciate. In their attempts to separate the church from Christendom and associate it with the poor, they need to be careful that they are not recreating a new Christendom.) But the church, as a community within the community, can bear witness to the real values of what Driver has called *communitas*, and can be a means whereby human values within the secular community can be rebuilt.[63] I fear that since no other institution within the black community is able to encompass all groups and all classes and all tribes and different ideologies within it, if the church fails to do this then Sipho cannot be helped.

> The Church must be a sample of the kind of humanity within which e.g. economic and racial differences are surmounted. Only then will she have anything to say to the society which surrounds her about how these differences must be dealt with. Otherwise her preaching to the world a standard of reconciliation which is not her own experience will be neither honest nor effective.[64]

Jesus, I believe, can be a Saviour for Sipho; can offer what no other person in Sipho's context can offer. Jesus shows that God cares for Sipho, with all the poor and rejected and humiliated 'little people' of the world. He also shows that the potential is there for Sipho not to be a 'little person' any more, but to grow in openness to the empowering Spirit of God within him. He serves as teacher, as model, as example, as encourager in a more powerful, more complete and more radical way than any one else for Sipho. He has already served that function for many black heroes in the South African situation. Jesus is not just a simple 'hero' in human history; he is the catalyst for many who have followed after and lived following his pattern. There is no guarantee that the battle will be won in the short term. There is, however, a promise that like those other black heroes, individuals can rise above the situation to protest and to refuse to be rubbish. Yet if that witness is to continue, it will depend upon the church, or at least upon some within the church (since, being part of this world, the church as an institution must often fail) to continue to give living witness to the truth of these promises.

There is a painful ambivalence about the reality of the witness of the church. Potentially, because the church is so central an institution in black life, it can keep alive the saving work of Jesus. In fact it has in part done so, and the list of heroes past and present in the struggle bears witness to that. And in part – since the church has contributed to the development of apartheid – it has failed. I do not think we can get out of this ambivalence by saying that only the 'church of the poor' is the true church, or using some such device. The church is composed of sinful, fallible human beings. The

Afrikaans churches have been churches of the poor in their time, and became churches of the oppressors. The English churches have had their share in oppressive colonial administration. The black churches will no doubt face their own temptations in years to come. A faithless church does render the actual relevance of Jesus to Sipho of less account. It is very serious that this should be so, but it is obviously true.

A salvation which is entrusted to human hands will never be certain, or final. The salvation which is offered to Sipho in Jesus is true salvation, and yet is not final or complete or even sure. He, or others, may not grasp it. Jesus is, in Driver's words, 'a party to ethical development, not its norm or its completion'.[65] There is a provisional quality to the salvation which Jesus brings, precisely because the church, and we ourselves, may not choose to live in its light. Yet I hope that we can see that Jesus does meet the needs which I suggested earlier were paramount for Sipho and for others like him. Jesus is Saviour.

We should emphasize at this point that he is Saviour because he acts with the Spirit's power. That is, we could and should say that *God* is Saviour. Jesus' concern for the poor arises from his conviction that *God* is concerned for the poor, and his words and deeds showing and offering salvation to the poor are words and deeds which express the loving purposes of *God*. God alone saves us, and yet Jesus saves us and in turn we save ourselves because of what Jesus has done for us.

The salvation which we are offered is, then, not a salvation from our poverty and political weakness, but a salvation from helplessness and impotence in the face of poverty and political weakness.

Salvation – frequently and even characteristically – is not deliverance from alien constrictions making ultimately for death, but the redemption of the constrictions themselves.[66]

We return here to the idea of sacrifice and representation. Certainly the life and death of Jesus is a sacrifice, and a representative sacrifice at that – not as 'one, perfect, sufficient sacrifice and atonement for sin': I have suggested that this kind of atoning sacrifice is unnecessary and untenable – but in the way that the Gospels record him as speaking of his own death: 'Greater love has no man than this, that a man lay down his life for his friends.'[67] Jesus is not a substitute for us, for we will have to follow in his steps. But because he was for us the new human, the 'man for others', the pioneer of first fruits of our salvation, we can truly say that he lived and died for us, on our behalf, representing both the purposes of God and the potential of humankind.

Frances Young comments that the imagery of sacrifice permeates the New Testament and the early church.[68] She describes the various concepts of sacrifice found in the Old Testament and in the Graeco–Roman world. Since Jesus died in the way he did, some sacrificial interpretation of that death was inevitable. Young does not propose to try to go back to the early church or the pre-Christian concepts of sacrifice but believes nevertheless that the world of modern literature – she refers to Steinbeck's *To a God Unknown* and to Golding's *Lord of the Flies* – shows that there is still an atavistic awareness of the need for sacrifice.

This is surely true in South Africa. The dead heroes of the struggle are remembered in much the same way as martyrs in the early church. Their deaths are not only a matter of mourning and sadness but have considerable energizing power for those who come after. Tertullian's phrase about the blood of the martyrs being the seed of the church is just as true of the struggle now as it was then of the early church.

Buthelezi's comments quoted earlier about the power of Good Friday for black people refer to the way in which Jesus' offering of himself is thus more than a model to be followed. It is a sort of catalytic action, a sacrifice which triggers off then and now a change in the balance of things.

Is this a sufficiently coherent account of how Jesus saves? Does it fit the facts that we have, both about the historical Jesus and about our own circumstances? Does it provide a sufficiently weighty account of salvation to be worth bothering with? I think so. I suspect that in fact it is the model which most black Christians in South Africa follow explicitly anyway. Jesus is a most significant key – for many, *the* most significant key – for change and for new life in their situation.

Yet in this model it is not necessary that Jesus be ontologically divine. In fact a Chalcedonian Christology would weaken this account of the work of Jesus. To return to our questions from the earlier part of the book, therefore, we do not need to be burdened with the mystery of how Jesus can be understood as fully God and fully human. The account of Jesus which sees him to be human and not divine except in the sense of being filled with the Spirit of God to a very special degree is not only easier to understand and believe in, but also provides a more useful model of salvation in a situation of oppression. It seems a better christology. In another age, in other circumstances, this might no longer be the case, and our paradigm will need to shift yet again. Jesus is indeed saviour; yet our understanding of how he saves will never be final and complete.

It is therefore entirely appropriate that the traditional formulae, e.g. of the Nicene Creed and of the substitutionary language of much Christian liturgy, etc., be preserved and used still. It is not at present helpful to understand the formulae in a literal way, but their use reminds us of past models and paradigms and that our own understanding is ephemeral and linked to our own circumstances. Don Cupitt suggests that ordinary Christians, i.e. those without formal theological training, do in fact demythologize the language of the Prayer Books all the time and find no great difficulty in doing so.[69] The classic images and phrases and vocabulary of Christianity need to be preserved as part of our awareness of and dialogue with the past. The meaning we place upon them, however, needs to be one which is of current and pragmatic significance to us now.

A final issue: does perhaps the model pander to the lowest common denominator of rationalistic conscience, making the faith easier to swallow for university-educated agnostics, but emotionally unsatisfying and thin, offering only grim duty?

I am not so sure that duty has to be grim. Richard Holloway, in an address to the Australian Catholic Renewal Conference, recounted evocatively his own youthful desire to give himself utterly and heroically to God: evocatively because it paralleled so closely my own dreams and hopes. I suspect that these are dreams and longings which many young people have had, and which have had to be tempered, like Holloway's and my own, with the somewhat more ordinary and fallible grind of daily experience.

But the dream and the longing do not disappear. Holloway describes some of the heroic Anglo-Catholic slum priests. To those whom he mentions each of us will have our own favourites to add. I quote him at some length.

These men were known in their generation, yet there were countless others who were not, yet who laboured just as well, just as heroically . . . And what can we learn from all this? Well, I speak mainly for myself in what I want to say in conclusion. I am more and more troubled by the gap between our Christian profession of belief and the actual reality of our lives. The Christian faith is about sacrifice and loss and heroism. It is about a God who loved the world so much that he gave his only-begotten son, and that act of self-emptying has always been the hallmark of authentic Christianity. We see it especially in the great call to the monastic life, with its great counsels of poverty, celibacy and obedience. We see it when men and women are led to offer themselves in service to the poor of the world. And we see it in the quieter heroism that characterizes the ordinary life lived for God. I may be wrong, but I do not see much of that heroism or self-abandonment in today's Church . . . it is a truly horrifying thing that we have done. We have taken the vast and wintry summons of God, the great organ note of self-abandonment that sounds through the Bible, and we have put it on tape, and we let it play through our stereo system while we get on with our own little tasks about the house. The Lord has roared from Zion, and we are content because we got it on a cassette.[70]

I have obviously taken a different line on incarnation from that of Richard Holloway. But the person of Jesus who gives himself to the Father and the Father's poor with such abandonment and whole-heartedness is surely as powerfully attractive to us as it was to those who knew him in the flesh. The call to 'duty' is no dry, dull, desiccated call, but one filled with passion and romance. It is God's call. Like Holloway's 'grand organ note' it reverberates through creation, it resonates in our very being. Answering it we become more fully alive, more fully ourselves. In this model, Jesus is still a person to live for, to die for, he is still the central vision of our lives.

Notes

Introduction

1. John Hick (ed), *The Myth of God Incarnate*, SCM Press and Westminster Press 1977.

2. Thomas F. Torrance, *The School of Faith*, James Clarke 1959, p. 263.

3. See below p. 59ff.

4. John Sobrino, *Christology at the Crossroads*, Orbis Books and SCM Press 1978, p. 19.

5. Edward Schillebeeckx, *Christ; the Christian Experience in the Modern World*, SCM Press and Crossroad Publishing Company 1980, p. 63.

6. Ibid., p. 76.

7. Ibid., p. 65.

8. Ibid., p. 29.

9. Alan Paton, who coined the phrase with the title to his novel, believed in this hope until his death in 1988.

I Jesus Human and Divine

1. G. Bray, 'Can We Dispense with Chalcedon?' *Themelios* 3.2, January 1978. p. 2.

2. C. F. D. Moule, *The Origin of Christology*, Cambridge University Press 1977.

3. M. Green, *The Truth of God Incarnate*, Hodder & Stoughton 1977, p. 17.

4. John 10.30.

5. Moule, *Origin* (n. 2), pp. 136ff.

6. J. L. Houlden, *Connections*, SCM Press 1986, p. 100.

7. G. Kittel & G. Friedrich, abridged G. Bromiley, *Theological Dictionary of the New Testament*, Eerdmans 1985, p. 763.

8. Matthew 14.33.

9. C. S. Lewis, *Christian Reflections*, Collins 1981, p. 157.

10. E. L. Mascall, *The Secularization of Christianity*, Darton, Longman & Todd 1965, p. 226; *Theology and the Gospel of Christ*, SPCK 1977, p. 70.

11. D. Cupitt, *The Debate about Christ*, SCM Press 1979, p. 72.

12. A. M. Farrer, in H. W. Bartsch, *Kerygma and Myth*, SPCK 1953, p. 220.

13. Moule, *Origin* (n. 2), p. 6.

14. Ibid., p. 7.

15. J. D. G. Dunn, *Unity and Diversity in the New Testament*, SCM Press and Trinity Press International ²1989, p. 263.

16. Ibid., p. 307.

17. J. D. G. Dunn, *Christology in the Making*, SCM Press and Westminster Press 1980, p. 266.

18. J. L. Houlden, *Patterns of Faith*, SCM Press 1977, p. 7.

19. Houlden, *Connections* (n. 6), p. 39.

20. Ibid., p. 44.

21. Edward Schillebeeckx, *Jesus*, Crossroad Publishing Company and Collins 1979; *Christ*, SCM Press and Crossroad Publishing Company 1980.

22. Schillebeeckx, *Jesus* (n. 21), p. 21.

23. Ibid., p. 54.

24. Ibid., p. 387.

25. Ibid., p. 56.

26. Ibid., p. 406–440.

27. Ibid., p. 62.

28. W. Pannenberg, *Basic Questions in Theology* 1, SCM Press and Westminster Press 1970, p. 8.

29. W. Pannenberg, 'Did Jesus Really Rise from the Dead?', *Dialog* 4, 1965, p. 135.

30. P. Lapide, *The Resurrection of Jesus*, Augsburg Publishing House 1983, pp. 127, 128.

31. Ibid., p. 152.

32. P. Hinchliff in A. E. Harvey, *God Incarnate* SPCK 1981, p. 92.

33. F. Watson, in '"Historical Evidence" and the Resurrection of Jesus', *Theology* XC, no. 737, September 1987, pp. 365ff.

34. Schillebeeckx, *Jesus* (n. 21), p. 641.

35. Watson, '"Historical Evidence"' (n. 33), p. 372.

36. It is true that many, from the Chalcedonians on, have perceived other reasons for believing in the Trinity apart from the need to make sense of believing in a divine Jesus without being polytheistic.

37. Schillbeeckx, *Jesus* (n. 21), p. 564.

38. Athanasius, ed. R. W. Thomson, *de Incarnatione* Oxford University Press 1971.

39. Ibid., p. 183.

40. Ibid., p. 259.

41. Ibid., p. 263.

42. Ibid., p. 265.

43. A. Grillmeier, *Christ in Christian Tradition* 1, Mowbray ^{2}1975, p. 315.

44. Ibid., p. 311.

45. C. Brown, *That You May Believe*, Eerdmans 1985, p. 109.

46. M. F. Wiles, *Working Papers in Doctrine*, SCM Press 1976, p. 119.

47. Plato, *The Dialogue of Plato* 1, Random House 1892, Phaedo 103–105.

48. Anselm, 'Cur Deus Homo?', in E. R. Fairweather (ed.), *A Scholastic Miscellany: Anselm to Ockham*, Library of Christian Classics, SCM Press and Westminster Press 1956.

49. Grillmeier, *Christ in Christian Tradition* (n. 43), p. 308.

50. J. S. Macarthur, *Chalcedon*, SPCK 1931, p. 141.

51. K. Rahner, *Theological Investigations* 1, Darton, Longman & Todd 1961, p. 149.

52. E. L. Mascall, *Whatever Happened to the Human Mind?*, SPCK 1980, p. 28.

53. K. Runia, *The Present-Day Christological Debate*, IVP 1984, p. 103.

54. Wiles, *Working Papers* (n. 46), p. 99.

55. J. Macquarrie, *Principles of Christian Theology*, SCM Press and Scribners 1966, pp. 4ff.

56. Ibid., p. 17.

57. In Harvey, *God Incarnate* (n. 32).

58. Wiles, *Working Papers* (n. 46), pp. 17ff.

59. S. R. Sutherland, *God, Jesus and Belief*, Blackwell 1984, p. 5.

60. Schillebeeckx, *Jesus* (n. 21) p. 578.

61. B. L. Hebblethwaite, *The Incarnation*, Cambridge University Press 1987, p. 130.

62. Ibid., p. 25.

63. Ibid., p. 28.

64. A. McGrath, *The Enigma of the Cross*, Hodder & Stoughton 1987, p. 70.

65. Hebblethwaite, *Incarnation* (n. 61), p. 48.

66. Ibid.

67. Mascall, *Theology and the Gospel of Christ* (n. 10), pp. 151ff.

68. See below, p. 244.

69. E.g. in 'Is Belief in God Rational?' in C. F. Delaney, *Rationality and Religious Belief*, University of Notre Dame Press 1979.

70. A seventeenth-century Archbishop of Armagh famous for his dating of the creation at 6000 years ago.

71. B. L. Hebblethwaite, *The Problems of Theology*, Cambridge University Press 1980, p. 12.

72. M. F. Wiles, 'Does Christology Rest on a Mistake?', In S. W. Sykes & J. P.Clayton, *Christ, Faith and History*, Cambridge University Press 1972.

73. J. N. D. Kelly, *Early Christian Doctrines*, A. & C. Black [2]1960, p. 171.

74. G. O'Collins, *Interpreting Jesus*, Geoffrey Chapman 1983, p. 184.

75. 'Kenosis' means 'emptying' (from Phil. 2.7): Jesus 'emptied himself, taking the form of a slave'.

76. E. Brunner, *The Mediator*, Lutterworth Press 1934, p. 352.

77. Mascall, *Theology and the Gospel of Christ* (n. 10), p. 135.

78. Hebblethwaite, *Incarnation* (n. 61), p. 22.

79. Ibid., p. 67.

80. Ibid., p. 3.

81. Ibid., p. 65.

82. Ibid., p. 75.

83. Ibid., p. 68.

84. Ibid., p. 8.

85. T. V. Morris, *The Logic of God Incarnate*, Cornell University Press 1986, p. 94.

86. E.g. Matthew 23.

87. G. Vermes, *Jesus the Jew*, Fontana Books 1973, p. 36.

88. Mark 7.26–40.

89. Luke 2.46–50.

90. John 2.4.

91. S. W. Sykes, in Sykes & Clayton, *Christ, Faith and History* (n. 72), pp. 65, 66.

92. Mascall, *Theology and the Gospel of Christ* (n. 10), p. 133.

93. Hebblethwaite, *Incarnation* (n. 61), p. 63.

94. Schillebeeckx, *Jesus* (n. 21), p. 59.

95. Cupitt, *Debate* (n. 11), p. 37.

96. Morris, *Logic of God Incarnate* (n. 85).

97. P. & L. Badham, *Immortality or Extinction?*, Macmillan 1982, p. 57. I think that in fact Morris has isolated a relatively minor emphasis in the Badhams' book.

98. See below, p. 62.

99. Hebrews 4.15.

100. Hebrews 5.8, 9.

101. See below, p. 63.

102. Sutherland, *God, Jesus and Belief* (n. 59), p. 16.

103. Rosemary Radford Ruether, *Faith and Fratricide*, Seabury Press 1974.

104. H. Maccoby, in R. L. Brahan, *The Origins of the Holocaust*, Boulder: Social science monographs and Institute for Holocaust studies of the City University of New York 1986, p. 5.

105. Romans 1.21.

106. K. Rahner, In J. Hick & B. L. Hebblethwaite, *Christianity and Other Religions*, Collins 1980, pp. 52ff.

107. Ibid., p. 71.

108. Hebblethwaite, *Incarnation* (n. 61), p. 160.

109. See below, p. 123.

110. Moule, *Origin of Christology* (n. 2).

111. W. Cantwell Smith, *Towards a World Theology*, Macmillan 1981.

112. A. M. Farrer, *Love Almighty and Ills Unlimited*, Collins 1962, p. 129.

113. Morris, *Logic of God Incarnate* (n. 85), p. 170.

114. Alan Richardson (ed.), *A Dictionary of Christian Theology*, SCM Press 1969; Alan Richardson & John Bowden (eds.), *A New Dictionary of Christian Theology*, SCM Press 1983 (US titles *Westminster Dictionary* . . ., same dates).

115. O'Collins, *Interpreting Jesus* (n. 74), p. 182.

116. Ibid., p. 183.

117. E.g. J. A. T. Robinson, *The Human Face of God*, SCM Press and Westminster Press 1973.

118. *Theology* LXXVIII, No. 664, October 1975, p. 554; *Theology* LXXXIV, No. 700, July 1981, pp. 243ff.; *Religious Studies* 14, 1978, pp. 223ff.

119. A. M. Farrar, *Faith and Speculation*, A. & C. Black 1967. p. 154.

120. Ibid., p. 155.

121. A. M. Farrer, *Saving Belief*, Hodder & Stoughton 1964, p. 43.

122. A. M. Farrer, *The End of Man* SPCK 1973, p. 142.

123. M. F. Wiles, *God's Action in the World*, SCM Press 1986.

124. Ibid., p. 26.

125. Hebblethwaite, *Incarnation* (n. 61), p. 99.

126. Cupitt, *Debate* (n. 11), p. 20.

127. Morris, *Logic of God Incarnate* (n. 85), p. 151.

128. See below, p. 63.

129. J. W. de Gruchy, *Standing by God in his Hour of Need*, Pretoria: University of South Africa 1986, p. 3.

130. Ibid., p. 12.

131. D. Bonhoeffer, *Letters and Papers from Prison*, SCM Press and New York: Macmillan ²1971, p. 360.

132. L. Roberts, *The Achievement of Karl Rahner*, Herder & Herder 1967, p. 105.

133. K. Rahner, In G. McCool, *A Rahner Reader*, Darton, Longman & Todd 1975, pp. 83ff.

134. H. E. W. Turner, *Jesus the Christ*, Mowbray 1976, pp. 4, 5.

135. K. Rahner, *Theological Invesigations* 11, Darton, Longman & Todd 1974, p. 13.

136. Sutherland, *God, Jesus and Belief* (n. 59), p. 135.

137. McGrath, *Enigma* (n. 64), p. 48.

138. Ibid., p. 53.

139. See W. J. Abraham, *An Introduction to the Philosophy of Religion*, Prentice-Hall 1985, p. 88ff., for a very helpful summary of Plantinga's position.

140. Morris, *Logic of God Incarnate* (n. 85), p. 32.

141. Ibid., p. 18.

142. Ibid., p. 104.

143. Ibid., p. 107.

144. See above, p. 29.

145. Hebblethwaite, *Incarnation* (n. 61), p. 35.

146. Ibid.

147. L. Hodgson, *The Doctrine of the Trinity*, Nisbet 1943.

148. Hebblethwaite, *Incarnation* (n. 61), p. 38.

149. E.g. I Cor. 12.27.

150. Hebblethwaite, *Incarnation* (n. 61), p.136.

151. Ibid., p. 41.

152. Ibid., p. 36.

153. See above, p. 34.

154. See below, p. 141.

155. Hebblethwaite, *Incarnation* (n. 61), pp. 33, 34.

156. Ibid., p. 63.

157. Ibid., p. 72.

158. K. Ward, 'Incarnation or Inspiration – A False Dichotomy', *Theology* LXXX no. 676, July 1977, pp. 251–5.

159. B. L. Hebblethwaite, *Theology* LXXX, no. 678, November 1977, p. 444.

160. See below pp. 144–5.

161. Hebblethwaite, *Incarnation* (n. 61), p. 28.

II Salvation

1. Edward Schillebeeckx, *Jesus: An Experiment in Christology*, Crossroad Publishing Company and Collins 1979, p. 657.

2. Ibid., p. 575.

3. Ibid., p. 604.

4. John Sobrino, *Christology at the Crossroads*, Orbis Books and SCM Press 1978. p. 8.

5. Ibid.

6. William James, *The Varieties of Religious Experience*, Penguin Books 1982, p. 20.

7. Ibid., p. 238.

8. Ibid.

9. Ibid., p. 239.

10. Ibid., p. 237.

11. Edward Schillebeeckx, *Christ: The Christian Experience in the Modern World*, SCM Press and Crossroad Publishing Company 1980, p. 63.

12. *Baptism, Eucharist and Ministry*, Faith and Order Paper No. 111, World Council of Churches 1982, p. 18.

13. Paul Badham, 'A Critique of the Lima Report', *Expository Times* 97 no. 10, July 1986, p. 294.

14. Ibid.

15. Kai Nielsen, *An Introduction to the Philosophy of Religion*, Macmillan 1982.

16. John Macquarrie, *God Talk: An Examination of the Language and Logic of Theology*, SCM Press 1967, p. 18.

17. Schillebeeckx, *Jesus* (n. 1), p. 603.

18. Alan Richardson, 'Salvation', in G. A. Kepler et al, *Interpreter's Dictionary of the Bible*, Abingdon Press 1962, p. 172.

19. Ibid.

20. James, *Varieties of Religious Experience* (n. 6), p. 239.

21. Juan Luis Segundo, *The Liberation of Theology*, Orbis Books and Gill & Macmillan 1977, p. 8.

22. *Sic*. Would all liberationists agree that war is a sin?

23. Rosemary Radford Ruether, *To Change the World: Christology and Cultural Criticism*, SCM Press and Crossroad Publishing Company 1981, p. 19.

24. José Míguez Bonino, *Revolutionary Theology Comes of Age*, SPCK 1975, p. 78.

25. J. Andrew Kirk, *Liberation Theology: An Evangelical View from the Third World*, London: Marshall, Morgan & Scott, 1979, p. 36.

26. Ruether, *To Change the World* (n. 23), p. 28; Sobrino, *Christology at the Crossroads* (n. 4), p. 35.

27. Donald G. Bloesch, *Jesus is Victor*, Abingdon Press 1976, p. 82.

28. Dietrich Bonhoeffer, *Ethics*, SCM Press and New York: Macmillan 1955, p. 92.

29. Ibid., p. 96.

30. *South African Statistics 1988*, Pretoria: Republic of South Africa 1988, pp. 1–5.

31. See below pp. 123ff.

32. *Race Relations Survey* Johannesbury: South African Institute of Race Relations 1982, p. 449.

33. *Race Relations Survey, 1987/1988*, Johannesburg: South African Institute of Race Relations 1988, p. 151. These figures do not take into account children in the 'independent' homelands such as Transkei, Venda, etc., which would considerably worsen the comparison.

34. Richardson, *Interpreter's Dictionary* (n. 18), p. 168.

35. Including ibid.; E. M. B. Green, *The Meaning of Salvation*, Hodder & Stoughton 1965; and Werner Foerster/Georg Fohrer, '*sozo, soteria, soter, soterios*', in G. Friedrich, *Theological Dictionary of the New Testament* 7, Eerdmans 1971.

36. See John F. A. Sawyer, *Semantics in Biblical Research: New Methods of Defining Hebrew Words for Salvation*, SCM Press 1962.

37. '*Sozo* etc.', *TDNT* (n. 35), p. 974.

38. Ibid., p. 976.

39. Ibid., p. 977.

40. Richardson, *Interpreter's Dictionary* (n. 18), p. 169.

41. Green, *Salvation* (n. 35), p. 46.

42. Richardson, *Interpreter's Dictionary* (n. 18), p. 173.

43. Ibid., p. 176.

44. Green, *Salvation* (n. 35), p. 45, 46.

45. Richardson, *Interpreter's Dictionary* (n. 18), p. 171.

46. Green, *Salvation* (n. 35), p. 30.

47. Ibid., p. 33.

48. R. C. Denton, 'Redemption', in G. A. Kepler, *Interpreter's Dictionary of the Bible* (n. 18), p. 22.

49. A. M. Hunter, *Introducing New Testament Theology*, SCM Press and Westminster Press 1957, p. 13.

50. '*Sozo*, etc.', *TDNT* (n. 35), p. 992.

51. G. B. Caird, *Saint Luke*, Penguin Books 1963, p. 130.

52. C. F. D. Moule, in E. Bammel & C. F. D. Moule, *Jesus and the Politics of His Day*, Cambridge University Press 1984, pp. 91ff.

53. Flavius Josephus *Antiquities* XVIII, 3.1, 3.2, 4.1.

54. John Howard Yoder, *The Politics of Jesus: Vicit Agnus Noster*, Eerdmans 1972.

55. J. P. M. Sweet, in *Jesus and the Politics of His Day* (n. 52), p. 9.

56. Richardson, *Interpreter's Dictionary* (n. 18), p. 178.

57. Edward Schillebeeckx, *Christ. The Christian Experience in the Modern World*, SCM Press and Crossroad Publishing Company 1980, p. 634.

58. M. Cassidy, *I Will Heal Their Land*, Pietermaritzburg, South Africa: Africa Enterprise 1974, p. 14.

59. Many who are known to me personally, mostly African women, spring to mind.

60. *The Kairos Document: Challenge to the Church: Theological Comment on the Political Crisis in South Africa*, Johannesburg: Skotaville 1986, p. 29.

61. I do not think that the modern secular state of Israel is a manifestation of the peaceful and righteous kingdom that was promised!

62. Albert Nolan, *Jesus before Christianity: The Gospel of Liberation*, Cape Town: David Philip 1976, p. 4.

63. F. W. Dillistone, *The Christian Understanding of the Atonement*, Nisbet 1968 reissued SCM Press 1984, p. 23.

64. Dillistone, *Atonement* (n. 63), p. 27.

65. Oliver C. Quick, *Doctrines of the Creed*, Fontana Books 1963, p. 234.

66. Albrecht Ritschl, *A Critical History of the Christian Doctrine of Justification and Reconciliation*, Edinburgh: Edmonton & Douglas 1872.

67. Quick, *Doctrines* (n. 65), p. 225.

68. John Macquarrie, *Principles of Christian Theology*, SCM Press and Scribners 1966, p. 284.

69. *Hymns Ancient and Modern Revised*, No. 214.

70. Gustaf Aulen, *Christus Victor*, SPCK 1931, p. 97.

71. Sam K. Williams, *Jesus' Death as Saving Event*, Scholars Press 1972, p. 107.

72. C. H. Dodd, *The Epistle of Paul to the Romans*, Fontana Books 1959, p. 101.

73. Leon Morris, *The Apostolic Preaching of the Cross*, Tyndale Press 1965.

74. John Baillie, *The Place of Jesus Christ in Modern Christianity*, T. & T. Clark 1929, p. 152.

75. See above, p. 106.

76. Anselm, 'Cur Deus Homo?', in E. R. Fairweather (ed.), *A Scholastic Miscellany: Anselm to Ockham*, Library of Christian Classics, SCM Press and Westminster Press 1956, p. 141.

77. Ibid., p. 111.

78. Ibid., p. 120.

79. Ibid.

80. ibid., p. 108.

81. Ibid., p. 111.

82. Ibid., p. 148.

83. Hastings Rashdall, *The Idea of Atonement in Christian Theology*, Macmillan 1919, p. 355.

84. See above, p. 87.

85. Baillie, *Place of Jesus Christ* (n. 73), p. 165.

86. Aulen, *Christus Victor* (n. 70).

87. Ibid., p. 71.

88. Ibid., p. 76.

89. Macquarrie, *Principles* (n. 68), p. 287.

90. Ibid., p. 206.

91. Aulen, *Christus Victor* (n. 70), p. 66.

92. G. B. Caird, *Principalities and Powers*, Oxford University Press 1956.

93. Aulen, *Christus Victor* (n. 70), p. 73.

94. See above pp. 32, 33.

95. *Race Relations Survey 1987/1988*, Johannesburg: South African Institute of Race Relations 1988, p. 8.

96. Allan Boesak at the Assembly of the World Council of Churches, Vancouver 1983.

97. Allan Boesak, *Farewell to Innocence*, Johannesburg: Ravan Press 1977, p. 45.

98. Desmond M. Tutu, in J. W. de Gruchy & C. Villa-Vicencio, *Apartheid is a Heresy*, Cape Town: David Philip 1983, p. 47.

99. Desmond M. Tutu, in John Webster, *Bishop Desmond Tutu: The Voice of One Crying in the Wilderness*, Mowbray 1982, p. 88.

100. Maurice Wiles, *God's Action in the World*, SCM Press 1986.

101. René Metz & Jean Schlick, *Liberation Theology and the Message of Salvation*, Pittsburgh: Pickwick Press 1978, pp. 52, 53.

102. See below, pp. 130ff.

103. *The Kairos Document* (n. 60), p. 24.

104. See above, pp. 42, 43.

105. Oscar Cullmann, *Christ and Time: The Primitive Christian Conception of Time and History*, SCM Press and Westminster Press 1951, p. 84.

106. E. J. Payne, in A. W. Ward, G. W. Prothero & S. Leathes, *The Cambridge Modern History* 1, Cambridge University Press 1902, p. 11.

107. B. Diaz, *The Conquest of New Spain*, Penguin Books 1963, p. 176.

108. See D. Carrasco, 'The Hermeneutics of Conquest', in *The History of Religions* 28.2, November 1988, p. 157.

109. P. Maylam, *A History of the African People of Southern Africa from the Early Iron Age to the 1970s*, Cape Town: David Philip 1986, p. 121.

110. 'A Young Black Man', *The Argus*, 6 November 1976, quoted by J. de Gruchy, *Cry Justice*, Collins 1986, p. 119.

111. I. D. MacCrone, *Race Attitudes in South Africa*, Johannesburg: Witwatersrand University Press 1937, p. 6.

112. Ibid., p. 41.

113. H. Giliomee in H. W. van der Merwe, *Looking at the Afrikaner Today*, Cape Town: Tafelberg 1975, p. 4.

114. Meiring et al., in S. van der Horst, *Race Discrimination in South Africa*, Cape Town: David Philip 1981, p. 187.

115. J. W. de Gruchy, *The Church Struggle in South Africa*, Cape Town: David Philip, 1979, p. 117.

116. R. Buis, *Religious Belief and White Prejudice,*, Johannesburg: Ravan 1975, p. 11.

117. *Hymns Ancient and Modern*, no. 573.

118. MacCrone, *Race Attitudes* (n. 111), p. 113.

119. Ibid., p. 127.

120. Julian Cobbing, 'The Mfecane as Alibi: Thoughts on Dithokong and Mbolompo', *Journal of African History* 29.3, 1988, pp. 492, 493.

121. Dr E. P. J. Kleynhans, at that time (1978) Moderator of the Nederlandse Gereformeerde Kerk, quoted in J. H. P. Serfontein, *Apartheid, Change and the N.G. Kerk*, Emmarentia, Transvaal: Taurus 1982, p. 64.

122. Nederduitse Gereformeerde Kerk. There were three white Dutch Reformed churches in South Africa, of which the N.G.K. is the largest. Recently there was a further breakaway of the even more politically conservative Afrikaans Gereformeerde Kerk.

123. Serfontein, *Apartheid* (n. 121), p. 63.

124. Quoted by J. Bird, *Annals of Natal*, Vol. 1, Pietermaritzburg, South Africa: P. Davis 1888, p. 459.

125. Calvin, *Institutes of Religion*, ed. J. T. McNeill, Library of Christian Classics, SCM Press and Westminster Press, p. lix.

126. Borchenhagen in 1880, quoted by H. Giliomee in van der Merwe, (n. 113), p. 14.

127. Quoted in ibid., p. 27.

128. In 1966 the Dutch Reformed Church said firmly that 'differentiation and diversity was established under God's providential determination, and was maintained in the face of sinful and wilful striving for uniformity at Babel'. The state is therefore 'justified in taking legislative action and prohibiting racial mixing' (*Human Relations in South Africa*, Cape Town: Dutch Reformed Church 1966, p. 8). It spoke of the role of Christian 'trusteeship' and 'guardianship' over undeveloped peoples (ibid., p. 4). But by 1986 it said that 'the conviction has gradually grown that a forced separation and division of peoples cannot be considered a Biblical imperative. The attempt to justify such an injunction as derived from the Bible, must be recognized as an error and be rejected (*Church and Society: A Testimony of the*

Dutch Reformed Church, Bloemfontein: Dutch Reformed Church 1986, p. 47).
It said that the invisible unity of humans should be made visible in the church
(ibid., p. 15). However, it also said that 'in contrast to the social structures
emanating from creation, only the Church is a product of God's recreation',
thus implying that this visible unity is unlikely to be achieved in the secular
state, and that the Bible is not concerned with national or political policies.
'Whether or not to maintain a national (= racial) identity is determined by a
people's own commitment to the preservation of its cultural values' (ibid.,
p. 20).

129. J. Kinghorn, *Die N G Kerk en Apartheid*, Johannesburg: Macmillan 1986.

130. Ibid., p. 39.

131. A. Kuyper, quoted in W. A. de Klerk, *The Puritans in Africa*, Rex Collings
1975, p. 204.

132. Ibid., p. 258.

133. D. F. Malan, quoted in van der Horst, *Race Discrimination* (n. 114), p. 189.

134. A. P. Treurnicht, quoted in de Klerk, *Puritans* (n. 131), p. 259.

135. Rashdall, *Idea of Atonement* (n. 82), p. 446.

136. Ibid., p. 438.

137. Ibid., p. 440.

138. Ibid., p. 444.

139. See above p. 27.

140. See above p. 113ff.

141. Rashdall, *Idea of Atonement* (n. 82), p. 447.

142. Ibid., p. 442.

143. Quick, *Doctrines* (n. 65), p. 227.

144. Ibid., p. 228.

145. Macquarrie, *Principles* (n. 68), p. 286.

146. Rashdall, *Idea of Atonement* (n. 82), p. 455.

147. Jürgen Moltmann, *The Crucified God*, SCM Press and Harper and Row 1974,
p. 48.

148. Ibid., p. 65.

149. Ibid., p. 183.

150. Ibid., p. 33.

151. Ibid., p. 87.

152. Ibid., p. 127.

153. Ibid., p. 138.

154. Ibid., p. 140.

155. Ibid., p. 146.

156. Ibid., p. 150.

157. Ibid., p. 149.

158. S. G. F. Brandon, *Jesus and the Zealots*, Manchester University Press 1967.

159. Moltmann, *Crucified God* (n. 147), p. 161.

160. Ibid., p. 173.

161. Ibid., p. 228.

162. In fact, although he speaks of the Trinity, he makes so little mention of the
role of the Holy Spirit that, in this book at least, he is really operating with a
binitarian rather than trinitarian idea.

163. Ibid., p. 245.

164. Ibid., p. 193, my emphasis.

165. Ibid., p. 249.

166. Jürgen Moltmann, *Theology of Hope: On the Ground and the Implications of
a Christian Eschatology*, SCM Press and Harper and Row 1967.

167. Moltmann, *Crucified God* (n. 147), p. 52.

168. Ibid., p. 250.

169. Ibid., p. 251.
170. Ibid., p. 219.
171. Ibid., p. 149.
172. Ibid., p. 152.
173. See above, p. 81.
174. A. McGrath, *The Enigma of the Cross*, Hodder & Stoughton 1987, p. 83.
175. Ibid.
176. See above, p. 36.
177. Vincent Taylor, *The Atonement in New Testament Teaching*, Epworth Press 1940.
178. Ibid., p. 271.
179. Ibid., p. 247.
180. Ibid., pp. 246, 247.
181. Ibid., p. 19.
182. Ibid., p. 258.
183. Ibid., p. 283.
184. Ibid., p. 303.
185. Ibid., p. 307.
186. Ibid., p. 309.
187. In addition to *The Atonement in New Testament Teaching* see also *Forgiveness and Reconciliation*, Macmillan 1946, and *Jesus and his Sacrifice*, Macmillan 1937.
188. Frances M. Young, *Sacrifice and the Death of Christ*, SPCK 1975 reissued SCM Press 1983.
189. Dillistone, *Atonement* (n. 63).
190. Ibid., p. 69.

III   Salvation as Liberation

1. See A. Nolan, 'The Option for the Poor in South Africa', *New Blackfriars* 67, no. 787, January 1986, pp. 5ff, for a helpful discussion of this point.
2. P. Freire, *Education for Critical Consciousness*, Sheed and Ward and Seabury Press 1973, pp. 41ff.
3. G. Gutierrez, *A Theology of Liberation*, Orbis Books and SCM 1974, pp. 36, 37.
4. E.g. B. M. Couch in S. Torres & J. Eagleson, *Theology of the Americas*, Orbis Books 1976, pp. 305–7.
5. J. Maritain, *Integral Humanism*, University of Notre Dame Press 1973.
6. In M. Walsh & B. Davies, *Proclaiming Justice and Peace*, Collins 1984.
7. In W. M. Abbott, *The Documents of Vatican II*, Geoffrey Chapman 1966, pp. 199ff.
8. D. McCann, *Christian Realism and Liberation Theology*, Orbis Books 1981, p. 147.
9. Gutierrez, *Theology of Liberation* (n. 3), p. 36.
10. Quoted by McCann, *Christian Realism* (n. 8), p. 165.
11. Ibid., p. 131.
12. A. Fierro, *The Militant Gospel*, Orbis Books and SCM Press 1975, p. 239.
13. G. Gutierrez, in R. Gibellini, *Frontiers of Theology in Latin America*, Orbis Books and SCM Press 1979, p. x.
14. G. Gutierrez, quoted in McCann, *Christian Realism* (n. 8), p. 156.
15. H. Assmann, *Theology for a Nomad Church*, Orbis Books 1976, p. 79.
16. G. Gutierrez, *Theology of Liberation* (n. 3), p. 11.
17. J. L. Segundo, *The Liberation of Theology*, Orbis Books 1976, p. 94.
18. G. Gutierrez, *Two Theological Perspectives*, Orbis Books 1978, p. 247.
19. Gutierrez, *Theology of Liberation*, (n. 3) p. 291.

20. Fierro, *Militant Gospel* (n. 12), pp. 388–394.

21. J. Miguez Bonino, *Doing Theology in a Revolutionary Situation*, Orbis Books and SPCK 1975, p. 134.

22. See above, p. 120.

23. S. J. Croatto, *Exodus*, Orbis Books 1981, p. 28.

24. J. Miranda, *Being and the Messiah*, Orbis Books 1977, p. 34, 35.

25. R. Alves, in Gibellini, *Frontiers of Theology* (n. 13), p. 301.

26. Miguez Bonino, *Doing Theology* (n. 21), p. 136.

27. Gutierrez, *Theology of Liberation* (n. 3), p. 234.

28. Ibid., p. 167.

29. L. Boff, in Torres & Eagleson, *Theology of the Americas* (n. 4), p. 298.

30. J. Sobrino, *Christology at the Crossroads*, Orbis Books and SCM Press 1978, p. 353.

31. S. Trinidad, in J. Miguez Bonino, *Faces of Jesus*, Orbis Books 1983, p. 59.

32. Segundo, *Liberation of Theology* (n. 17), p. 111.

33. Ibid., p. 95 n. 5.

34. Ibid., p. 111.

35. Ibid., p. 112.

36. P. Ricoeur, *Interpretation Theory*, Texas Christian University Press 1976, p. 30.

37. Ibid., p. 44.

38. Ibid., p. 79.

39. Ibid., p. 75.

40. Ibid., p. 52.

41. Segundo, *Liberation of Theology* (n. 17), p. 108.

42. Ibid., p. 118.

43. Ibid., p. 116.

44. Ibid., p. 117.

45. Ibid., p. 121.

46. Fierro, *Militant Gospel* (n. 12), p. 195.

47. E. Norman, *Christianity and the World Order*, Oxford University Press 1979.

48. McCann, *Christian Realism* (n. 8), p. 200.

49. H. Marcuse, *One Dimensional Man*, Ratledge and Beacon Press 1964, p. 20.

50. Che Guevara, quoted by O. Bullock & A. Stallybrass, *The Fontana Dictionary of Modern Thought*, Fontana Books [2]1981, p. 274.

51. H. Marcuse, *Eros and Civilization*, Vintage Books 1962, p. 73.

52. McCann, *Christian Realism* (n. 8), p. 217.

53. Segundo, *Liberation of Theology* (n. 17), p. 212.

54. Ibid., p. 236.

55. See above, p. 164.

56. Norman, *Christianity and the World Order* (n. 47), p. 25.

57. See Couch in Torres & Eagleson, *Theology of the Americas*, (n. 4) pp. 305–7.

58. See above, p. 120.

59. M. H. Ellis, *Toward a Jewish Theology of Liberation*, Orbis Books and SCM Press 1987, pp. 74, 75.

60. See above, pp. 121–2.

61. Fierro, *Militant Gospel*, (n. 12), p. 146.

62. McCann, *Christian Realism* (n. 8), p. 196.

63. M. Machovec, *A Marxist Looks at Jesus*, Fortress Press 1976, p. 108.

64. McCann, *Christian Realism* (n. 8), p. 204.

65. Ibid., p. 194.

66. Ibid., p. 196.

67. Fierro, *Militant Gospel* (n. 8), pp. 306, 307.

68. Ibid., pp. 307–310.

69. Quoted in ibid., p. 164.

70. Ibid., p. 366.

71. Ibid., p. 126, see J. Miguez Bonino, *Christians and Marxists*, Eerdmans 1976; J. Miranda, *Marx and the Bible*, Orbis Books and SCM Press 1974.

72. R. Niebuhr, *An Interpretation of Christian Ethics*, Harper and Row 1935, p. 113.

73. Quoted in McCann, *Christian Realism* (n. 8), p. 31. From this, Niebuhr developed his key idea of a New Testament ethic which cannot fully be implemented in an imperfect world but which must be taken seriously as a continual judgment on our interim policies.

74. Fierro, *Militant Gospel* (n. 12), pp. 208–10.

75. D. W. Ferm, *Third World Liberation Theologies*, Orbis Books 1986, p. 111.

76. K. R. Popper, *The Open Society and Its Enemies*, Vol. 2, Routledge and Kegan Paul ²1966.

77. Fierro, *Militant Gospel* (n. 12), p. 109.

78. Gal. 3.27, 28; I Cor. 12.13.

79. John 12.8.

80. Fierro, *Militant Gospel* (n. 12), p. 336.

81. Ibid., p. 330.

82. Norman, *Christianity and the World Order* (n. 47), p. 19.

83. Gutierrez, *Theology of Liberation* (n. 3), p. 232.

84. Miguez Bonino, *Christians and Marxists* (n. 71), p. 152.

85. J. H. Cone, 'An Introductory Note on the Essay "God is black"', unpublished paper.

86. B. Moore, *The Challenge of Black Theology in South Africa*, C. Hurst and John Knox Press 1974.

87. A. Boesak, *Farewell to Innocence*, Johannesburg: Raven 1977.

88. *The Kairos Document*, Johannesburg: Skotaville ²1986.

89. M. Motlhabi, in I. J. Mosala & B. Tlhagale, *The Unquestionable Right to be Free*, Johannesburg: Skotaville 1986, p. 38.

90. B. Goba, in Mosala & Tlhagale, *Unquestionable Right* (n. 89), p. 68.

91. See Moore, *Challenge of Black Theology* (n. 86).

92. G. Setiloane, *African Theology*, Johannesburg: Skotaville, 1986, p. 43.

93. In M. Motlhabi, *Essays in Black Theology*, Johannesburg: Ravan 1972, p. 7.

94. In G. S. Wilmore & J. H. Cone, *Black Theology*, Orbis Books 1979, p. 483.

95. A. Mokoena, 'African Culture', *Pro Veritate*, May 1977, p. 1.

96. S. Maimela, in Mosala & Tlhagale, *Unquestionable Right* (n. 89), p. 105.

97. Boesak, *Farewell to Innocence* (n. 87), p. 5; D. M. Tutu, in J. W. de Gruchy, *Cry Justice*, Collins 1986, p. 12.

98. Goba, in Mosala & Tlhagale, *Unquestionable Right* (n. 89), p. 57; see also *Journal of Theology for Southern Africa* 31, June 1980, p. 23.

99. L. Sebidi, *Doing Theology in a Divided Society*, unpublished paper.

100. B. Goba, unpublished thesis.

101. B. Tlhagale, in Mosala & Tlhagale, *Unquestionable Right*, p. 126; I. J. Mosala, ibid., p. 175; T. A. Mofokeng, ibid., p. 125.

102. T. A. Mofokeng, *The Crucified among the Crossbearers* Kampen: J. H. Kok 1983, p. 18.

103. E.g. Goba in Mosala & Tlhagale, *Unquestionable Right* (n. 89), p. 66.

104. A. Mpunzi, in Motlhabi, *Essays* (n. 93), p. 112.

105. Boesak, *Farewell to Innocence* (n. 87), pp. 96, 97.

106. S. Dwane, 'Christology and liberation', *Journal of Theology for Southern Africa* 35, June 1981, p. 30.

107. *Kairos Document*, p. 10, F. Chikane in de Gruchy, *Cry Justice* (n.97), p. 72.

108. J. H. Cone, *Black Theology and Black Power*, Seabury Press 1969, p. 29.

109. K. E. Mgojo, 'Prolegomenon to the Study of Black Theology', *Journal of Theology for Southern Africa* 21, December 1977, p. 21.

110. Boesak, *Farewell to Innocence* (n. 87), p. 16.

111. Goba, in Mosala & Tlhagale, *Unquestionable Right* (n. 89), p. 65.

112. I. J. Mosala, unpublished Ph D thesis, also Mosala & Tlhagale, *Unquestionable Right* (n. 89), p. 176ff.

113. F. Chikane, 'The Incarnation in the Life of the People in Southern Africa', *Journal of Theology for Southern Africa* 51, June 1985, p. 46.

114. D. M. Tutu, 'Church and Nation in the perspective of Black Theology', *Journal of Theology for Southern Africa* 15, June 1976, p. 6.

115. M. Buthelezi, 'Violence and the Cross in South Africa', *Journal of Theology for Southern Africa* 29, December 1979, p. 52.

116. Mofokeng, *Crucified among Crossbearers* (n. 102), p. 28.

117. Buthelezi, Violence (n. 115), p. 52.

118. B. Goba, *An Agenda for Black Theology*, Johannesburg: Skotaville 1988, p. 40.

119. S. Biko, in Moore *Challenge of Black Theology* (n. 86), p. 41.

120. S. Dwane, *Christology and Black Experience*, Pietermaritzburg: Federal Seminary 1980, p. 10.

121. S. Biko, in Motlhabi, *Essays* (n. 93), p. 23.

122. See above pp. 121, 122.

123. S. Maimela, in Mosala & Tlhagale, *Unquestionable Right* (n. 89), p. 110.

124. Ibid., p. 111.

125. M. Buthelezi, in Mosala & Tlhagale, *Unquestionable Right* (n. 89), p. 156.

126. F. Chikane, in ibid., p. 50.

127. S. Maimela, *Proclaim Freedom to My People*, Johannesburg: Skotaville 1987, p. 117.

IV Conclusions

1. W. Pannenberg, *Jesus – God and Man*, SCM Press and Westminster Press 1968, p. 39.

2. T. F. Driver, *Christ in a Changing World*, Crossroad Publishing Company and SCM Press 1981, p. x.

3. See above, p. 81.

4. O. C. Quick, *Doctrines of the Creed*, Collins 1938, p. 226.

5. See above, p. 139.

6. I Cor. 9.27.

7. W. Wink, *Violence and Non-violence in South Africa*, Philadelphia: New Society publishers 1987, has some ideas on this point.

8. Phil. 4.8.

9. Albert Schweitzer, *The Quest of the Historical Jesus*, A. & C. Black [3]1954 reissued SCM Press 1981.

10. Julian of Norwich, *Revelations of Divine Love*, Penguin Books 1966, p. 225.

11. P. Newman, *A Spirit Christology*, University Press of America 1987.

12. Mark 1.15. See also A. M. Hunter, *Introducing New Testament Theology*, SCM Press 1957, pp. 25ff.

13. J. H. Yoder, *The Politics of Jesus*, Eerdmans 1972, pp. 16, 17.

14. Ibid., p. 24.

15. Ibid., p. 115.

16. Ibid., p. 66.

17. Ibid., p. 76.

18. H. Falk, *Jesus the Pharisee*, Paulist Press 1985.

19. Luke 16.8.

20. See above p. 142.
21. See above p. 136.
22. Yoder, *Politics of Jesus* (n. 13), p. 98.
23. Ibid., p. 112.
24. Mark. 8.34; Matt. 16.24.
25. Luke 9.23.
26. Col. 1.24; Phil. 1.29.
27. Yoder, *Politics of Jesus* (n. 13), p. 97.
28. Ibid.
29. Wink, *Violence and Non-Violence* (n. 7).
30. Ibid., p. 51.
31. For example, the declaration by the Anglican Lambeth Conference in 1988 that it could not condemn the use of violence by South African liberation movements, or the 'Lusaka statement' of May 1987: 'While committed to peaceful change we recognize that the nature of the South African regime which wages war against its own inhabitants and neighbours compels movements to the use of force along with other means to end the oppression.' Although not all the participants at the Lusaka meeting were church representatives, the Anglican church at least said that it 'accepted the Lusaka document', whatever that means, while at the same time urging consideration of the Wink line.
32. Rom. 12.2.
33. Matt. 10.42.
34. Luke 9.58.
35. Quoted by Anselm Hughes, *The Rivers of the Flood*, Faith Press 1961, p. 123.
36. D. M. Tutu, in J. W. de Gruchy, *Cry Justice*, Collins, 1986, p. 95.
37. D. Nineham, in J. Hick (ed.), *The Myth of God Incarnate*, SCM Press and Westminster Press 1977, p. 186.
38. J. A. T. Robinson, *Honest to God*, SCM Press and Westminster Press 1963, p. 74.
39. Nineham, in Hick (ed.), *Myth of God Incarnate* (n. 37), p. 203.
40. D. Sölle, *Christ the Representative*, SCM Press 1967, p. 115.
41. Ibid., p. 116.
42. Yoder, *Politics of Jesus* (n. 13), p. 63.
43. Newman, *Spirit Christology* (n. 11), p. 179.
44. See above, pp. 60ff.
45. E. J. Tinsley, in Alan Richardson (ed.) *A Dictionary of Christian Theology*, SCM Press 1969, pp. 165, 166.
46. Driver, *Christ in a Changing World* (n. 2), p. 32.
47. C. Hickling, 'Towards a Definition of Salvation', *Faith and Unity* XIX.3, Summer 1975, p. 42.
48. Ibid., p. 43.
49. H. Scott Holland, quoted by D. Nicholls in G. Rowell, *Tradition Renewed*, Darton, Longman & Todd 1986, p. 144.
50. Mark 8.31; 9.31; 10.33.
51. Quick, *Doctrines* (n. 4), p. 207.
52. quoted in I. J. Mosala & B. Tlhagale, *The Unquestionable Right to be Free*, Johannesburg: Skotaville 1986, p. 164.
53. Newman, *Spirit Christology* (n. 11), pp. 69ff.
54. John V. Taylor, *The Go-Between God*, SCM Press 1972.
55. Yoder, *Politics of Jesus* (n. 13, p. 107.
56. See above pp. 131–2.
57. Newman, *Spirit Christology* (n. 11) , p. 147ff.
58. Ibid., p. 205.

59. Thursday afternoons were traditionally the maids' half day in South African households. Many churches hold their Women's Auxiliary or Mothers' Union, etc., meetings on Thursday afternoons.

60. Driver, *Christ in a Changing World* (n. 2), p. 165.

61. Ibid., p. 166.

62. Newman, *Spirit Christology* (n. 11), p. 135.

63. Driver, *Christ in a Changing World* (n. 2) p. 151.

64. Yoder, *Politics of Jesus* (n. 13), p. 154.

65. Driver, *Christ in a Changing World* (n. 2), p. 24.

66. Hickling, 'Definition of Salvation' (n. 47), p. 43.

67. John 15.13.

68. F. Young, *Sacrifice and the Death of Christ*, SPCK 1975 reissued SCM Press 1983.

69. D. Cupitt, *Taking Leave of God*, SCM Press and Crossroad Publishing Company 1980, p. 58.

70. R. Holloway, *Suffering, Sex and other Paradoxes*, Morehouse-Barlow 1985, p. 141.

Index